CRICKETING
REMINISCENCES

Reproduced by permission from an Oil Painting by J. Ernest Breun.

W. G. Grace

'W.G.' CRICKETING REMINISCENCES & PERSONAL RECOLLECTIONS W.G. GRACE

INTRODUCTION BY E.W. SWANTON

The Hambledon Press,

35 Gloucester Avenue,
London NW1 7AX.

1980

First Published 1899
Reprinted 1980

ISBN 0 950 6882 0 7

Printed and bound by
Redwood Burn Limited
Trowbridge & Esher

CONTENTS

ILLUSTRATIONS

W.G. — THE MAN AND THE LEGEND

E. W. SWANTON

ONE could make a good case for the proposition that more has been written about Dr. W. G. Grace than any sporting figure in history — even of almost any Englishman of his day in any walk of life. To an extent, of course, this was an accident of time, for his early manhood coincided with a country-wide explosion of interest in games and sports and a corresponding regimentation in the form of new ruling bodies, international fixtures, and the founding of clubs innumerable, covering many forms of exercise.

As it happened, cricket could boast a greater antiquity than most popular pastimes at the time of W.G.s emergence on the scene. In the villages of Kent, Sussex, Hampshire and Surrey the roots of cricket were already centuries deep. The coming of the railways had brought the game to the cities, and was beginning to stimulate county rivalries. In the Marylebone Club, playing on the ground which had been laid out for it at St. John's Wood by Thomas Lord half a century before, cricket had a natural headquarters in the heart of Empire.

What was needed was a focal figure — and if ever the hour produced the man it did so in the person of W.G.

In more than just the physical aspect W.G. was larger than life. Learning the game by long and assiduous boyhood practice with his parents and the whole ample family of Graces and Pococks in the Downend orchard, he was taken in 1864 just prior to his 16th birthday on his first tour, and, after making 170 and 56 not out at Hove, scored 50 against MCC on his first appearance at Lord's. The following summer, still a few days short of 17, he played the first two of his 85 matches for the Gentlemen, and at Lord's was on the winning side. What precocity!

Over the span of the following 35 years he exercised over the cricket world a sway both unique and unrepeatable. He began remarkably young, and his command lasted, despite increasing girth, over an unusually long period. He was just coming up to 47 when, in 1895, in a sudden return to the brilliance of his youth, he performed the unthinkable and scored 1000 runs in the month of May. In 1899, a month before his 51st birthday, he led England against Australia for the last time, having by then built an imperishable monument of achievement that is the more remarkable the more closely one examines and compares it with the records of his contemporaries. It must be borne in mind, too, that in the 'seventies he combined his cricket with medical training and afterwards had to answer the demands of his practice as a parish doctor — though in the summer he eased the strain by employing a 'locum'. The idea, once common, that he was a doctor only by courtesy does not stand examination.

As I say, it could well be that no sportsman of any age has been the subject of more "column inches", ranging from the press of the day to every sort and degree of cricket literature, than W.G. — and who else, by the way, has ever been identified almost exclusively by his initials alone sixty years and more after his death? *A Bibliography of Cricket* lists 44 publications of one kind or another with which his name is associated. Yes, but of narrative books ostensibly *by* W.G. there are only two, this, published in 1899, and a previous one entitled "Cricket" eight years earlier.

W.G. was clearly as averse from writing about the game as he was from talking formally about it, and there is no disguising that in the case of these Reminiscences and Recollections, if the thoughts were those of W.G., their written expression was the work of a collaborator, the journalist Arthur Porritt. They are none the less valuable for that, since if there had been no one at hand with the patience and pertinacity of Porritt there would have been no book; W.G. was failing on his own to produce the book for which he had contracted. There is indeed evidence that, loath as he was to undertake the labour of composition, W.G. was willing enough to be associated with the responsible efforts of others, since in the MCC library may be found the text of his other book — and, surely, not such a full or satisfactory one as this —

also ghosted yet written from first to last in his own firm, legible hand.

If it had not been for Cowden Clarke we should not have Nyren's immortal pen-pictures of the cricketers of his time. The romantic history of Hambledon would be all but forgotten. Porritt is not a chronicler in that class: far from it. He has however drawn from W.G., and recorded pleasantly enough in the conventional style of the day, not only memories of his cricket life, but sketches of many of his fellow-players, the whole spiced with good practical advice on the game. The Hambledon Press is owned by a young student of cricket history, Mr. Martin Sheppard, who should be congratulated surely on bringing this old book once again into circulation, and neatly timing its arrival moreover to coincide with the centenary of the first of all Test Matches in England, wherein, inevitably, our hero made the first of all hundreds for his country.

There is much that a modern biographer might have hoped to persuade his subject to reveal, but he would have been hard pressed, for W.G., according to Porritt, despite his exceptional practical qualities was 'a singularly inarticulate man'. He 'accepted me as his collaborator with the utmost heartiness', wrote Porritt in his own reminiscent book *The Best I Remember* 'and although the task of getting the material from him was almost heart-breaking, I enjoyed the work immensely'. What does come through in this joint effort is W.G's innate modesty — as shown, for instance, in his description of 'another funny experience at Canterbury in 1876'. The joke was that when MCC followed on, late on the second afternoon, 329 behind, W.G., going in first, decided (according to Bernard Darwin's *W. G. Grace*) that 'we'll make it warm for them this time'. This he did to the tune of scoring 344 in six hours, thus drawing the match with plenty to spare. One wonders whether by the end of it Lord Harris, Kent's captain, was quite appreciating the humour of the situation. This, by the way, was the start of that phenomenal seven days wherein he followed the 344 with 177 against Notts at Clifton and then 318 not out at Cheltenham against Yorkshire: 839 in the three innings, once not out.

Porritt assesses thus his personality:

'About Dr. W. G. Grace there was something indefinable — like the simple faith of a child — which arrested and fascinated me. He was a big grown-up boy, just what a man who only lived when he was in the open air might be expected to be. A wonderful kindliness ran through his nature, mingling strangely with the arbitrary temper of a man who had been accustomed to be dominant over other men.'

Darwin quotes with approval a close friend of the Old Man saying much the same thing: 'W.G. was just a great big schoolboy in everything he did'. Darwin goes on: 'He had all the schoolboy's love for elementary and boisterous jokes: his distaste for learning; his desperate and undisguised keenness; his occasional pettishness and pettiness; his endless power of recovering his spirits. To them may be added two qualities not as a rule to be found in schoolboys; a wonderful modesty and lack of vanity; an invariable kindness to those younger than himself, "except", as one of his most devoted friends has observed, "that he tried to chisel them out l.b.w." '

Here perhaps is the essence of W.G., to which it needs only to be added that there seemed not to be anyone who knew him who was not devoted to this spontaneous, unaffected countryman who became and remained over the last three decades of the reign of Queen Victoria, with the possible exception of the Prince of Wales, the best known man in England.

INTRODUCTION

A PRELIMINARY LOOK ROUND

REMINISCENCES of thirty-five years—it is a long innings I have before me. As I buckle up my pads, pull on my batting-gloves, and take up my bat, or rather my pen, I am painfully conscious that my eye cannot long remain undimmed, that my muscles must soon lose their elasticity, and that in a year or two my name, like that of so many of the companions of my youth, will drop out of the "averages." Some one has said that only an old man writes reminiscences, and it may be true ; but as some one else has said, old men have one advantage—they know as much of the future as young men, and they know a great deal more of the past. It is on the past I have to dwell in this volume—the future of cricket can take care of itself. The game has taken deep root in the hearts of the British people, and wherever the English language is spoken, wickets are pitched and cricket is played. In the thirty-five years during which I have been in the field I have seen cricket jump by leaps and bounds into popular favour ; I have watched its development with the greatest interest, have seen it pass through critical times, and, as best I could, have done my share to make the game of games the national pastime of the British people.

I take up my pen with reluctance, for writing is not a recreation I care for. Nature, training, temperament, and predilection combine to make me prefer the open air, and even now I would sooner enter on a long day's leather-hunting than write a single chapter of reminiscences. But the chapters must be written. I have promised, and must fulfil that promise.

How and where shall I begin these reminiscences—by reviewing the dim memories of forty years ago, when in my Gloucestershire home I was first initiated into the mysteries of cricket, or by a few rambling observations more or less anecdotal, and perhaps wholly disconnected? The latter course may commend itself to my readers, and to them I submit. Whatever my book may be, whatever its literary defects and manifest shortcomings, I know that the public, who have for so long encouraged and stimulated me by their generous appreciation of my endeavours in the cricket-field, will be indulgent even if they are critical. On that confidence I rest.

"Yours must have been a grand life," a man said to me once, "always playing cricket." Well, perhaps it has been. It would ill become me to say that a cricketer's life is not a happy one. There may be—there are—drawbacks and disadvantages, but they all have their compensations, and I at least can say, after thirty-five years in the cricket-field, that the joys have far exceeded the pains, and that I look back along the vista of years now growing dimmer and dimmer and rejoice that my nerve, eyesight, and physique have served me so long to participate in the delights which cricket affords. A cricketer's life is a life of splendid freedom, healthy effort, endless variety, and delightful good fellowship.

A friend of mine who was at the Oval a few days ago overheard one man say to another, " I wonder if old W. G. really likes playing cricket," and his companion wondered also. If these lines should meet the eyes of either of those gentlemen, I want to assure them that I never liked cricket more than I do now, and that the only regret I entertain is that my career is ending instead of beginning.

What a flood of reminiscences pours into my mind as I think of the men who at one time or another have been my comrades in the cricket-field ! Some who were veterans when I was a youngster are dead, and perhaps are forgotten in the mists of memory ; some who were of my own age have dropped out of active cricket, though they still shoulder their bats to "show how fields were won " ; while others have given us their sons to carry on the family traditions. Glancing back, it seems to me as if the cricket-field was a panorama with scenes ever changing, and faces ever new passing before my eyes.

I have stayed on in the cricket-field while two or three generations have sprung up, had their day, and ceased to be. How many generations of bowlers I have played with and against I scarcely like to calculate. In the late sixties there were Tinley, Tarrant, Jackson, Grundy, Willsher, and Freeman ; in the early seventies, Southerton, Alfred Shaw, Martin McIntyre, and Morley ; in the late seventies, Ulyett, Allan Hill, Barnes, Tom Emmett, W. McIntyre, Watson, Mycroft, and A. G. Steel ; in the early eighties, Peate, Crossland, C. T. Studd, Flowers, Humphreys, and Barlow ; in the late eighties, Lohmann, Briggs, Attewell, Davidson, and Peel ; in the early nineties, J. T. Hearne, S. M. J. Woods, Mold, Tyler, Sharp, and Martin ; and now, in this closing half of the nineties, we have Richardson, Mead, Cuttell, C. J. Kortright, C. L. Townsend, F. S. Jackson, Rhodes, and Lockwood. Roughly speaking, each decade sees the rise and fall of two generations of bowlers ; so I am the survivor of seven different generations.

And then the batsmen of my time ! What a catalogue their names would make if I began with George Parr, and went through the intervening years, naming one after another of the men like Daft, Carpenter, and Hayward, who were the giants of my boyhood, Jupp, Ephraim Lockwood, Tom Humphrey, and George Ulyett, who were in their prime in the seventies, and the great army of batsmen who during the last twenty years have been my fellow cricketers!

In the thirty-five years over which my memory sweeps, cricket has undergone many changes. The game we play to-day is scarcely like the game of my boyhood. There have been silent revolutions transforming cricket in many directions, improving it in some ways, and in others robbing it of some elements of its charm.

If some old champion of the early Victorian days—say Alfred Mynn, who was the Kent "crack" in the days when cricketers played in white tall hats—could by some dispensation pay a visit to Lord's when some great match is in progress, he would, I doubt not, stand amazed at the metamorphosis fifty years have effected in cricket. The very ground itself would bewilder him. He played on open commons, with rude tents as dressing-rooms, and the vast enclosure and palatial pavilion would dazzle his senses. Then the smooth turf and billiard-table wickets would amaze the old bowler, who triumphed on bumpy pitches. And then the crowds. How he would marvel at the vast fringe of spectators, exceeding in thousands the hundreds who watched his most brilliant deeds! But the changes in the game itself would perhaps hold him spell-bound. The high delivery of modern bowlers would horrify the famous trundler of the good old days, when to deliver the ball from above the level of the shoulder was as heinous an offence as throwing is to-day—perhaps more so, for umpires in Mynn's day were not afraid to "No ball" an offender. The altered style of batting would scarcely surprise him less, and I can imagine the old man doubting his eyesight if he saw a batsman hitting fast bowling with absolute confidence and ease. In his time, he would remind us, fast bowling was treated more reverently, and batsmen were content to play back, and be thankful if they scored behind the wickets. Yet the changes which would perplex this old man of the past have all taken place within my own recollection. I have watched all these gradual variations of the game begin as experiments, and then establish themselves as general practices.

And if Alfred Mynn, restored to life for the purpose, could, after visiting Lord's, travel over England from Berwick-on-Tweed to Land's End, he would find that cricket, which in his day was the game of the few, has become the pastime of all. He would find County Cricket, which in his time had scarcely any real existence, organised on a scale of elaboration which would take his breath away ; while the regular visits of Australian teams and return visits of English teams to Australia would make his confusion even worse confounded. When I compare the cricket of to-day with the cricket of the sixties, with which my earliest recollections are associated, I confess that the extent of the changes surprises even me.

I need not say that my connection with cricket has been close as well as prolonged. I have been in the thick of it from my childhood, living among cricketers and cricket enthusiasts, and taking an active part in what I may call the "politics" of the game. My closest ties have, of course, been with Gloucestershire cricket, but I have played at different times for South Wales, for the Marylebone Cricket Club, for the Gentlemen of England, for the United South, for the South of England, and for England. I have played on almost every important cricket-ground in the country, and on most of them have had the pleasure—for it is a pleasure—of scoring a hundred. Once I accompanied a team to Canada and America, and twice I have captained an English team in Australia. Wherever I have played I have found cricketers the best of good fellows and the truest of sportsmen. There is something in cricket, I think, which brings out the best elements of a man's nature. Perhaps my enthusiasm for the game tempts me to exaggerate its virtuous influences, but I certainly believe that no sport cultivates the manly attributes better than cricket. The conditions under which it is played, the absence of occasion for passion, the freedom from the gambling spirit, the confidence it engenders between men, the good fellowship it inspires, and the friendships which spring from participation in the game—all these combine to give cricket a unique place among sports.

I have had some curious experiences. Once, in Canada, I played in the dark, when it was next to impossible to see the ball ; once in Boston I played on a wicket which was a veritable quagmire ; and once in Australia I played on a cricket-ground whose surface would be put to shame by a decent macadam road in England. Only once I played under a *nom de plume*. It was in the sixties, before the appearance of my photograph in illustrated papers had made my features public property. At that time, on my frequent visits to London, I often stayed with some relatives in the neighbourhood of Tufnell Park. Once, when I was visiting there, William Absolon, who was captain of a club at Islington, invited me to play for him at Stratford against the Eastern Counties Club. On the way they said to me, "You must not let on that you are W. G. Grace, or they will object to your playing." Consequently I was put down as Mr. Green. I happened to be in good form and had scored 118 before my identity was accidentally disclosed. Then Ted Pooley, who afterwards became the famous Surrey wicket-keeper, casually strolled upon the ground, and someone said to him, "That fellow Green is knocking the bowling about all over the place." "No wonder," said Pooley, "it's Mr. Grace." That's the only time I ever tried to play *incognito*.

What a book could be written on the humours of cricket ! The game breeds some curious characters, or at least some curious characters find their way into the cricket-field : wags, wits, practical jokers, and humorists. Tom Emmett was one of them. His ready tongue was equal to any emergency, and his wit was always a match for any joker who took Tom in hand.

A hundred good stories are told of Tom Emmett. One of the best was an incident that happened to myself. I have told it before, but it bears repetition. I had been up to Edinburgh for a medical examination, and hurried back to London to play in an M.C.C. match. As I was walking towards Lord's Ground I overtook Emmett, who was also playing in the match. He knew why I had been to Edinburgh, and asked how I had got on. " Oh, all right, Tom," I said, " I have got my diploma," pointing to the roll I was carrying in my hand. The wicket that day was very wet, and when I was batting, Emmett, who was fielding at cover-point, slipped and fell backwards in trying to stop a hard hit of mine. As he seemed slow in getting to his feet I asked if he had hurt himself. " No," he said, as he pointed to an extensive mud mark on his trousers, " but I have got my diploma."

Then there was Martin McIntyre, a man whose good temper saved him from no end of scoldings. When he was out in Australia with my first team he fell a victim to Colonial hospitality, and I found on calling at his hotel late one night that Martin was still out. As I had insisted, as captain, that everyone in the team should go to bed early in view of the big match next day, I was annoyed, and prepared a sharp reproof for McIntyre. But when next morning I walked towards him on the field, Martin, who apparently expected a wigging, sealed my lips by saying, " It's all right, sir ; McIntyre has given himself a good talking to, and he says it won't happen again." I had to laugh, and then it was no use letting off my reproof. Poor McIntyre ! how he did enjoy himself on those up-country rough Australian wickets. His apologetic smile, when one of his fast balls knocked a batsman over, was simply beyond description. And then there was Edward Pooley, the good old wicket-keeper, who did not like having his hands damaged by fast bowling, and who always went with me to survey the wicket when the United South were playing a match, and invariably put on a knowing look and said, "A slow bowler's wicket to-day, sir," no matter what condition the ground was in. Another character of the cricket-field was William Barnes, the great Nottingham all-round professional, whose faculty for getting out of scrapes was remarkable. It is hard to believe that " Barney," as we called him, is dead, for even last year he was as full of life as ever. The cricket-field has still its bright spirits—though these old characters are gone—and will always have them, I hope.

Cricketing Reminiscences

CHAPTER I

EARLY RECOLLECTIONS

I HAVE frequently been asked if I was born a cricketer. I do not think so, because I believe that cricketers are made by coaching and practice, and that nerve, eyesight, physique and patience, although necessary, would not be of much use alone. Hereditary instinct is helpful, because it would be absurd to deny that successful cricketers often run in families. There are, for instance, the Austen Leighs, of whom five used to play at the same time for the Gentlemen of Berkshire ; the Lytteltons, seven of whom represented Eton ; and the Walkers, of whom six at one time or another appeared in the Gentlemen's Eleven v. Players. There are also the Rowleys, the Steels, the Studds, the Palairets, and the Fosters, to mention only a few of the most famous.

But if I was not born a cricketer, I was born in the atmosphere of cricket. My father, who was a keen sportsman, was full of enthusiasm for the game, while my mother took even more interest in all that concerned cricket and cricketers. When I was not much taller than a wicket I used to wonder what were the hard cuts, leg hits, and long drives, about which my father and brothers were constantly talking. As far back as I can remember cricket was a common theme of conversation at home, and there was great excitement in the house when some big match was coming off in the neighbourhood.

My father, Henry Mills Grace, was a Somersetshire man, but in 1831 he settled down as a doctor at Downend, a quiet village about four miles out of Bristol. He had a large practice, extending over an extensive radius, and the calls upon his time left him but little leisure for cricket. In those days few villages had cricket clubs of their own, and for a time my father had to content himself with occasional glimpses of the matches that took place at Clifton and Bristol. As his boys grew up he naturally wished to provide them with healthy, enjoyable recreation. He anticipated modern schoolmasters in the belief that it is wise to superintend boys' games as carefully as their lessons. So he prepared a cricket pitch on the lawn of Downend House, where my elder brothers laid the foundation of their cricketing careers. My father was one of the leading sportsmen in the district, and though a busy, hard-working man, he found time to indulge in a little cricket in the summer, and hunting in the winter. He was a friend of the Duke of Beaufort, father of the late Duke, and paid frequent visits to Badminton when hunting. He took great care that the foxes were preserved, and was so strict that he used to say that a man who would kill a fox would commit almost any crime. Right up to his death, at the age of sixty-three, he hunted every winter. He was a most abstemious man, never smoked, and drank nothing except a glass of wine with his dinner and a little whiskey and water at night. Curiously enough, all his sons took after him in one respect—we were all non-smokers. I ought to say that my brother, Alfred, who has been in the habit of hunting three or four days in the week with the Duke of Beaufort's or Fitz-hardinge's hounds, has acquired the habit of smoking at the covert-side. But we chaff him, and tell him he is a poor performer—so far as tobacco is concerned ; but he cannot be beaten in following the hounds across country.

It was my father who took the initiative in establishing the Mangotsfield Cricket Club, which was composed of people from the neighbouring villages, and played on Rodway Hill Common, just above the present Mangotsfield Station. About this time Mr. H. Hewitt, who was as keen a sportsman as my father, formed the West Gloucestershire Club, which played at Coalpit Heath. Both clubs soon became well known, but were eventually amalgamated, keeping the

name of West Gloucestershire, but playing at
Rodway Hill.   My mother's brother, Alfred
Pocock, was an enthusiastic member of the old
Mangotsfield Club, and taught me all my early
cricket.

My earliest recollections of any cricket match
are connected with a visit which William Clarke's
All England team paid to Bristol in 1854.   Clarke's
combination used to travel about the country,
playing matches against eighteen or twenty-two
players of different districts.   In this way a great
deal was done to stimulate interest in cricket, as
a visit from the All England team was a red-letter
day wherever they went.   My father organised
this match, and captained the local twenty-two.
The game took place in a field behind the Full
Moon Hotel, Stokes Croft, Bristol, and I remember
driving in to see the ground which my father's
gardener and several other men were preparing.
It was originally a ridge and furrow field, and
had been specially re-laid in the previous autumn.
The pitch was first rate, but the rest of the ground
was rough and uneven.   I was with my mother,
who sat in her pony-carriage all day.   I don't
remember much about the cricket, but I recollect
that some of the England team played in top hats.
My mother was very enthusiastic, and watched
every ball.   She preserved cuttings of the newspaper reports of this and most other matches, and
took great care of the score books.   I have several
of her scrap-books, with the cuttings pasted in,
and very useful I find them, because in those

days " Wisden's Annual" was not in existence,
and no proper record was kept. I see from the
score-book that my eldest brother, Henry, and
my Uncle Pocock played besides my father.

The All England brought down a first-class
team, consisting of A. Clark; Bickley, who was a
grand bowler ; S. Parr; Caffyn, the great Surrey
man ; George Parr, the famous Nottingham
cricketer ; Julius Cæsar, of Surrey fame, and one
of the very best all round cricketers of his day ;
George Anderson, the genial Yorkshireman, one
of the finest hitters of his time ; Box, the celebrated wicket-keeper ; J. B. Marshall, who was
a great supporter of cricket ; Edgar Willsher,
of Kent ; and W. Clarke, the slow underhand
bowler—most of whose names are still famous in
the annals of cricket. It is doubtful whether nine
men out of the eleven could have been excelled,
and as was only to be expected, the West
Gloucestershire twenty-two were beaten—by 149
runs.

I cannot recall any more cricket until the next
year, when almost the same team came down and
played a second match on the same ground. This
year my brother, E. M., played. W. Clarke, who
acted as secretary and manager of the All England Eleven, was present, but did not play, as his
eyes were troubling him. What makes me remember his presence was that after the match he
came up to E. M. and gave him a bat, because he
had long-stopped so well upon the rough ground.
E. M., who was only fourteen at the time, came

specially from school at Long Ashton to play in
the match, and everybody congratulated him.   It
was a great thing then to have a bat given you by
one of the All England players, and E. M. put it
up in front of the pony-carriage with great pride.
I see from the score-sheet that E. M. was given
out leg before wicket. I wonder if he was satisfied with the decision ?   In the first innings my
brother Henry was top scorer with 13, and in the
second my father with 16.   Uncle Pocock made
15.   There were no other double figures reached
by the West Gloucestermen, who made 48 in the
first innings and 78 in the second.   The fielding
ground was very rough, but the wicket was good,
as may be seen by the scores of the All England.
Julius Cæsar made 33 and 78 off his own bat.   Of
course, the All England team won again—this
time by a hundred and sixty-five.

The next thing I remember was a cricket week
in 1858 and 1859 at Badminton, the Duke of Beaufort's residence.   The celebrated I Zingari team
was invited down and played three matches—
v. Cirencester, Kingscote Club, and Gentlemen of
Gloucester.   In 1858 the Hon. Spencer Ponsonby
(now the Hon. Spencer Ponsonby-Fane) was
playing for the I Zingari, and so was Mr. J. L.
Baldwin, the founder of the club.   Next year Mr.
Harvey Fellows, the famous fast bowler, was one
of the team, and Mr. R. A. Fitzgerald, with whom
I went to Canada in 1872.

We drove over, and I remember that the Duke
entertained us very hospitably.   I also recollect

that the Duke was at that time training five couple of hounds for a match (which, however, never came off) of "horses against hounds." The hounds were to run against three horses carrying eight stone seven over the Beacon Course of four miles at Newmarket.

I learned the rudiments of cricket when quite a child. As small boys we played about the garden in a rough and ready way, and used to make the nurses bowl to us. In 1850 my father had moved from Downend House to the " Chestnuts," which was a great improvement, because it had two orchards, and the grounds were larger. My father laid out a cricket pitch in one of the orchards, which E. M., who was already a keen cricketer, improved by his own efforts. My father, my brother Henry, and my uncle Pocock practised at every spare moment, and we youngsters fielded for them from the time we could run about. Then they would give us a few balls, so I soon learned how to handle a bat. Uncle Pocock took special pains with me, and helped me a great deal, by insisting on my playing with an upright bat, even as a child. I soon got so fond of the game that I took every opportunity of playing, and when I couldn't play proper cricket, I used to chalk a wicket on a wall and get a stable-boy and one or two youngsters from the village to join me. So I got some sort of practice —sometimes with a broom-handle instead of a bat. We played all the year round, and at all hours of the day. I consider that a great deal

of my quickness of eye is due to the fact that the
boys with whom I played bowled a very large
proportion of fast underhand " daisy cutters,"
which used to jump about in a most erratic way,
and needed a lot of watching.   I also played fives,
a game which is good practice for the eye during
the winter months.

When I was at boarding-school cricket was
encouraged by the masters, and I used to play as
often as possible.   Then I began playing for the
West Gloucestershire Club, in which my father
was the leading spirit.   Of course, I used to go in
last, and if I got a run or two I thought I was
very lucky.   As early as 1857 I played three or
four innings for the West Gloucestershire Club.
I was then only a boy of nine, and I couldn't be
expected to do very much against the elevens we
played, which were composed of grown-up men.
As I grew older I played oftener, and in 1859 had
eleven innings, which realised twelve runs.

The year 1860 marks an epoch in my cricket
career.   On the 19th and 20th of July (I was then
in my twelfth year), I was selected to play for
West Gloucestershire against Clifton, which was
a keen rival of my father's club, and one of the
crack teams in our neighbourhood, as it is to-day.
I mention that particular match, because it was
the occasion of the first score I remember making.
I went in eighth (my brother E. M., who at this
time was in rare form, had already made 150, and
my Uncle Pocock 44) and added 35 before stumps
were drawn. My father and mother were delighted,

and both were very proud next day when I carried my score on to 51. I do not think my greatest efforts have ever given me more pleasure than that first big innings. In that year I had four innings, and made 82 runs. My average came down a good deal in 1861, when I played ten innings, and made only 46 runs, but it looked up a little the next season with five innings and 53 runs. But it was not until 1863 that I began to score with any consistency. That year was really the beginning of my serious cricket, for then I played in most of the West Gloucestershire matches. In 19 innings I made 350 runs, not against schoolboys, but against the best gentlemen cricketers of that time, many of them 'Varsity men, and capital players.

One of the most extraordinary matches I ever played in took place about this time. The story has been told before, but I think it will bear re-telling. My eldest brother Henry, who was in practice as a doctor at Kingswood Hill, was captain of a small club at Hanham, and frequently asked me to go over and play in matches against neighbouring village clubs. Over these matches a good deal of feeling usually sprang up, and not a little jealousy existed between the clubs. Victory was a great thing on the one hand, and defeat often a source of much annoyance on the other. My brother arranged a match between Hanham and Bitton, a village about a mile away. The Bitton team, knowing that we had a good eleven, secured some strangers, including one or two of the best men from Bristol, to help them. My brother E. M. put his cricket bag in the carriage, and came with us, pretending that we might be one short. When we arrived at the ground the captain of the Bitton eleven was delighted at E. M.'s appearance, and said, "Teddy, I am glad you've come. I think we shall give them a beating to-day." Without letting us know, E. M. had promised to play for the other side.

It was a wet day, and the wicket was very soft, but we commenced the match, and our side got the worst of it, E. M. taking most of the wickets. When the Bitton men went in a second time they wanted only ten runs to win the match. As E. M. went out to take his place at the wicket an old friend said, "I haven't seen a good hit to-day." E. M. laughingly replied, "All right, I'll show you one. I'll win the match with one hit." He tried to carry out his promise, and was bowled first ball by a shooter. We were glad to get E. M. out so cheaply, but never thought we had the remotest chance of winning the match. However, we began to feel very jubilant when three or four more wickets fell one after another without a single run being made. Some of the Bristol men had changed their clothes, thinking they would not have to bat. We chaffingly called out, "You had better get ready. You'll be wanted yet." Sure enough they were but they only walked to the wickets to walk back again. Only one man scored at all. He made three, and just when he looked like winning the match for them an excited partner ran him out. As the result of the match was now hanging in the balance the excitement became tremendous, especially as the Bitton men scored three off a bye. Ultimately, we got the whole eleven out for six, and so won the match by three runs. It was one of the closest finishes I ever saw.

But while I was making a local reputation, my brother E. M., who was seven years my senior, was doing great things all over the country. He was at his very best, and was making some wonderful scores. His first appearance in the Canterbury week made a great sensation. My father and mother always went to stay with friends at Canterbury during the cricket week, which in the sixties was even more interesting than it is now. While they were at Canterbury the secretary told my father that he was one man short, and asked him to let E. M. play. My father pointed out that it was scarcely worth while bringing him all the way from Gloucestershire for one match, but promised to send for him on condition that he was also allowed to play in the M.C.C. match. This request was acceded to, and E. M. was telegraphed for. He got to Canterbury on the second day just in time to have his innings, but he made a duck. In the second innings he retrieved his failure by scoring 56, which was described as a very fine performance.

This match was over at half-past two. In those days three matches were played, and as soon as one was over the next was commenced. Before the M.C.C. match commenced there was a slight dispute, some of the Kent players objecting to E. M. playing for M.C.C. as he was not then a member. The Kent secretary was away from the ground, but soon returned and explained that he had given leave for E. M. to play in the match. E. M. carried his bat through the M.C.C. innings for 192 not out, and took every single wicket in Kent's second innings. Some of the Kent cricketers may have wished their secretary had not been so generous, but all were probably delighted with E. M.'s magnificent play. Earl Sefton, President of the M.C.C., presented him with a bat to commemorate the occasion. His bowling exploit was rewarded by the Hon. Spencer Ponsonby (who had played against E. M. at Badminton), who sent him the identical ball mounted on an ebony stand with the following inscription on a silver plate :—

WITH THIS BALL
(PRESENTED BY M.C.C. TO E. M. GRACE),
HE GOT EVERY WICKET IN 2ND INNINGS, IN THE
MATCH PLAYED AT CANTERBURY,
AUGUST 14, 15, 1862,
GENTLEMEN OF KENT v. M.C.C.,
FOR WHOM HE PLAYED AS AN EMERGENCY, AND
IN WHICH, GOING IN FIRST,
HE SCORED
192 NOT OUT.

A score of 118 in the same year, made at Lord's

for South Wales against the M.C.C., established
E. M.'s reputation in first-class cricket, and at
that time he was as well known on cricket grounds
all over the country as I am now.

In 1863 I was selected as one of the 22 to
represent Bristol and District against the All
England team. I remember the match very well
—it was made memorable to me by a generous
act by Tarrant, the famous bowler. I was to go
in tenth, but the luncheon hour arrived just
before my turn came to bat. During the interval
Tarrant gave me a little practice. Curiously
enough, he was bowling when I opened my
innings. Whether I had got my eye in during
the luncheon hour, or whether he was kind
enough to send me down one or two loose balls
by way of encouragement, I don't know ; but I
knocked him about so freely that he was taken off,
and Tinley went on with underhands. Now at
that time I had a distinct partiality for lobs, and
I welcomed Tinley by sending his first ball to
the boundary. In trying to do the same with the
next I hit over it and was clean bowled. My
score of 32 made me quite a hero for the rest of
the season.

Another curious thing happened in that match.
In the second innings E. Stephenson (known as
the Yorkshire Stephenson, to distinguish him
from H. H. Stephenson, the celebrated Surrey
cricketer) came in and made a slight stand.
E. M., who was captain, gave the ball to me, and
said, " Pitch him one or two well up, and I'll go

and catch him in the long field." I followed
instructions, and Stephenson hit the very first
ball straight to E. M., who never dropped a catch
in those days. On that occasion the English
team had to follow on, and were ultimately beaten
by an innings and 20 runs.

It is perhaps interesting to record that this
match was played on Durdham Down, as was
the Gloucestershire and Devonshire match the
year before, and our first real County Match *v.*
Surrey in 1870. As the Down is an open
common no charge could be made to spectators.
Flags were put up to mark the boundary, and we
had no pavilion. In those days we had to dress
and lunch in tents. That was considered no hard-
ship in the sixties and seventies, though perhaps
we should regard it differently now. I sometimes
think that the modern conditions of cricket are
too luxurious. County cricket is made too
much of a business, and some of the best
elements of the game have consequently been
eliminated.

In 1863, George Parr took out an eleven to
Australia. E. M. went and did fairly, though he
was not at all well when he landed (which he
attributed to ship diet, not then as luxurious
as voyagers now enjoy), and was, moreover,
hampered by a whitlow on his finger, which
prevented him doing himself justice. While out
there he and Tarrant played—and won easily—
several single-wicket matches, which excited a
lot of interest. E. M. remained in Australia

longer than the rest of the team, and did not come back till the middle of the summer.

His absence in Australia gave me my first opportunity to play in a really big match. My brother Henry and I were invited to join in the annual tour of the South Wales team. I do not know what was my qualification for playing for South Wales, but we didn't trouble much about qualification in those days. Only a few weeks ago I had a letter from a gentleman saying that he played with me for the South Wales against Middlesex on the old county ground at Islington, and remarking that he never could tell why he played for South Wales, because up to then he had never been in Wales. He is not the only cricketer who could claim the same negative qualification for playing in that combination. Still, most of the players came from the West Country, and after all my brother and I were only divided from Wales by the Severn.

We came to London to play, and I made my first appearance at Kennington Oval on July 12, 1864. I secured four wickets in the first innings, and made 5 and 38 with the bat. After the Kennington match the captain of the South Wales told my brother that he didn't want me to play in the next match, which was at Brighton. Then, as now, it was always easier to get men to play at seaside resorts than in the provincial towns, and the Hove ground has always been very popular. But my brother Henry would not have me left out of the Brighton match, and insisted that I should play. I did, and went in first wicket down. When I had made 170 in the first innings and not-out 56 in the second, the captain did not repent that I had been included in the team. That was my first notable achievement away from home. The match was against the Gentlemen of Sussex, for whom those fine old cricketers, E. and W. Napper, were playing. Mr. W. Napper has often told me since that he ought to have captured my wicket, because when I had cut him three times to the boundary off successive balls he bowled me another which I also cut (but through Point's hands) to the boundary. Mr. Napper still thinks that Point ought to have taken that chance.

I made my first appearance at Lord's a few days later (July 22, 1864), playing for South Wales against the M.C.C. and Ground. It is a curious coincidence that on that day the first important match, Kent v. Notts, was played at the Crystal Palace, Sydenham, and now, thirty-five years later, I am arranging for more big matches on the same ground. I went in first wicket down and made 50. Mr. J. J. Sewell, father of Mr. C. O. H. Sewell, who now plays for Gloucestershire, was one of the South Wales eleven. He was a fine cricketer, a hard hitter, and a capital fieldsman in any position, but especially at coverpoint.

Mr. J. J. Sewell was a native of Cirencester, Gloucestershire, and went to school at Marlborough College, for which he played from 1860

to 1862. In the latter year he went in first against
Rugby at Lord's, and was top scorer with 50 out of
110. Marlborough won by an innings and 17 runs.
This was the fifth match between the two schools,
but the first which was won by Marlborough.
Mr. B. B. Cooper, who was captain of Rugby
afterwards, used to go in first with me for the
Gentlemen v. Players.

In 1862 Gloucestershire played Devonshire on
Durdham Down. This was the first county
match ever played in Bristol. Mr. Sewell and
my brother E. M. went in first and made 113
before they were parted, E. M. scoring 57 and
Sewell 65. Gloucestershire won by an innings.
Subsequently Mr. Sewell played for Middlesex,
and a few years later went to South Africa. It
will be remembered that his son came over with
the South African team in 1894, and, staying in
England to study the law, played for Gloucestershire. The local paper commented on the above-
mentioned Gloucestershire v. Devonshire match
as follows :—

" The county has thus made a good beginning,
and we hope they will long retain the laurels they
have so gallantly won, and who knows but in
time they may be fit antagonists for Cambridge,
Yorkshire, Kent, and even for Surrey itself. It
may appear presumptuous to speculate thus, but
we believe there is plenty of good stuff in the
district." The prophecy may have been presumptuous; however, in ten years we were not
only " fit antagonists " for the other counties, but

in 1876 and 1877 we reached the top of the tree, not losing a single match in either year.

Though the Gloucestershire County Club did not play regularly until 1870, my father frequently got up inter-county matches before that time. Those matches have never been generally chronicled, but they were played for five or six years, before first-class county cricket was established.

CHAPTER II

CRICKET IN THE SIXTIES

IT is no exaggeration to say that between 1860 and 1870 English cricket passed through its most critical period. The game itself was then in a transition stage, and it was quite a revolutionary period so far as its rules were concerned. A good deal of jealousy existed between the All England Eleven and the United Eleven, and there was constant bickering between the North and the South. Numerous schisms led to the display of much ill-feeling, and to a considerable extent jeopardised the progress of the rapidly expanding popularity of the game. Combinations and strikes among cricketers were almost painfully frequent. The unsatisfactory character of the law as to no-balling was a source of grievance until the law which forbade a bowler to raise his arm above his shoulder was amended, so that it merely prohibited the ball being jerked or thrown. This removed an obnoxious restriction and in a measure led to a complete metamorphosis in bowling.

It was during this decade that fast round-

arm bowling reached its highest point of perfection. Fast underhand bowling was just going
out as I began to play first-class cricket, and
Tarrant, Willsher, and Jackson—that remarkable
trio of formidable fast bowlers—were in the
heyday of their strength. Tarrant, who played
for Cambridgeshire, was generally known as
"Tear 'um," because he took such a long run
before delivering a ball, and gave himself the
appearance of ferocity. He was in every way
a remarkable bowler. His deliveries were very
straight and very fast—quite as fast, if not
faster, than Tom Richardson's. Jackson was a
native of Bungay, in Suffolk, but always played
for Nottingham. He was one of the few men,
not born in the county, who have played for
Nottingham, which has always loyally en-
deavoured to adhere to the birth qualification.
Jackson, like Tarrant, was a right-hand bowler.
He bowled at a great pace, the peculiarity of his
delivery being the extraordinary rapidity with
which the ball rose after striking the ground.
Although he did not take so long a run, or give
the impression of such a terrific speed as Tarrant
did, many people thought he was the faster
bowler. The fact was his delivery was very
deceptive, and batsmen new to his bowling were
often astounded and baffled by its actual pace.
That, indeed, was the secret of his success.
Willsher, who was a Kent man, was a left-
handed fast bowler, with a high action. His
delivery was the subject of much discussion,

and it was due to the fact that he was " no-
balled " that the rule was amended. He was one
of the most difficult left-hand bowlers that I have
ever had to play against. On bad wickets all
these three bowlers were almost absolutely unplayable.

The introduction of fast round-arm bowling had
led to some important changes in the arrangement
of the field. The fast bowlers gained the upper hand
over the batsmen, and most of the runs scored off
their bowling were made behind the wicket. Consequently, when they were bowling it was not
necessary to put fieldsmen in the long-field.
E. M. was almost the first to play out at the fast
round-arm bowling. Having a wonderful eye he
could hit forward the swiftest balls, and as he
constantly drove them over the bowler's head,
fieldsmen had again to be placed in the long-field.
When I began to play in first-class cricket, I
followed the same tactics.

During this decade, too, important clubs began
to pay special attention to the condition of their
grounds. Up to this time many of the principal
grounds were so rough as to be positively dangerous to play upon, and batsmen were constantly
damaged by the fast bowling. When the wickets
were in this condition the batsmen had to look
out for shooters, and leave the bumping balls to
look after themselves. In the sixties it was no
unusual thing to have two or three shooters in an
over ; nowadays you scarcely get one shooter in
a season. At this time the Marylebone ground

was in a very unsatisfactory condition—so unsatisfactory that in 1864 Sussex refused to play at Lord's owing to the roughness of the ground. When I first played there the creases were not chalked out, but were actually cut out of the turf one inch deep, and about one inch wide. As matches were being frequently played, and no pains were taken to fill up the holes, it is quite easy to imagine what a terrible condition the turf presented. Happily, the idea of cutting out the creases did not prevail for long. If I am not mistaken, the experiment was only tried for one season and then abandoned.

The period of reform and improvement at Lord's began, I think, in 1863, when my old friend R. A. Fitzgerald was elected honorary secretary of the M.C.C. Mr. Fitzgerald became paid secretary in 1868, and held the post of secretary thirteen years, resigning it on the ground of ill-health in 1877. An assiduous and energetic official, he initiated numerous improvements, both as regards the ground and the management of the club. His popularity may be judged from the fact that when he became secretary the membership of the M.C.C. was 651, while when he resigned it was 2080. In the year after his appointment (1864) a portion of Lord's ground (about 80 yards by 40) was levelled and returfed, and the whole premises were thoroughly repaired. That was the year in which the M.C.C. had a Jubilee match to celebrate fifty years' occupation of the present ground. In the evening Mr. Fitzgerald

presided at a dinner given in the pavilion to celebrate the occasion, when about forty gentlemen
were present. In 1865 two new wings were added
to the pavilion, and the roof was altered so that
spectators could view the match from that coign
of vantage. In every respect Lord's was improved,
although many years elapsed before the ground
attained its present state of perfection. Wickets
at the Oval were always much better than at Lord's,
where the clay in the soil has always handicapped
the ground men. It may surprise some people who
admire the existing green sward at Marylebone
when I say that within my recollection I could go
on to the pitch at Lord's and pick up a handful of
small pieces of gravel. That was very detrimental
to the wickets, as a ball would sometimes hit one
of the small stones and fly high in the air.

To show how crude the arrangements at Lord's
were in the old days, I may mention that it was
not until 1865 that the scorers were provided with
a covered box in which to do their work. Up to
that year the two unfortunate men had been
perched on high seats without any protection
whatever from sun or rain. Originally, of course,
in the early days of primitive cricket, scores were
kept by the cutting of notches in a stick, and the
scorers usually squatted themselves somewhere
near the umpire.

There were no fixed boundaries at Lord's when
I first played there. If the ball struck the pavilion
railings a four was allowed — although even
that rule was suspended one year — but every

other hit had to be run out. The institution of
boundaries came about in a curious way. As
interest in cricket extended and deepened the
crowds attending the matches increased rapidly.
Occasionally a ball would be hit among the
spectators, who would open to let it pass through
them, but often close again immediately. Fieldsmen frequently found it difficult to get through
the crowd to the ball. On one occasion Mr.
A. N. Hornby was out in the long-field at
Lord's, when a ball was driven among the spectators. As everybody knows, the Lancashire
amateur was a very energetic fieldsman, and as
he dashed after the ball he scattered the crowd
in all directions. One poor old gentleman, not
being sufficiently alert to get out of the way, was
thrown on his back and rather severely hurt.
The incident opened the eyes of the authorities
to the necessity for better regulations, and as the
result a boundary line was instituted. The good
example set by the M.C.C. in the matter of the
improvement of Lord's ground was followed by
other influential clubs, and a general system of all-
round reform became the order of the day.

Just about the time when I came to the front
in first-class cricket, a somewhat discreditable
intrigue was attempted against the M.C.C. It
was, in fact, an attempt to supersede the authority
of the club as the law-giving authority of the
cricket world—a position it has held ever since
the Hambledon Club was dissolved about 1791.
A proposal, emanating from the columns of the

Sporting Life, was made to institute a Cricket Parliament. It was suggested that the time had come when some more comprehensive and responsible form of government than that which had hitherto existed for the regulation of the national game had become necessary. It was argued that when the M.C.C. took upon itself the responsibility of being lawgiver for cricket the game was confined to a few of the Southern counties, and that as cricket had gradually extended to the North and was becoming popular all over the country, the *régime* of the M.C.C. ought to come to an end. To legislate for the vast cricket-playing community was, it was suggested, too great a task for a single club, such as the M.C.C., and the proposal was made that the onus of regulating the game should be put upon the shoulders of a more extended, responsible, and differently constituted assembly, to be composed of practical and business men from every part of the United Kingdom, who should be elected by the voice of their respective constituencies, and should have the opportunity periodically of discussing openly and dispassionately all matters and things appertaining to the game.

The actual proposal was that a Parliament should be established, to consist of an unlimited number of members, who should be elected annually or otherwise as might be thought expedient, and who should have power to frame a general code of rules and to make all necessary by-laws. This led to a long discussion, which occupied the columns of the *Sporting Life* for some time, and gave a number of would-be reformers (who in most cases were careful to write under a *nom de plume*) an opportunity to air imaginary grievances against the M.C.C. Of course this was nothing but an attack upon the Marylebone Club, but happily for cricket the agitation collapsed, and the proposal came to nothing.

Nothing is easier than to get up an agitation of this kind, but it is lucky for the game of cricket that this and other attempts to overthrow the M.C.C. have been futile. One ground of complaint emphasised by the agitators was that the M.C.C. did not, even at Lord's, enforce the laws which it promulgated. As far as my experience goes this was a distinct mistake, because at Lord's the laws are always carried out to the letter. There is less time wasted between the innings at Lord's than there is at any other important ground. Play always begins punctually at Marylebone, and the regulations are rigidly adhered to. Of course the one vexed question concerning the law prohibiting throwing has caused trouble at Lord's, but the interpretation of that law is a matter of opinion — one cricketer or umpire regarding as perfectly fair bowling what another would condemn as throwing.

My own personal feeling is that the laws and regulations of cricket generally could not have been entrusted to better hands than those of the M.C.C. The club has always set a high standard to the cricket world, and has never refused to consider reasonable suggestions from responsible cricketers. It has acted with the impartiality of the High Court of Appeal, and has always safeguarded the best interests of the game, without unduly interfering with the rights and liberties of cricketers, individually or collectively. In cricket the classical maxim that he governs best who governs least applies as completely as it does in national life. A judicious conservatism—born of a dread of change which is not improvement—has always guided the counsels of the M.C.C., and if it had done nothing else than successfully resist some of the ridiculous proposals which have from time to time been noisily advocated, it would have done splendid service to our national game. If the M.C.C. had listened to the agitations which have been sprung upon it during the last thirty years there would have been continual alteration of the rules, and finality or fixity would have been impossible. Legislative tinkering would have been fatal to cricket, and the M.C.C. has, I think, shown its wisdom by throwing its influence against precipitate action.

The years 1865 and 1866 stand out in my memory as especially eventful. In the former year an interesting match was played at Bath between eighteen of the Lansdowne Club (one of the oldest in the district) and the United All England Eleven, which was a rival combination to William Clarke's All England team. The scene of the match was the Sydenham Fields, Bath, and the wicket was pitched on land now occupied by the Midland

Railway Goods Station.   E. M., who was batting
this season with particular vigour and freedom,
played a grand innings of 121.   He got well hold
of one ball, and knocked it clean into the river ; but
he was eventually magnificently caught at long leg
by G. M. Kelson, the well-known Kent amateur, who
was playing for the Eleven.   The All England
scored 99 and 87.   A peculiar point about the
match was that my brothers, E. M. and Henry, and
myself took every wicket in both innings.   E. M.'s
score of 121 was almost an epoch-making event,
as such achievements against the All England
team were almost unheard of.

One of my best matches, as far as bowling is
concerned, was an encounter between the Gentlemen of the South of England and the Players of
the South, which took place at the Oval the same
year.   The Oval is a ground on which I would
always much rather bat than bowl, but on this
occasion Mr. I. D. Walker and myself took all the
wickets between us.   In the first innings Walker
took four and I got five ; in the second, Walker
captured two, and I secured the remaining eight.
I have a memento of this match still, for the
Surrey Club had the ball mounted and inscribed,
and presented it to me.   E. M. did not play on
that occasion owing to ill-health.

It was at the Oval, on September 28, 29 and
30, that a memorable incident occurred, in a
match between eighteen Gentlemen of the South
of England and the United South of England
Eleven, which was played for the benefit of the

bowlers connected with the Kennington ground. Jupp, who was the stonewaller of the time, was batting, and the bowlers were all perplexed as to how to get him out.   Both Mr. I. D. Walker and E. M. had been bowling lobs for some time without any success, when E. M. said : " I'll give him a high toss."   So saying, he bowled a high underhand ball, which soared right over Jupp's head, and fell on the top of the bail.   This incident caused a considerable sensation.   The spectators expressed their dissatisfaction very freely, and for a little while it looked as if there was going to be a riot.   Some of them called out to Jupp not to go out, and it looked as if blows were going to be exchanged.   One or two of the Gentlemen armed themselves with wickets as weapons of defence. The game was suspended for some time, but eventually the troubled waters were calmed, and the innings was resumed.   While I do not think it was wise to bowl such a ball, there was nothing in the rules to forbid it, and so, of course, it was perfectly fair.   The extraordinary part of the episode was that the ball should fall on the wicket. I suppose such a thing would not occur once in a thousand times.

It was the custom of the Surrey Club in the sixties to give a bat to any one who made 50 runs in a first-class match at the Oval.   On this occasion, E. M. made 64 and 56, and so had a couple of bats presented to him.   It was announced that these made the seventy-fifth bat with which he had been presented up to that time.

The year 1866 was one of my greatest scoring seasons in the early days of my cricket. I made 173 not out for The Gentlemen of the South v. The Players, and 224 not out against Surrey, whilst playing for England.

It was in 1866 that I played for the first time at Sheffield. The occasion was an interesting one also, because it afforded me my first experience of captaining an important team. The people of Sheffield were very anxious for E. M. to pay them a visit, but as he was studying medicine at the time and couldn't go he suggested that they should invite me in his stead. The suggestion was adopted, and the match was played on the Hyde Park ground at Sheffield. The ground stood on the top of a high hill, and I began to despair of the cab ever getting to the top. I captained eighteen colts of Notts and Sheffield against the All England team. George Parr was playing and scored 20, all made off leg hits. Nowadays we get very little leg-hitting, as the bowling is more accurate, and bowlers keep the ball as much as possible on the off-side; but Parr was a past-master in the art of scoring on the leg side, and it was a perfect treat to see him playing balls to leg with his consummate ease and skill. I made nine runs in the first innings, and 36 (out of 91) in the second. George Atkinson and J. C. Shaw were bowling, and as the All England team were anxious to catch the train to get away to some other part of the country, they begged me to get out. But I didn't see throwing away my wicket

in those days. Since then I have made many a
big score at Bramall Lane, which I don't mind
confessing is one of my favourite grounds. It
got into a bad state some years ago, but they
are getting it back to its former condition of
excellence.

Towards the end of the sixties my youngest
brother, G. F. Grace, began to come into prominence. As a boy he had shown marvellous aptitude
for the game, and in local matches around Bristol
frequently made scores of a hundred and upwards while quite a youngster. At the age of
nine he performed a great feat, taking thirteen
wickets while playing in a small match against
grown-up men. In 1866 he made his *début* in
first-class cricket, by playing at Canterbury for
The South of the Thames *v.* The North of the
Thames. Two years later, when seventeen years
of age, he made his first appearance at Lord's,
playing for England against the M.C.C. and
Ground. In this match G. F. and I played for
England, while E. M. was one of the M.C.C.
team.

In 1866 the Gentlemen, for the first time since
the institution of the Gentlemen *v.* Players match
at the Oval, defeated the professionals. In celebration of the event, each member of the team
was presented with a bat by Mr. W. Burrup, who
was then Secretary of the Surrey Cricket Club.
It was his custom to give a bat to every gentleman who scored fifty or more at the Oval, and it
was always an interesting sight to see him standing

on the pavilion step, bat in hand, awaiting the
retiring batsman who was to be the recipient of
the honour.

The first time I ever scored a hundred in each
innings of a match was in August 1868, when I
played at Canterbury for the South of the Thames
against the North of the Thames, my contributions being 130 in the first innings and 102 in the
second. I may add that I have since repeated
this achievement on three occasions. Notwithstanding my big score in each innings I was on
the losing side. The Rev. J. M. (now Canon)
McCormick was among our opponents, and
rendered yeoman service with scores of 137 and
27.

I scored a hundred for the first time in this
bi-annual encounter in the Gentlemen v. Players
match at Lord's in 1868, my contribution being
134 (not out) out of a total of 201. In the same
year, which was one of my best early batting
seasons, I made scores of 210, 130, 111, and 103.

A record, which remained unbroken for thirteen years, was established in May 1868 by Mr.
E. F. S. Tylecote, a Clifton College boy, who, in a
big-side match (Classicals v. Moderns), scored
404 (not out). This wonderful performance,
which took the boy three afternoons to achieve,
held the record until July 1881, when Mr. W. N.
Roe, playing for Emmanuel College Long Vacation v. Caius College Long Vacation at Cambridge, made 415 (not out). Four years later this
colossal score was exceeded by Mr. J. S. Carrick,

who scored 419 (not out) for the West of Scotland *v.* Priory Park at Chichester. But Mr. Carrick's triumph was short-lived, as in the very next season Mr. A. E. Stoddart, the well-known Middlesex amateur, compiled the gigantic score of 485 for Hampstead *v.* the Stoics. Mr. Stoddart's innings still holds the record as the highest individual score ever made in any match.

A team of Australian aborigines, captained by Charley Lawrence, visited England in 1868. Lawrence, who had been one of H. H. Stephenson's team, which made the first visit of English cricketers to Australia, had stayed behind and taught the aborigines how to play cricket. The team went up and down the country, playing matches against clubs, including several of the Counties, and acquitted themselves very well. The best all-round player of the team was Mullagh, but one or two others showed conspicuous skill at the game. In addition to playing cricket, they generally gave exhibitions of boomerang throwing in the towns they visited.

On May 14, 1869, I first played for the M.C.C., of which I had some time previously been elected a member. The match was played on the old Magdalen ground at Oxford, and I celebrated my inclusion in the club team by scoring 117. Since that time I have scarcely ever failed to represent the M.C.C. in its most important matches, and have had the honour of captaining its eleven on occasions too numerous to mention.

The most remarkable run-getting match in

which, up to that time, I had ever taken a part,
was an encounter between the Gentlemen of the
South and the Players of the South, at the Oval
in July 1869. The Players batted first, sending
in Pooley and Jupp to open their innings. These
two put on 142 runs for the first wicket, and their
side kept possession of the wickets until the
middle of the second day. By this time they had
compiled 475 runs, Charlwood heading the score-
sheet with 155. Mr. B. B. Cooper, the old
Rugby captain, and I were deputed to open the
Gentlemen's innings, and made the great stand
which for many years remained the record for a
first-wicket score. For three and three-quarter
hours we defied the bowlers, scoring at the rate
of nearly a hundred runs an hour. Change
after change was made in the attack, and then as
a last resort Mantle, who was by far the worst
bowler on the field, was given the ball. The
result was a proof of the truism that any change
is better than no change at all, for in the course
of six balls Mantle was lucky enough to dismiss
both Cooper and me. Our partnership had
realised 283 runs; Cooper, who scored 101,
having made one six, two fives, and six fours,
while in my contribution of 180 I had hit two
sixes, one five, and ten fours. When play ended
on the second day, the score stood at 306 for
two wickets. Next day we carried the total on to
553 before our innings closed, Mr. I. D. Walker
having hit the bowling about and scored 90.
We thus topped our opponents' score by 78 runs

The Players, who had about an hour and a half's batting, made such good use of their time, that they had run up 108 for one wicket before time was called.   Altogether in this extraordinary match 1136 runs were scored off 548 overs for the loss of 21 wickets, the average per batsman being over 50.   During the match no less than 15 different bowlers tried their hands, but the wicket was all in favour of the batsmen, and scoring was comparatively easy.

In the last two years of the decade under review, county cricket began to take a prominent place, and to excite great interest.   Nottingham and Yorkshire led, with Surrey running them close and Lancashire, Kent, Sussex, and Middlesex following, in something like the order in which I have placed them.

CHAPTER III

WITH R. A. FITZGERALD'S TEAM IN CANADA

I WAS one of a team of twelve amateurs who, towards the close of the English cricket season of 1872, visited Canada under the ægis of Mr. R. A. Fitzgerald, who was then Secretary of the M.C.C. Early in the previous year two Canadian gentlemen—Captain N. Wallace, since then a member of the Gloucestershire team, and Mr. J. C. Patteson—invited Mr. Fitzgerald to organise an amateur team for a tour in the Dominion. The invitation was really given at the instigation of a number of Canadian clubs, and the hope was expressed that the team would also visit the United States, and play a few matches there. Mr. Fitzgerald consented to undertake the formation of a team, and approached a number of leading gentlemen cricketers—myself among the number—on the subject. After many discouragements and a good deal of persuasion "Fitz," as we called him, induced the following representative cricketers to make the tour: W. G. Grace, A. Lubbock, Edgar Lubbock, A. N. Hornby, Hon. G. Harris (now Lord Harris), A. Appleby (the well-known left-handed Lancashire bowler), W. H. Hadow, C. J. Ottaway, C. K. Francis (now one of the Metropolitan Stipendiary Magistrates), F. Pickering, and W. M. Rose. Mr. Fitzgerald captained and managed the tour, which was one of the pleasantest experiences of my life.

We met at Liverpool on August 8, 1872 (I had to leave Canterbury in the middle of the cricket week, so as to catch the boat), and just before sailing a number of gentlemen— well-known cricketers in the Liverpool district —entertained us at luncheon at the Adelphi Hotel. We left the Mersey that afternoon by the steamship *Sarmatian*, which was then the latest addition to the Allan Line fleet, and a fine comfortable ship too. She was making her second trip when we were among her passengers. After crossing the bar of the Mersey and getting off the coast of Ireland we took in mails and a few more passengers off Lough Foyle. Then the bad sailors began to feel the first effects of the Atlantic billows. Up to that point we had been a happy party, but for a day or two several of the team were in the throes of *mal-de-mer*, and made no appearance in the saloon. I think Harris and I were the worst victims, for before we were on deck again the others had got their sea-legs, and were in sufficiently good spirits to subject us to some merciless chaff when we sat in the leeward under a boat hanging in the davits. We both made up our minds that if the captain would only lower

a boat for us we would try to get back to old
England again. But the Atlantic behaved itself
in the most exemplary manner, and both Harris
and I threw off our sea-sickness and began to
enjoy the voyage. We were all greatly interested
in seeing some gigantic icebergs as we approached
the Newfoundland coast, but they were a long
way off, and we were very glad of it too, as icebergs are not pleasant things to encounter. None
of us were sorry when we got past the lighthouse
at Belle Isle and into the placid waters of the
St. Lawrence.

We reached Quebec on August 17, after making
the fastest passage of the year (2656 miles in nine
days one and a half hours) and one that has
seldom been beaten since. We were met at the
wharf by Mr. Patteson, who as I have said was
one of the initiators of the tour. We had some
difficulty in finding quarters, as unfortunately all
the hotels in the city were crowded. One hotel
offered to let us have rooms if we were not very
particular ; but I have always found that cricketers
are very particular so far as their rooms are concerned. The Club took charge of some of us,
and friends took in others, and though it was
annoying to have to hunt for accommodation
we ultimately got comfortably settled. Some of
the officials of the Toronto Cricket Club,
and other clubs in different parts of the
Dominion, had come down to Quebec to give
us a welcome, and we were very hospitably
entertained. Lord Dufferin, who was then

Governor of Canada, invited us to dinner at the citadel.

After leaving that function Fitzgerald and I, along with two or three others, started off in the small hours of the morning for a fishing and shooting expedition above the Falls of Mont-morenci, which are close to Quebec, and which impressed us greatly until we saw Niagara, and had our impressions of the smaller Falls effaced by the grandeur of the ' mighty thunderer of waters." Chartering a "calash" and tandem we drove about eighteen miles (we were assured that it was only about ten miles, but Canadian miles are so long that the distance was nearer twenty), along a bush track which was in a horrible condition and made us all apprehensive for our safety. We arrived at the clearing in the early morning. Having breakfasted, the shooting party went off in one direction while Fitz and I commenced fishing in a very delightful stream. The water was rather low, but in places there were pools, and between them the current ran swiftly. We had a capital day's sport, but I do not think that on that occasion, at all events, it was the result of any special skill in casting the line, as I who had never got a trout with a fly rod in my life (although I had often hooked them in a small stream with the toothsome worm) hardly ever threw my line without securing a rise. In fact, as soon as the fly touched the water the fish dashed greedily at it, and we hauled them in as rapidly as could be. By noon we had had quite

enough of it, having secured 130 trout, most of
them small, but now and again running to about
a pound.

The shooting party fared less happily. They
got wandering aimlessly about, and, thinking they
were perfectly free in any direction, trespassed
on some private land, and were confronted by an
indignant and stalwart virago. She was armed
with a stout stick, and ferociously threatened to
lay it about them if they didn't clear off from her
land ; so they beat a retreat. Altogether though
they covered a good many miles they got very
little sport. Indeed, they only saw one unfortunate small bird which was scarcely worth powder
at all, and which they " bagged " as it sat basking
on a rock. Our return to Quebec was fraught
with difficulties, as the track, which had seemed
bad enough in the night time, appeared worse in
the daylight. It was so rough that we congratulated ourselves when we got to Quebec that we
had come over such a road with our limbs whole.
When we reached the Stradacona Club, about five
o'clock in the evening, we learned that the other
members of the team had been entertained at
a champagne luncheon. We were all very
hungry, and soon made up for lost time. Before
sundown we had a little cricket practice on the
ramparts.

The most notable feature of Quebec is the
great rock which rises abruptly out of the St.
Lawrence to the height of several hundred feet.
It was on this rock, known as Abraham's Heights,

that Montgomery was killed in the famous siege of Quebec. The spot where he met his death is marked by the words " Here Montgomery fell," painted in large letters half way up the precipitous slope of the rock. A capital story is told concerning this spot. A somewhat obtuse American, standing on the deck of a Canadian liner which was passing down the St. Lawrence under the shadow of Abraham's Heights, asked a comrade who was looking at the rock through a binocular what the words were. His friend replied : " it says, ' Here Montgomery fell.' " " Wall," said the American, apparently blissfully ignorant of Canadian history, but impressed with the steepness of the rock, ' it's no wonder he did."

We left Quebec for Montreal later in the same evening, crossing the St. Lawrence to the Grand Trunk Depôt. Here we met with our first accident. One member of the team, on whom misfortunes had an unhappy knack of falling, tripped over a plank on the landing stage, which had been damaged by fire a few days previously, and dropped his dressing-case through a hole. It fell into the mud and water about twenty feet below the landing-stage, and as the train was on the point of departure the bag was never recovered, or, at least, we never heard of it being recovered. But that was not the worst of it, as he injured his knee, and was thereby prevented from playing in our first match. A friend had provided a private sleeping car for our night journey, but we thought that the best part of that car was " Parker," the man who controlled the bar, and who gave us during our journey an introduction to the peculiar beverages which the Americans call " cock-tails," and of which they concoct an endless variety.

On August 21st we arrived at Montreal. We had taken the trouble to have the best of the trout we had caught on the previous day packed in ice for our own consumption in Montreal, but in the bustle the fish got left behind. The heat in Montreal was very intense, although the summer was far advanced. One of our first acts was to visit the cricket ground, which is just at the foot of the mountain, and of which we did not think very much. Indeed, we made a good many complaints about the ground, which was in a deplorable condition. Luckily, some heavy thunderstorms improved the wicket, and by dint of hard work it was made fit to play upon, though it was bad enough in all conscience. We took the opportunity to get a little practice, and then occurred the second accident in our chapter, Francis being struck on the head with a ball which laid him low for a short time. Captain Fitzgerald, having only twelve men at his disposal, and finding two of them already *hors de combat,* put a stop to further practice that afternoon. While I was practising I hit a ball out of the ground over a neighbouring fence, and the ball could not be found. We all went to look for it, and, to my astonishment, I found a melon-bed in the garden. The fruit was growing luxuriously in the open air

—a thing which I had never seen before. The gardener politely cut the ripest and best of the melons and presented it to me, and I carried it off the ground in high exultation. Whether he kept the ball in exchange for the melon I don't know ; if he did he got the best of the bargain, as I found later that melons were very cheap in Montreal.

The first match of our tour was a three days' encounter with twenty-two of Montreal. We had an easy victory. In our first innings we made 255, towards which I contributed 81. Our lob bowler, Rose, proved much too good for the Colonials, who scored only 48 and 67.

One of the Montreal papers, in referring to my innings, said : " Mr. Grace is a large-framed, loose-jointed man, and you would say that his gait is a trifle awkward and shambling, but when he goes into the field you see that he is quick-sighted, sure-handed, and light-footed as the rest. He always goes in first, and to see him tap the ball gently to the off for one, draw it to the on for two, pound it to the limits for four, drive it beyond the most distant long leg for six, looks as easy as rolling off a log." I have had my style and appearance variously described at different times by newspaper reporters, but that reference is, perhaps, the most curious I have ever had made to myself.

On the evening of the first day of the match we were banqueted, and I made my first appearance as an after-dinner speaker. I had to reply to a

toast to "The Champion Batsman of Cricket-
dom," and our Captain Fitz, in his amusing book,
"Wickets in the West, or the Twelve in America,"
records my maiden effort as follows : "Gentlemen, I beg to thank you for the honour you have
done me. I never saw better bowling than I have
seen to-day, and I hope to see as good wherever
I go." We had another dinner on the second
night, this time at the St. James's Club, the
members of which kindly invited us to be their
guests. The people of Montreal took a very keen
interest in all our movements, and large crowds
assembled to watch the match. The newspapers
paid great attention to all our doings. Their
reports of the matches were very funny, if not
very accurate. Neither the reporters nor the
spectators seemed to understand the game very
thoroughly, and we were often amused at the
excitement when a catch was made off a bump
ball.

From Montreal we travelled to the Dominion
capital, Ottawa, where we took up our quarters
at the Russell House, and were very well looked
after by the proprietor. Canadian hotel-keepers
seem to keep their bars open all night, and I was
awakened about half-past two one morning by an
exciting discussion which was going on in the
bar. Recognising the voice of Farrands, whom
we took out as our umpire, I listened to the conversation, and overheard a gentleman bragging
about his own cricketing abilities, and declaring
that he had scored freely off Freeman's bowling.

Farrands would not listen to this assertion, and bluntly told the man that Freeman would knock him, bat and all, right through the wickets in a couple of overs. I believe that if I had not made my appearance and pacified the disputants, who were getting very excited, a row would have been inevitable. I poured oil on the troubled waters, and when I left the scene of the controversy Farrands was enjoying the hospitality of his antagonist.

Next day we commenced our match against twenty-two of Ottawa, and again we won a single innings victory. The wicket was certainly better than it had been at Montreal, and as I was in good form I made 73, the top score of our innings. Rose and Appleby did the mischief with their bowling against the twenty-two.

Of course, we were entertained in Ottawa—we could not move anywhere in Canada without being entertained, as the people were so hospitable. Once more I was called on to reply to a toast, and once more I cannot do better than quote Fitzgerald's report of my utterance : "Gentlemen, I beg to thank you for the honour you have done me. I never saw a better ground than I have seen to-day, and I hope to see as good wherever I go." I have a lively recollection of this particular banquet, because among the delicacies of the *menu* was a haunch of bear. Naturally, never having tasted this rarity, we all thought we would sample it. It looked all right, appetising enough in its way, but it was terribly tough, and the taste was abominable. I quite believe that that haunch never came off a wild bear; in fact, I think it was a relic of some poor superannuated show animal whose dancing career was ended. It was quite impossible to get one's teeth through it, and though the taste for bear may perhaps be cultivated, like the taste for olives, I fought shy of the delicacy ever afterwards.

While in Ottawa we were asked, as everybody who visits Ottawa is asked, to " do the slides." Shooting the slides really means sliding down the rapids of the Ottawa River on a lumber raft. We were comfortably assured that there could be no danger, as the lumber was always firmly secured when picnic parties were doing the shoots, and so most of the party accepted the invitation. It is exciting work for the first time, and makes a pleasant diversion, but it is a pastime of which one soon tires. As Fitzgerald said, the peril all told is not equal to a real slide on a bit of orange-peel on a London pavement.

Journeying *via* Lake Ontario, one of the most amazing of Canada's inland seas, we next stopped at Toronto, where we found a well-prepared ground ready for our encounter with twenty-two of Toronto. The interest in our tour was even keener here than at Montreal or at Ottawa, and the crowd of spectators was greater than had hitherto been attracted by our matches. A flower-pot stand, with accommodation for 2000 onlookers, had been specially erected for the occasion, and much better accommodation was provided for the cricketers than we had previously enjoyed. For the first time, for instance, we found soap and towels provided in the pavilion for our use, and as the climate was sultry we greatly appreciated the thoughtfulness which prompted this provision. I recollect this match principally because I was lucky enough to make my first century in Canada on this occasion—my share of the English score of 319 being 142. Again we were easily victorious, winning for the third time in three matches by an innings. Against Rose and Appleby's bowling the Toronto twenty-two compiled only 97 in the first innings and 117 in the second. The match excited great interest. One gentleman, who had come down from the country to witness the encounter, got himself introduced to me in order to offer me a couple of young bears to take home to England. I could not quite see to what use I could apply the creatures when I got them home, so I declined the seductive offer.

At Toronto we had another banquet—that goes without saying. This time the members of the Royal Canadian Yacht Club were our hosts. Here I perpetrated my third speech, reported by Fitzgerald thus : "Gentlemen, I thank you for the honour you have done me. I have never seen better batting than I saw to-day, and I hope to see as good wherever I go."

Our visit to Toronto was made extremely pleasant by the hospitality of the people. We were entertained somewhere and somehow nearly every night. The Toronto Club invited us to a banquet, and of course I had to get on my legs again to respond to a toast. Fitz reports my fourth speech as follows : " Gentlemen, I have to thank you for the honour you have done me. I never met such good fellows as I met to-day, and I hope I shall meet as good wherever I go." I may say that my ·speech was received with rapturous applause. Mr. W. H. Smith, afterwards the leader of the House of Commons, was present at this banquet, and also spoke. Hospitality was literally showered upon us. Indeed, the people seemed unable to do enough to make our visit pleasant and memorable. The Lieutenant-Governor gave a ball in our honour, and an excursion was arranged by Mr. and Mrs. Cumberland to Lake Simcoe, and Couchising. Altogether, we did not get much breathing time between a constant succession of festive and social engagements.

To finish up the week's sojourn, the Toronto Club organised a scratch match of teams selected from the English twelve and the Toronto cricketers. I captained one side, consisting of six Englishmen and five Canadians, and Fitzgerald captained the other, which was similarly constituted. Like most scratch matches it was productive of excellent fun, although the play was not of the order of strict cricket. My eleven made 168 (of which Lord Harris made 65) and 119, and Fitz's side scored 165 and 63. I ran out to meet a ball in my first innings and got stumped, and in the second innings, just when I was well set, and scoring freely, my opponents, who thought they had had enough of me for that day, bribed the umpire to give me out lbw, and I retired discomfited, much to their amusement and my own disgust. Throughout our stay in Toronto the weather was splendid, and we were reluctant to leave the city when the day of departure came.

Leaving Toronto, and still travelling westward, we made a short stay at London (Ontario), where we played a match on the old Barracks ground against twenty-two of London. We made 89 and 161, and they compiled 55 and 65, Appleby and Rose proving invincible with the ball. There was no lack of entertainment for us in London, whose citizens were not going to be behind Toronto, Ottawa, and Montreal in their welcome to us.

Our last sojourning place in Canada was Hamilton, where we had the experience of finishing a match in the dark, to which our opponents consented, so as to expedite our departure for Niagara. By this time, of course, the summer was rapidly waning, and the evenings shortening, and as there is no twilight to speak of in Canada, darkness fell suddenly upon us while we were playing. It was so dark that we could hardly see where the ball went, and I remember I bowled the last man out with an underhand sneak. We gave the twenty-two of Hamilton a thorough beating, for while we made 181, they only managed to put together 86 and 79. The captain of the Hamilton team entertained us at his house, and a large company assembled in our honour. Again I was made spokesman of our team in response to one of the toasts, and if Mr. Fitzgerald does not misreport me I said : " Gentlemen, I have to thank you for the honour you have done me. I have never seen prettier ladies than I have seen to-day, and I hope I shall see as pretty wherever I go."

The Canadian tour was a triumphal success in every way. Never did twelve cricketers work together in greater harmony and with more perfect *esprit de corps*. From the day we left the Mersey to the day we got back to Liverpool there was not a single hitch, nor one moment's bad feeling. I have spoken since to several members of the twelve, who have subsequently been to Australia, the Cape, and other places, with cricketing teams, and they all with one accord say that they never experienced such a harmonious tour. I attribute the credit for this very largely to the man we had as our captain. Poor old Fitz smoothed all the rough places with his unfailing tact, geniality, and businesslike ability ; and looking back to the tour, over a vista of nearly thirty years, it stands out in my memory as a prolonged and happy picnic.

Most of the cricketers we encountered in Canada were gentlemen who had gone out from England and settled in the Dominion for business and professional purposes. I have every reason to believe that our visit had a beneficial effect in the direction of cultivating cricket sentiment in Canada, though the Canadians have not gone ahead with the game as the Australians have. The batting of the teams we met in Canada did not attain a high standard—they seemed incapable of facing our bowlers, and fell victims to easy balls, which ought to have been severely punished— but nothing else could perhaps be expected. It must be said, however, that we met some excellent bowling, and that the fielding of the Canadians was very creditable.

It is a curious fact that while we were in Canada Fitzgerald never lost the toss, and yet with one exception we beat our opponents by an innings and some runs to spare.

As in the case with most travellers seeing the Falls for the first time, our first impressions of Niagara were in the nature of a disappointment. We were disposed to discount the majesty of the great cataract—like the Irishman who, when asked if he did not think it was wonderful that so many million tons of water should go pouring over the precipice, replied, " Wonderful ? No ! for, begorra, what's the hindrance ? It might have been wonderful if it had gone up the precipice." But this feeling soon vanished, and the awe-inspiring grandeur of the Falls grew upon us, and increased day by day until we left the vicinity. Of course we visited all the points of interest, and amongst other things were photographed, with the Horseshoe Fall as a background. The photograph hangs in my room as

I write, and conjures up many happy reminiscences of our Niagara experiences.

Several of the influential Canadians, who had fêted us during our visits to the cities of the Dominion, accompanied us to Niagara, and stayed at the Clifton House Hotel, where we had taken up our quarters. Some of the younger members of The Twelve thought it would be only right if we showed our appreciation of their kindness by returning their hospitality in some small way which would be agreeable and enjoyable to all ; so we gave a ball at the hotel, but unfortunately—or as some of us thought very fortunately—the ball took place on a Saturday night, and dancing had to stop at midnight.

CHAPTER IV

WITH THE TEAM IN AMERICA

LEAVING Niagara on September 16, we crossed into the United States, and entered on the second portion of our tour. We took train first to Albany, and then steamed down the Hudson to New York. We were not greatly prepossessed by our first glimpse of New York. The first thing that struck me in the city was that each hotel—we stayed at the Brevoort House—had its own oyster-bar. We found this exceedingly convenient, and soon became good customers, for the oysters were excellent.

We opened our tour in America with a match on the Hoboken Ground in New Jersey against twenty-two of the St. George's Club. To reach the ground from New York we had to cross the river, and for the first time in my life I saw a vehicle driven on to a ferry boat, and then driven off on reaching the other side. For this match we had an excellent wicket—it was prepared by Stubberfield, the old Sussex professional, who had an engagement out there—and we had another easy victory, our score being 249, of

which I made 68, while our antagonists totalled
only 66 and 44. In the first innings Rose and
Appleby did all the bowling, and in the course of
some chaff some one said that I could get the
St. George's men out even quicker than Rose.
Anyway, I went on bowling with Appleby in the
second innings, and we succeeded in getting rid
of the entire twenty-two for 44 runs. Great
interest was evinced by a certain section of the
people in this match, but cricket was not then, as
it is not now, a very popular game in New York.
George and Henry Wright, the famous baseball
players, were included in the St. George's twenty-
two, and were the best scorers of their side, while,
of course, their fielding was—as the fielding of all
baseball players is—simply magnificent.

Our visit to America was the third which had
been paid by English cricketers—George Parr
having captained a team which visited the States
in 1859, and Willsher having taken out another
team in 1868. Some of the comments of the
New York newspapers were extremely amusing.
Ottaway, for instance, was described as "a tall,
lithe, sinewy man, with a splendid reach, and an
eye that can detect at a glance the course about
to be pursued by the invading sphere of com-
pressed leather."

We were just as hospitably entertained in
America as in Canada, and at one of the banquets
in New York they made me make another speech.
In the words of Fitzgerald again, my speech
runs:—"Gentlemen, I have to thank you for the

honour you have done me. I have never tasted
better oysters than I have tasted here to-day, and
I hope I shall get as good wherever I go."

I think it is rather too bad of Fitz to have
perpetuated my first utterances in this way, but I
daresay that the reports are not libellous. I make
no pretensions to oratory, and I would any day
as soon make a duck as a speech.

After leaving New York our first stopping
place was Philadelphia, where we had the best
cricket of our tour. Our impending visit had
been quite a source of excitement in Philadelphia,
where cricket has a strong hold on public sentiment. Our reception was of a most enthusiastic
order. We were dined and fêted as we had been
throughout our tour, but in addition we were
made welcome in various other ways. Stalls
were placed at our disposal at Mr. Fox's theatre,
and upon our arrival the band struck up with
"God save the Queen," whereupon the whole
audience rose and cheered vociferously. We
returned the compliment when the orchestra
struck up "The Star Spangled Banner." An
official handbook was published, and a handsomely bound copy was presented to each of the
twelve. The programmes of the Cricket Fête
appeared on every blank wall, and announced
that a spacious grand stand had been erected for
the occasion, that a restaurateur had been engaged,
that the band from Navy Yard would play at
intervals, that telegraphs of the score would be
posted, and that the names of the English players

would be exhibited on large canvas strips as they "take the bat."

Great attention had been bestowed on the wicket for our match with twenty-two of Philadelphia, which proved a sharp tussle and ended amid a scene of great excitement. Fitz lost the toss—he never won the toss as long as we were in the United States—and the Americans scored 63 in their first innings. We had expected a bigger total, but the ground did not play very well. When we began our innings we found that with twenty-two superb fieldsmen constantly on the alert it was no easy task to get the ball away. Moreover, the bowling of Charles Newhall and Mead, who opened the attack, was particularly good, and Ottaway and I, who were the first to bat for the English team, experienced no small difficulty in making runs. When I had made 14 Newhall bowled me out. I have heard many a great shout go up in various parts of the globe at my dismissal, but I never remember anything quite equal to the wild roar that greeted my downfall on this occasion. Newhall and Mead bowled unchanged throughout the innings, and dismissed us for 105 runs. Throughout the innings their bowling was admirable. Newhall, who was a right-handed fast bowler, was one of the best trundlers I ever played against ; whilst Mead, a medium pace left-hand bowler, kept up a wonderfully good length. In the second innings the Philadelphians made 74, Dan Newhall, a brother of the bowler, being the top scorer with

15. Then came the tug of war. We wanted 33 runs to win, and as we had a whole day in which to get them, we commenced our innings first thing next morning pretty sanguine of victory, though the wicket was worn, and we were not, after our first experience, disposed to under-estimate the strength of the bowling. I had made a run off Newhall's third ball in the first over, when Ottaway's middle stump was sent flying by a fast ball, and there was another out-burst of cheering of a most vociferous order. This was one wicket, one run. A. N. Hornby, who joined me at the wicket, made one good leg hit for 3, when another roar of applause rent the air—the Lancashire man being caught at short-leg. This was two wickets for eight—certainly not a very promising start. Alfred Lubbock took the vacant place, and though we were at the wickets together for some time, we could not get the ball away, the bowling and fielding being so excellent. It was risky work doing it with twenty-two men in the field, but we stole a run or two. Then came another long interval during which the scorers were idle. Ball after ball was sent down, which we could do nothing beyond playing, and maiden over followed maiden over in un-broken monotony. At last Lubbock slipped a ball for three, and I got one to leg for another three.

By this time we had been three-quarters of an hour at the wicket, during which time we had compiled 15 runs. The wicket was crumbling, and getting worse and worse. Newhall's bowling rose dangerously, and Mead, as usual, kept up a splendid length. Between them they kept us stationary in our places for another spell, and then Alfred Lubbock fell a victim to Newhall— caught and bowled. Three wickets, 15 runs. Hadow was my next partner, and he opened his score by making three, but my end came immediately afterwards, as I was caught in the slips for seven runs, which had taken me nearly an hour to make. This is about the slowest pace at which I ever remember scoring. My dismissal was followed by a tremendous roar of applause. Hats and umbrellas were tossed high in the air by the excited spectators, whose delight for a few moments seemed to know no bounds. Four wickets, 18 runs. Things began to look serious, but Hadow and Harris, who were now partners, put a slightly different complexion on the game. They had carried the score on to 29, and we in the pavilion breathed more freely, as victory seemed in sight. Unfortunately, Harris, in trying to drive the ball from Newhall, skied it, and was caught at cover-point for a very useful and timely contribution of 9. Half our wickets were now down for 29, but as we only wanted 4 more runs to win, we did not begin to despair. To our horror, however, Hadow directly after this succumbed to Mead. Six wickets, 29 runs—so stood the score on the telegraph board. Only 4 runs were wanted, but we none of us now felt sure of victory. Francis followed, going in, as Fitz said, to do or die. He didn't—he died. Seven for 29.

The excitement, which had been growing intenser every moment, was now extraordinary. The atmosphere was electrical. I never remember seeing a team or a crowd of spectators more excited. They were in rhapsodies, and could scarcely keep still. The quietude amid which each ball was bowled was almost deathly, and no wonder, for thirteen successive maiden overs had been bowled and not a run had been secured for half an hour, during which time three wickets had fallen. Appleby walked quietly in, and joined Edgar Lubbock, who had taken the place of Francis at the wicket. By this time we were prepared for the worst, and we fully expected Newhall to bowl Lubbock. Luckily the ball, instead of hitting his wicket, hit his leg, and so at last we scored another single—a leg-bye, which lifted our score into the thirties. The tension, which was getting painful, was relieved at last by Appleby, who opened his shoulders and let out at an overpitched ball from Newhall, thus winning the match with a boundary hit. We all agreed that a glorious finish like this was almost worth going to America to witness, and, from the cricketer's point of view, it was the most memorable event in our tour. The only drawback was, our regret that both sides could not win, because the Philadelphians, by their plucky fight, deserved the victory quite as much as we did.

The prolongation of the Philadelphian match

made it necessary for us to rush off to catch the train for Boston, where we were due next day, and as a consequence we were unable to wait to drink the health of our opponents, a circumstance which we deeply regretted, and for which the Philadelphia press gave us an undeserved censuring next morning. The worst of it all was that, though we got in bad odour for our apparent lack of courtesy, we also missed the train for Boston, and thus earned a double reprimand, as the Bostonians were annoyed at our non-arrival. As a matter of fact, we reached Boston so late that we could not play at all on the day upon which it had been arranged that the match should open. This necessitated a curtailment of our original programme. It had been arranged that we were to go to Harvard University, but when we got to Boston we were unwashed, unkempt, and unfed, and these wants, requiring immediate attention, involved the abandonment of the trip to Harvard. Moreover, as we did not arrive at Boston until the morning of the 26th, and we were to sail from Quebec for Liverpool on the 28th, our time was so short that we had to play a one-day match only.

Our Captain, Fitzgerald, was not in the best of health, and having some business in Boston he entrusted the captaincy to me. When we got to the baseball ground, on which the match was played, we found it in a very deplorable condition, heavy rain having been falling all through the night. The wicket itself was not very bad, but where short slip, point and mid-off had to stand

there was a perfect quagmire. Some idea of the
condition of the turf may be judged from the fact
that between twenty and thirty bags of sawdust
had to be bestowed upon the ground before it
was fit for the match. Notwithstanding this precaution some of the fieldsmen stood ankle deep in
sawdust and slush. Our opponents were twenty-
two of Boston, and we got nineteen of them out
for 26 runs, when Linder put quite a different
complexion on the innings. He hit up well, and
carried out his bat for 17, the total reaching 51
before the last wicket fell. We began our innings
disastrously, and when Fitzgerald arrived on the
scene, thinking that perhaps only a few wickets
had fallen, he was astounded to find that
eight of our men were out for 39. Out of this
meagre total I had made exactly two-thirds,
having twice hit the ball out of the ground, for
each of which I was only allowed four, although
they were honestly worth six. Eventually we
were all dismissed for 51—a tie. In went the
Bostonians for their second innings, but Appleby
and I dismissed the twenty-two for 43 runs in the
course of an hour and a half's play. The one
incident of the innings was a splendid hit out of
the ground by Wright, the baseball player, who,
being a native of Boston, was one of our opponents. It was getting late, and darkness would
soon be upon us, but everybody was anxious that
we should go in again. We only wanted 44, so it
was decided that we should finish the match if
possible.

The wicket was getting worse and worse, the fieldsmen were sinking deeper and deeper in the mud, and the light was fading rapidly. Our start was again disastrous. Two wickets went down for 7, four wickets for 8, five wickets for 11 (by this time it was almost dark), six for 19, and then we appealed to the umpire for leave to abandon the match on the ground of darkness. The umpires decided against us, and Fitzgerald went in. A few minutes afterwards a full pitched ball hit him on the toe—he declared it might just as well have hit him in the face for all he could see of it—and the umpire then decided that it really was too dark to go on. Time was called, and in the darkness and damp we concluded the last match of our tour in the West. As a tie in our first innings was followed by our making half our opponent's score for the loss of half our wickets, we agreed that the "honours were easy." The match was altogether a very curious struggle, and I have often thought it was very lucky that darkness did come on, otherwise I am sure that we should have been beaten.

After the match George Wright presented each of the English twelve with a baseball. I have mine still, and preserve it as an interesting relic of the wind-up to a memorable tour.

A few hours later we were *en route* to Quebec and home. As we passed through Maine we came under the veto of the famous Prohibition Laws of that State, and had the curious experience of being absolutely unable to get, for love or moncy, anything stronger by way of refreshment than thick soup, washed down with weak tea and indifferent coffee. What impressed itself most vividly upon my mind during that journey through the woodland country were the first rays of sunlight in the early dawn, falling on the variegated foliage of the forests, which were now resplendent in their full autumn tints. The colouring was rich and deep, and the beauty of the scene as the sun rose above the woodlands was a sight never to be forgotten. We had spent five weeks in Canada and America during the season, which the people of the West call their "Indian Summer," but nothing so perfect in its beauty as the landscape changing every moment before our eyes as we sped towards Quebec had come under our observation.

We left Quebec on our homeward voyage on September 29, and on October 7 we were once more in Old England, our return trip being made in the *Prussian*. The Atlantic put on its best manners, and no one suffered much from sea sickness with the exception of Harris. The voyage was uneventful, but thoroughly enjoyable. The night before we arrived at Liverpool we ordered sardines on toast, as usual, for supper, but the significant fact was brought to our knowledge that the ship's supply of sardines had already been demolished. From that fact readers with any experience of the sea will naturally assume that our appetites were not dulled by the pangs of sea-sickness.

CHAPTER V

FIRST VISIT TO AUSTRALIA

As the result of overtures made to me in the spring of 1873 I agreed to form a team to visit Australia at the end of that year. The invitation came from a number of gentlemen connected with the Melbourne Club—the M.C.C. of Australia —who cabled to me inquiring, "Can you, will you, bring a team at the end of the year?" I consented, and set myself the task of selecting and engaging a representative team for the tour. Though the Melbourne Club did not undertake the financial responsibility, certain of its members, and other gentlemen keenly interested in cricket, formed themselves into a syndicate to promote the interests of the team. Some time before I had entered into another and more enduring engagement, and I was to be married in the autumn of 1873. The future Mrs. Grace, however, consented to our marriage taking place a few weeks before the date of departure for Australia, so that the tour might be regarded as an extension of our honeymoon.

Throughout the cricket season of 1873 I was

busily engaged in preparing for the tour, and I soon realised the difficulties which lay in the way of the undertaking. It was harder in those days than it is now to get together a good team for an extended absence from England, particularly in the case of first-class amateurs. At first I had great hopes of securing Mr. W. Yardley and Mr. A. N. Hornby, but at the last moment both these well-known cricketers found themselves unable to undertake the trip. I invited Tom Emmett and Alfred Shaw to include themselves in my combination, but neither could comply with my request. Pooley and Pinder were not available for the tour, so I had to fall back upon Mr. J. A. Bush, the Gloucestershire amateur, as wicketkeeper. At last these initial difficulties were overcome, and we arranged to sail from Southampton on October 23, in the P. and O. steamer *Mirzapore*. The team, as finally constituted, consisted of W. G. Grace (captain), G. F. Grace, J. A. Bush, F. H. Boult, W. R. Gilbert, A. Greenwood, R. Humphrey, H. Jupp, J. Lillywhite, M. McIntyre, W. Oscroft, and J. Southerton. We met at Southampton, and a party of Gloucestershire friends, consisting of my mother, Mrs. Gilbert, Colonel Bush (Mr. J. A. Bush's father), and my old schoolfellow, Jack Lloyd, came to see us off. Another party, consisting of Messrs. Alcock, Burls, and Oelrichs, joined us on our way to Southampton on a similar pretext. We were a merry party at dinner on the night before sailing, although some of the team did not like the idea of leaving England for the first time.

The voyage to Australia was an even more formidable undertaking in the seventies than it is now, and we were fifty-two days on shipboard before we reached Australia. Some of the team were good sailors, and some were bad, but good or bad we all breathed more freely when we left the Bay of Biscay behind us. We called at Gibraltar, and then steamed into the Mediterranean, where two days later we experienced a terrific storm, which lasted a little more than a day. After the rain had passed over, and the thunder and lightning had ceased, the wind blew a hurricane for some time. The brilliant rays of the sun fell on the foam which was flying before the wind and produced one of the most lovely sights I ever remember in the form of hundreds of miniature rainbows. This spectacle recalled to my mind a similar phenomenon caused by the sun shining on the spray at Niagara Falls—a sight which impressed itself vividly on my memory during my Canadian tour twelve months previously. On November 1 we arrived at Malta, where we spent a few hours on shore, very glad after our experiences in the hurricane to feel our feet once more on *terra firma*.

Alexandria, our next stopping-place, did not strike us favourably. Of all the filthy places I ever saw, Alexandria, or at least some of it, was far and away the worst, and I heard of its bombardment years later without any regret that

I should never see it again in its former condition. The British Consul came on board and tried his utmost to persuade us to make a short stay and play a match at Alexandria, undertaking to send us down by special train in time to catch the *Mirzapore* at Suez. I reluctantly declined the offer, feeling it safer to avoid all risk of being left behind in case any accident or unforeseen difficulty might have frustrated the plan of rejoining the ship.

We had pleasurable anticipations of sailing through the Suez Canal, but we were disappointed with De Lesseps' great engineering achievement. In those days ships did not use search-lights, and could consequently only steam through the Canal by daylight—pulling up at night till dawn. Our progress through the Canal was tediously slow, and we soon got tired of the monotonous stretches of sand which meet the eye on both sides. It was very foggy, but our captain, wishing to get to Suez as quickly as possible, proceeded in spite of the fog, a course which prolonged instead of shortening our voyage, as we had the misfortune to take the wrong side of a buoy, get stuck in the mud, and be detained the best part of a day.

On reaching Point de Galle on the southern coast of Ceylon we had to leave the *Mirzapore* and tranship to the *Nubia*, a smaller steamer, with which we were not at first prepossessed, but which took us safely and comfortably to Melbourne. On December 8 we arrived at King

George's Sound, where we went on shore and had several hours for cricket practice while the ship was coaling. Some of the natives gave us an exhibition of the art of throwing the boomerang. I tried my hand, but failed again and again, when suddenly the boomerang flew away down the cricket ground, fell a few yards in front of one of the players, took a second flight with increased velocity, and just missed the head of one of the members of the team. It was a narrow escape, as another foot would have involved an inquest.

The remaining six days of the voyage passed rapidly. The weather was extremely cold, and although it was then the Antipodean midsummer we were glad of our great-coats. We reached Melbourne a little before our time on December 13, and found a number of the promoters and leading Victorian cricketers assembled to welcome us. We were soon ensconced in our hotel, glad to be on dry land after seven weeks at sea. Mr. McArthur, President of the Melbourne C.C., kindly put his carriage at the disposal of Mrs. Grace and myself, and all through our stay spared no pains to enhance our comfort. In the afternoon we went down to see the Melbourne Cricket Ground, and then drove across to the South Melbourne Club, where a match—the final round of a cup contest—was in progress. About 7000 spectators were on the ground, and when we arrived they cheered enthusiastically.

As I was being shown round one of the players remarked, "You see we manage our crowds

better than you do in England. Our spectators are
impartial and good-tempered. We never experience any unpleasantness on our cricket grounds."
Within a quarter of an hour this remark was
refuted in a curious way. One of the umpires
gave a decision displeasing to the batting side—
which wanted just a few runs to win the cup—
and a wrangle ensued, in the course of which the
spectators broke into the ground. Ultimately the
players left the field, abandoning the match in its
unfinished condition. This, I am sorry to say, was
a foretaste of some experiences which subsequently fell to our lot. It was a manifestation of
the spirit which still unfortunately seems to survive in Australia, though not in so malignant a
form as in the seventies.

I may say here, in parenthesis, that Australia
has always been deficient in the matter of good
umpires, and though we in England are by no
means perfect in this respect, the Australians are
a long way behind us. In those days professional
umpires were almost unheard of in Australia.
Any one who took an intelligent interest in cricket
was thought good enough to umpire. Consequently inexperienced men had the delicate and
onerous duty thrust upon them, with the result
that no confidence was placed in their judgment
and scant respect was paid to their decisions. I
attribute the friction which has frequently arisen
during the visits of English teams to Australia to
the fact that even at the present time Australia is
not well provided with good umpires.

When I first played in Australia there were not sufficient important matches to keep capable umpires employed. The matches between Victoria and New South Wales were the only really important events in the cricket calendar—there was no South Australian team then. Even now, except when an English team visits Australia, first-class matches are few and far between, though, of course, there is plenty of club cricket. In England we draw our umpires from the ranks of professional cricketers of long experience, who have retired from active participation in the game; but in Australia they have not professional cricketers in sufficient numbers to keep up the supply of efficient umpires. It is not always recognised that the duties of an umpire call for uncommon intelligence, decisive judgment, and intimate acquaintance with the laws and customs of the game. It is too often assumed that because a man has been a good cricketer he is sure to make a good umpire, but I contend that this is no criterion, and that a more necessary qualification for an umpire is that he should have a good head on his shoulders, and should have had constant practice at this special branch of work.

One of the first things that struck me in Melbourne was that good wickets in Australia would not be the invariable rule. In the interval between landing and beginning our first match, we got some practice on the M.C.C. ground. Two or three days before the match I inquired of the groundman whether the wicket for the match was being prepared. " Oh," he answered, " we'll select a pitch and put the roller on it on the morning of the match, and that will be all right." I knew that a good deal depended on the condition of the wicket, and that the worse it was the less chance we had of success. As all cricketers know, a bad wicket brings all players down to a certain level, and I did not take to the idea of having the selection of the wicket left till the eleventh hour. Consequently I saw the authorities of the club, with the result that, by dint of rolling for two or three days, we ultimately got a very decent wicket. This incident in Melbourne rather put me in mind of the M.C.C. at home, for at that time " the powers that be" at Lord's thought a few hours' attention was enough for any wicket. I take upon myself the credit of having shown the Australians how to prepare a wicket, and of disabusing their minds of the idea that a good wicket can be obtained without special care and preparation. The lesson was not wasted on the Australians, and no one could wish to play upon better wickets than are now secured at Melbourne, Sydney, and Adelaide.

Cricket was in its infancy in Australia in 1873 —though two English teams had previously visited the Colony, and the Colonials had benefited from their experiences with them—and many of the best players we met in our tour were gentlemen who had learned all their cricket in England, and had gone out to settle under the Southern Cross. Mr. B. B. Cooper, who, with

me, made the record in 1869, when against the
Players of the South we compiled 283 for the
first wicket, formed one of the 18 of Victoria,
against whom we played our first match. Our
antagonists won the toss and kept us out in the
field industriously leather hunting while they
made 266. B. B. Cooper with 84 was the top
scorer, the other principal contributors being
Conway with 32 and Boyle with 30. We began
our innings and had a run of misfortune, being
dismissed for 110.   Allan and Boyle (both of
whom visited England with the first Australian
team in 1878) and old Sam Cosstick shared the
bowling honours. We had to follow on, and
again we did poorly. Our second innings closed
for 132, and the match ended in a single innings
victory for the Victorians. I made 23 and 51
not out, but no one else except Jupp, my brother
G. F., and Lillywhite, offered any serious resist-
ance to the bowling. The match excited great
interest, 40,000 spectators paying half a crown
apiece for admission during the three days. We
were naturally disappointed at our early defeat,
but we attributed it to the unquestionable fact
that we were not in proper form. Moreover, we
were certainly weak in bowling on this occasion,
as our regular bowlers were conspicuously ineffective. I blamed myself for not going on
sooner, as I took ten wickets for 49 runs, while
my brother, G. F., got four for 35. Southerton
secured one wicket at a cost of 41 runs, Lillywhite two for 49, while McIntyre had 47 made off

his bowling without capturing a wicket. Obviously our men were not up to their standard, and the match, though disappointing, was subsequently redeemed by a succession of victories.

From Melbourne we went up to Ballarat, a journey of about a hundred miles, made wearisome by dust, heat, and slow travelling. The ground at Ballarat is called the Oval, and it carried on Kennington Oval traditions so far as the wicket itself was concerned. There was nothing left to be desired. We won the toss in this match, which was against twenty-two of Ballarat, among whom were Mr. T. W. Wills, of Rugby fame, Allan, Cosstick, and Gaggin (who had played against us at Melbourne, and followed us up to Ballarat). We made good use of our opportunities, and profiting from the perfect condition of the wicket, which was not surpassed in excellence throughout the tour, we ran our score up to the creditable total of 470. I made 126, and my brother G. F. 112. Oscroft, who scored 65, lost his wicket by a stroke of ill-luck. Just when he seemed safe for a century, G. F., who was batting with him, skied a ball to point, and thinking that the ball was certain to be caught never left his ground, though Oscroft ran down the wicket. As luck would have it, point missed the catch, but atoned for his blunder by returning the ball smartly to the bowler, who promptly put the wicket down. Oscroft was run out, while G. F., who ought to have been caught, continued his innings.

I remember that Bush amused the spectators while he was making his score of 23 runs by pretending to run when backing up, and by stealing some short runs. This so exasperated the fieldsmen that they threw in frantically, and so helped our total. It was about the hottest day in which I ever played cricket. The heat was almost unbearable, dry, sultry, and exhausting. The temperature was about 100° in the shade. Some wooden seats placed around the ground for the spectators became so hot in the sunshine that the people could not sit upon them. Mr. W. H. Figgins, with a very creditable 53, was the highest scorer for the twenty-two, who did very well. They made 276 runs in their only innings, and retained possession of the wicket until within a few minutes of the time for close of play. The match was consequently left undecided. It is worth recording that when stumps were drawn the wicket was still as true as a billiard-table. Our total of 470 far exceeded the highest score ever made in Australia by an English visiting team, and my own individual score of 126 was for a short time the record innings of any Englishman visiting the Colony.

On the Sunday—which we spent at Ballarat— we had our first experience of an Australian dust storm. A hot wind swept over the city, scorching everything up, and clouds of blinding dust whirled along the roads and streets. It was thoroughly unpleasant, as the whole town was in darkness while the storm raged. On this Sunday Hum-

phrey met with an accident, which deprived us of
his services in the two succeeding matches. He
went for a drive into the bush country, and was
thrown out of the trap, falling on the stump of a
tree, and straining the muscles of his thigh.

Our troubles began in earnest when we turned
our backs upon Ballarat, and our faces towards
Stawell, where we were to play our next match.
The journey of 74 miles had to be made in an
old-fashioned Cobb's coach over a rough bush
track, quite undeserving of the name of road. At
the outset there were difficulties to overcome.
When they saw the vehicle in which they had to
make the journey several members of the team
flatly refused to take their seats, and were
only, after much coaxing, prevailed upon to do
so. We left Ballarat at 8.30 A.M. The first
fifteen miles were through cultivated country, and
the roads were tolerably decent, but for the
remaining sixty miles we endured agonies. The
horses laboured along up to their hocks in white
dust, with which we were literally cloaked, so that
we looked for all the world like so many millers
as we sat on the jolting and rickety vehicle.

To break the monotony of the journey, two
members of the team, who had guns with them,
amused themselves, if not their comrades, by
banging at the magpies and parrots as we went
along. It seems rather cruel to kill the lively
and entertaining parrot, but as they are as plentiful in Australia as sparrows are in London the
offence was perhaps not very serious. The

secretary of the Stawell Cricket Club, and a few
other cricket enthusiasts in the neighbourhood,
came twenty miles from home to meet us at
Ararat.   Four miles off Stawell itself it seemed as
if the whole town had turned out *en masse* to
greet us.   As we approached the crowd cheered
wildly, and two brass bands struck up a welcom-
ing strain.   The horses in one of the waggonettes
at once took fright, and overturned the vehicle.
Luckily, though the trap was smashed to atoms,
no one was injured.   Stawell was reached at
8.30.   We had been twelve hours on the road,
travelling under the most uncomfortable conditions, but our reception made us forget the
trials and troubles of the long drive.

At that time Stawell was a small, but rich,
mining centre of about 8000 inhabitants, and on
the following day most of the professionals in our
team inspected the North Cross Reef Gold Mine,
which was reputed to be the best paying mine in
Victoria.   My cousin, W. R. Gilbert, and I hired
a buggy and drove about ten or twelve miles to a
lagoon in the bush, where we had a fine day's
sport with our guns.   On the way we came across
an Irish settler, a wonderfully hospitable old man,
who, when we made ourselves known to him,
could scarcely do enough for us.   He showed us
where to find the best sport, and then left us for
about a couple of hours, returning with a big
basket of luscious peaches, which he had ridden
over to a neighbouring squatter's to procure for
us.   Gilbert and I were in hopes of bagging

a kangaroo, but no such luck came our way that day.

Our match against twenty-two of Stawell began next morning, under conditions by no means inspiriting. The ground was in a deplorable condition. Here and there were small patches of grass, but the greater part was utterly devoid of any herbage. We were not surprised to hear that the field had only been ploughed up three months before, and that the grass had been sown in view of our visit. The wicket was execrable, but there was no help for it — we had travelled seventy miles through bush and dust to play the match, and there was no option but to play.

Of course the cricket was shockingly poor, and the match a ludicrous farce. How bad the ground really was may be judged from the fact that one slow ball actually stuck in the dust, and never reached the batsman. It was ridiculous to play on such a wicket, but we were in for it and went through with it. Jupp and I batted first, and adopted slogging tactics. There was really nothing else to do, but the result was that in seventy minutes we were all out for 43 runs. If all the catches we gave had been held our total would have been still smaller. We were not sorry when our innings ended, as the wicket was one of the class which I have described, as bringing all players, good and bad, down to one level. Our opponents, who were more accustomed to such wickets, kept us in the field for a couple of hours, and made 71. McIntyre did the bowling for us, taking nine wickets for 10 runs. It is scarcely worth while recording the progress of the play, though it should be stated that we were beaten by ten wickets. A plague of flies, which swept over the field while play was in progress, added to our discomforts in this remarkable match.

As the match finished in two days, a single wicket match between six of our professionals and twelve of the Stawell team was arranged for the third day. The wicket was worse, and the cricket more grotesque than ever. In response to the 29 made by the twelve the six English professionals scored 2—made by McIntyre with one hit. I went off for some more shooting in the bush, along with one or two of the other members of the team, and we were not surprised, though we were amused, to hear on our return what had happened during the day. Some of the Stawell people apparently thought that our men did not try to do their best; but with the ground in such a state, it was almost astonishing that any runs were scored at all. If the ball was hit in the air it travelled all right, but if it was sent along the ground it could not possibly reach the boundary.

Another depressing drive across the bush country fell to our lot when we left Stawell for Warrnambool. We took it in two stages, journeying first to Ararat, where we spent the Sunday, and then proceeding to Warrnambool.

On the Sunday the rain, which was very much wanted, fell in torrents, and when we started at 4.30 A.M. on Monday for our ninety-one miles drive we found the tracks in an appalling state. They were bad enough in all conscience when we traversed them *en route* to Stawell, but the rain had converted the dust into thick mud, in which the wheels sank almost to the axles.

Of all my travelling experiences that coach drive to Warrnambool was the most unpleasant. Rain fell pitilessly all the time, and we were soon drenched to the skin. The first thirty-one miles took five hours and a quarter, and though we changed horses now and again our progress was exasperatingly slow. On leaving Hexham, where we halted for dinner, we came to a slight incline. Here two of our horses jibbed, and refused to budge. B. B. Cooper (who made the runs against us at Melbourne, and distinguished himself by a pair of spectacles at Stawell), Lillywhite, Jupp, Southerton, McIntyre, and Humphrey stayed at Hexham to lighten the load. We managed to make the horses convey the rest of us to Warrnambool, which we reached at half-past eleven at night, after a ride of nineteen hours. We were wet through, and our cricket bags and portmanteaus were soaking. Notwithstanding the rain a large number of the people at Warrnambool, who expected us to arrive in the afternoon, had gone out to meet us, but as we made no appearance they assumed that our coaches had broken down.

But if we were not met on the road we were most hospitably received at the hotel, and I remember how thankful we were to find fires in our bedrooms. I had just gone to sleep when a bang at the door made me jump up. In answer to my inquiry I was told that some one wanted to speak to me. It was a reporter from one of the papers ; but, as may be imagined, I did not think that midnight was the right hour for a man who had been travelling all day in the rain to encounter an interviewer. Though such journalistic enterprise deserved a better reward I did not receive the intruder with any kindly feeling, and turned him away with very little " copy."

After the bumping and jumping of the comfortless coach over muddy tracks and in persistent rain we were not in very fit condition for cricket, and our match against twenty-two of Warrnambool was not a brilliant display. Our opponents included B. B. Cooper, Allan, Wills, Gaggin and Conway, who throughout our tour followed us from place to place, and seemed prepared to regard themselves as representatives of any district in the Australian continent. The ground was sodden, and played slowly, which was perhaps a happy circumstance, as from its rough appearance it might have been dangerous to play upon if the wicket had been dry and fiery. It was incomparably superior to the wicket at Stawell, and the cricket partook less of the burlesque order. There was a very large com-

pany of spectators, a stand having been erected
for the ladies, and a band was in attendance to
enliven the proceedings. We lost the toss again,
and the twenty-two, in their first innings, were
dismissed for 68 runs. The last seven wickets
fell for seven runs, Southerton doing the hat
trick. It was in every respect a bowler's wicket,
and our total of 104 was not, on the whole, a poor
achievement. Jupp carried out his bat for 58—
one of the best innings he ever played. Allen's
bowling was remarkably destructive, his record
being 26 overs for 28 runs and six wickets. The
wicket had improved by the second day, but
Southerton and Lillywhite, who were in great
form, were almost unplayable. Our fielding maintained a high level throughout, and we won the
match by nine wickets—our first victory in
Australia.

To fill out the time on the second day, Bush,
Gilbert, my brother, and I played a single-wicket
match against Ten of Warrnambool, but time was
called before we arrived at any decisive result.
On the third day another scratch match was
arranged. The club authorities had, it appeared,
let the selling of refreshments to a contractor, and
in the agreement had used the words "for three
days," instead of "for the match"; consequently
they had to provide something for the third day.
The six English professionals, along with five of
the local cricketers, played a team of eighteen,
who went in first, scored 88 before a wicket fell,
and finally made 172. To this the eleven responded

with 26, of which Greenwood contributed 16, while the other five Englishmen did not break their ducks. At Warrnambool we were occasioned some annoyance by the card-sharpers and professional gamblers, who swarmed on the ground, and plied their trade in complete disregard of the police, who seemed to have no power to suppress the nuisance.

The amateurs of the team amused themselves on the third day at Warrnambool by fishing and shooting. It was here that I had my introduction to kangaroo-hunting, which proved extremely interesting and not a little exciting. The way the stockmen ride when kangaroo-hunting was a revelation. Some of us stood aghast at the recklessness with which they dashed through the bush. I was much impressed with the bush ponies. They are extraordinarily clever creatures, and if you leave their heads alone they will go galloping across scrub and bracken, reaching up to their girth, and though fallen trees may be lying about in all directions they will pick their course with perfect certainty. The kangaroo is either hunted down with rough greyhounds, or ridden down by stockmen, who are so clever in the pursuit that they will gallop alongside a kangaroo till it is tired out, and then catch it by the tail without dismounting. The kangaroo has one deadly weapon of defence—a terrible claw on its hind foot, and the hunter must be careful not to get in front of the animal, or he may be ripped up. In some places kangaroos are driven into stockades, expressly made for the purpose, and there killed by the stockmen.

After a splendid day's sport in the bush we left Warrnambool, then a pretty seaside village, for Melbourne, making the sea voyage in one of the small coast steamers. This was another unpleasant journey. The steamer was abominably uncomfortable—the stench of the oil from the machinery pervading the whole vessel—while the pitching and tossing in the rough sea we encountered soon made us all feel ill. We were sixteen hours on the boat, and till then I had never spent so wretched a night on board ship.

After a day or two in Melbourne, where I rejoined Mrs. Grace, who had stayed with friends during our up-country excursion, we embarked for Sydney. A large crowd saw us off at Melbourne, but we were no sooner outside Hobson's Bay than we came in for more rough weather, and had all to retreat to our cabins.

As we steamed through the Heads on the 22nd of January we were enchanted with the beauty of Sydney Harbour, and no less delighted with the welcome we received. Several steamers, crowded with people, came out to meet us, and greeted us with ringing cheers, which were renewed from five or six thousand voices as we drew alongside the wharf. A public breakfast was ready for us at Tattersall's Hotel, and then came the inevitable toasts, which, in my opinion, are carried to an extreme in Australia. In the afternoon we drove over to the Albert Ground, which has long since been built over, though the present ground has the same designation. It was in splendid condition, green and smooth, but the turf was rather carpety, which is more advantageous to bowlers than batsmen.

The match in Sydney (the fifth of our tour) was against Eighteen of New South Wales, and here I saw Spofforth for the first time. The "demon" was at that time quite a youngster, but he was a very fair bowler, and he took two of our wickets for 16 runs in the second innings. Though I was lucky in the toss, we did not take full advantage of our opportunity, for, with eighteen reliable men fielding in perfect style, we found runs hard to get, and were all disposed of for 92. The catch at square leg which dismissed my brother G. F. was one of the sort it is not easy to forget, the fieldsman taking it brilliantly while running hard. Coates, the slow left-hand bowler, played havoc with our wickets, six falling to him for 29 runs. My cousin, W. Pocock, son of my Uncle Pocock to whom I have often expressed my indebtedness in these reminiscences, was one of our opponents, and he did a good deal towards winning the victory for New South Wales. In each innings I was caught out by the same man from the same bowler, a coincidence which does not often happen. The tremendous shout of jubilation which went up along with hats, caps, umbrellas, walking-sticks, when I was sent back to the pavilion, reminded me of the similar scene at Philadelphia, which has already been described in a previous chapter. The match, which ended in our defeat by eight wickets, was one of the pleasantest we played in Australia.

Once again, to fill up the time, we played a single wicket match—seven Englishmen against twelve of New South Wales. The twelve, who batted first, scored 29. I went in first for the Englishmen, and won the match without assistance, as my score of 28 and a couple of byes produced the desired 30.

The people of Sydney entertained us regally, as, indeed, did the people of Australia generally, and one of the most delightful excursions to which I have been a party was a picnic down Sydney Harbour the next day. We were taken in a launch to explore the charming nooks and coves in the Bays, and if we were impressed by our first glimpse of the splendid harbour, we were enraptured by the exquisite views which were brought under our notice that afternoon. In every respect the picnic was a triumphant success. The arrangements were perfect, the weather faultless, and the means provided for us to amuse ourselves were innumerable. It was a most enjoyable day, and one which, during the twenty-five years which have elapsed since, has always provided a subject for pleasant retrospection.

Our next match ought, according to our programme, to have been played at Maitland, but the heavy rains had occasioned serious floods in the district, and the cricket ground was entirely

submerged. This fixture was consequently can-
celled, and in its place the promoters arranged
for us to go to Bathurst. The change of arrangements was by no means unwelcome to us, as it
obviated the necessity for another of the short
sea voyages, of which we had already had a surfeit.
Apart altogether from the discomfort occasioned
us by these coasting trips, the constant attacks of
sea-sickness to which they subjected the members
of our team seriously affected our cricketing
form. In many respects the teams which have
subsequently visited Australia have been less
severely handicapped than we were by the in-
conveniences attending travelling in the Colony.
Since 1874 locomotion in Australia has been
greatly facilitated, and teams which now visit the
Colony are relieved from the fatigue and worry
occasioned us by the primitive means of transit
which obtained at the time of my first visit.

Many of the leading cricketers of Sydney
accompanied us to Bathurst, while others, including the Governor—Sir Hercules Robinson—and
a party of his friends, followed in our wake and
witnessed the match. On this journey we had
an experience of slow railway travelling, which,
however, proved infinitely more agreeable than
our travelling adventures in the lumbering coaches
in the bush and the tossing little steamers of the
coast. To reach Bathurst we had to cross the
Blue Mountains, the magnificent range of Australian Alps which rear their heads to the sky
about forty miles from Sydney. We began the

ascent by running round one of the mountains, and then by zigzagging up the slope of another. The curves were so sharp that the engine could not turn them, but pulled us along one portion of the line and shunted us up the next. The railway, which has been described as a freak of engineering, did not inspire us with much confidence. The gradients were in places very steep, and at times our sensations were curious, as we were painfully conscious that the snapping of a coupling would send us careering down the precipitous slope to certain death. When we reached the summit, and looked backwards over the track, we could not restrain our astonishment that such an ascent was possible. For some miles the railroad took us along the summit of the mountains, through most picturesque and impressive scenery. At one moment we were on the edge of a magnificent but dreadful gorge, and at another deep down in a darksome cutting. I rode on the engine in ascending the mountain, and was invited to repeat the experiment on our descent, but I declined the privilege. Five miles from Bathurst we came to the railway terminus, and were met by a cavalcade of horsemen, carriages, and every variety of vehicle. For the rest of our journey we were accompanied by a brass band and a body-guard of excited pedestrians. Eventually we reached Bathurst about six o'clock, having been nine hours on the journey of one hundred and forty miles.

The cricket ground at Bathurst was certainly

rather primitive. Luckily the wicket had been
well watered, though they seemed to have been a
little afraid of using the roller, which, as we found
previously and subsequently, was a fault common
to most Australian groundsmen. There was
nothing extraordinary in the cricket in our match
with twenty-two of Bathurst, but very keen
interest was taken in it, and we had the usual big
luncheon and numerous speeches. When driving
past the cricket field one of the Australian
gentlemen made a bet with Mrs. Grace that I
would not hit the ball out of the ground, and at
first sight I did not think I should manage it.
However, I made up my mind to do my best to
win the wager—which was for a pair of gloves—
and I went in for hitting. I got hold of one ball,
full in the bat, and sent it right over the scoring
box, but, unfortunately, it landed just inside the
ground, and so Mrs. Grace lost her bet. The
scoring-box, by the way, was made of a frame-
work of wood, with branches of the native gum-
tree as roofing. Eventually we won the match
by eight wickets. Governor Wells, of Western
Australia, was present throughout the match.

In the evening we were entertained in the
Town Hall at a banquet, at which the Mayor
was in the chair, and afterwards we adjourned
to the ball-room, where dancing was kept up
until the small hours of the morning. During
our visit to Bathurst my wife and I were the
guests of Mr. Frank Suttor, who did everything
a man could do to make us comfortable. One

morning he arranged for me to have a little quail shooting, which was all the more enjoyable, because I had not to walk more than two hundred yards from his house before I entered the paddock—in which thistles were growing almost to the height of my head. The birds were plentiful, and we had excellent sport, bagging twenty-two couples in about two hours.

On the return journey to Sydney we had another delightful glimpse of the picturesque mountain country. Our second match in Sydney was against a combined fifteen of Victoria and New South Wales, and it proved one of the most important events in our tour. We batted first, and when I had scored nine I was dismissed—to the huge delight of the vast concourse of spectators. Our first innings, which realised 170, was redeemed by a fine display by M'Intyre. The combined fifteen made an indifferent show against the bowling of Southerton and Lillywhite, who bowled unchanged throughout the innings, which closed for 98. Luckily for us, the fifteen had just saved the follow-on, which in those days was caused by a deficiency of 80 runs.

The excitement began with our second innings. I was in form, had a good go at the bowling, and twice I hit the ball outside the chains. I soon felt sure that we had the match well in hand, and told our men to hit out, regardless of their wickets. With three hours to play the fifteen went in, wanting 309 runs to evade defeat.

Two courses were open to them—to play to draw,
or to lose the match. They selected the former
and adopted defensive tactics, but we were intent
on victory, and did our level best. We succeeded
in the fight against time, for though the batsmen
played to keep up their wickets rather than to
score runs—as may be judged from the fact that
one stonewaller was at the wickets more than
an hour for 2—we pulled off the victory by
218 runs.

At one moment it seemed as if we were to be
robbed of a hard-earned win by an ugly incident.
Some of the spectators raised noisy objections to
a decision given by one of the umpires. The
batsman who had been given out left the wicket
and the next batsman came in. Then the first
batsman, acting apparently on advice given him in
the pavilion, returned to the wicket, and, repu-
diating the decision of the umpire, claimed the
right to continue his innings. The curious sight
was witnessed of three batsmen being at the
wickets at the same time. To this unconstitutional
proceeding we naturally entered an emphatic
protest, and as the batsman refused to budge I
took my team off the field. It was only when we
reached the pavilion that the authorities succeeded
in persuading the batsman to abandon his ridiculous attitude. We then resumed play, and won
the match amidst intense excitement. Mr. Bush,
our wicket-keeper, performed his duties in this
match, as indeed he did throughout the tour,
with distinct credit to himself, and greatly to our

advantage, his contribution to our success in the last moments, when the result was hanging in the balance, being invaluable. At the close of play we had quite an ovation in front of the pavilion. The spectators stood closely packed together, cheering vociferously, and refusing to be satisfied until one by one we had all appeared and bowed our acknowledgments. It was like the scene at Kennington Oval, when at the close of an exciting match the Surrey crowd masses itself in front of the pavilion and shouts for the heroes of the day.

With this match we ended our tour in New South Wales. We were loath to say good-bye to Sydney, which we liked as a city, and in which we had been entertained with generous kindness —in excess even of that accorded us in our previous stopping-places, which is saying a good deal. Another choppy sea voyage on our way to Melbourne put the whole team *hors de combat* for two days. In the third day the storm subsided and the sea calmed down, and we crawled on deck again. I espied some sacks of oysters which were going down to Melbourne. One of the stewards whom I consulted said that he dared not touch the oysters, but after a little argument he told me that if I liked to buy a whole sack I could do so. We struck a bargain, and in less time than it takes to write it we had half a dozen stewards hard at work opening oysters and cutting bread and butter, while we entertained the poor sea-sick passengers to a feast of stout and oysters. The sack, which cost me about fifteen shillings, contained so many that even after we had made an oyster supper a plentiful supply was left for the stewards.   We had no sooner reached Melbourne than we started on another journey to Sandhurst, one of the gold settlements of Victoria. Here we played a team of twenty-two, which was unique in one respect—every man who played was an actual resident in the district.   The heat was dreadful, and the ball got up dangerously on the dry, crumbling wicket.   Again I was in hitting form, and made 52 in the first innings and 72 not out in the second.

Several interesting episodes were connected with our next match, which took place at Castlemaine.   When I was batting I hit a ball high in the air towards the boundary.   The fieldsman, in bringing off a good catch, fell over the ropes, whereupon I appealed to the umpire, who at once gave me "not-out," on the ground that the ball was caught out of bounds.   An ordinary boundary hit was regarded as four, but a hit over the ropes counted five, and the scorers naturally wanted to know with how many runs they should credit me.   To our surprise the umpire refused to allow us more than the single which we had run before the ball was caught.   As I had a keen suspicion that I ought to have been given out I did not argue out the point, though I was greatly amused by the inconsistency of the umpire, who happened to be our own man.

The Australian umpire, not to be outdone, gave an

equally ridiculous decision. One of the batsmen, who had ventured out of his ground, was plainly stumped by Mr. Bush, but much to every one's astonishment was given "not-out." This was a decision we could scarcely accept, but in response to our request for an explanation the umpire promptly said, "Ah, Mr. Bush, I was watching you then, and when you took the ball the tip of your nose was in front of the wicket, and, as you know, rule 35 says that if any part of a wicket-keeper's person be over or before the wicket the striker shall not be out if he is stumped." Of course we could not dispute the decision after this ingenious explanation ; so the batsman went on with his innings.

A still more amusing episode, of which Mr. Bush was again the hero, took place in our second innings. When only a few runs were needed to win the match Bush joined Mr. Gilbert, who was set and batting well. The two batsmen agreed to steal runs wherever possible—in fact, to adopt tip and run tactics. As the wicket was as bad as it could possibly be, I am not sure that it was not the best thing they could do. They had been batting a few minutes when Bush received a fast ball, which shot as he thought between his legs and the wicket. Gilbert cried, " Come on, Frizzy " (which was our familiar nickname for Bush), and they ran as hard as they could for four runs. To his dismay Bush then discovered that the ball had really bowled him, and that the bail had been off while they had been dashing between the wickets.

Needless to say, Bush never heard the last of that episode, and was chaffed unmercifully about it all through the tour.   Gilbert won the match for us by a brilliant innings.   I had only one ball, and I did not really want any more on such a wicket, which made the bowling bump about in a perilous fashion.   As a writer describing the match at the time said, "The most merciful escape was that none of us was killed.   For myself I had no more pleasing experience of the Australian tour than the end of this match. M'Intyre was thoroughly at home as he played merrily about the ribs of those Castlemaniacs, and enjoyed himself in a pure and innocent fashion to the full."

While at Castlemaine we had a little experience, which we had no desire to repeat, of the recklessness of Australian four-in-hand drivers.   The road from the hotel to the cricket ground was exceedingly hilly, and down some of these declivities, which no English driver would descend without his brake full on, and his skid pan fixed, the Australian driver let his horses " rip," as he called it, which meant giving them their head and letting them go galloping down at a breakneck pace.   One or twice we were in mortal terror of our lives, and dismounted with feelings of relief when the coach came to a standstill.

We went back to Melbourne to play our return match against Victoria.   As the Victorian Eighteen had beaten us on the first occasion the committee decided to play a team of fifteen, but the experiment was a failure, as we won by seven wickets, and found it a comparatively easy task. After the match we filled out the afternoon by playing against Eleven of the Victorians, so as to give an exhibition of what we could do with only eleven in the field. I think the Melbourne people were pretty well satisfied, as Jupp and I made 140 before we were parted. When time was called we had lost five wickets for 250 runs, all made in two hours and a half. My individual score on this occasion was 126. In this match one of the Australian bowlers, finding that he could not get my wicket, lost his temper, and deliberately threw at me, an act which no one afterwards regretted more than the offender, except, perhaps, the players on his own side.

A visit to Tasmania was the next event in our programme. We crossed from Melbourne to Launceston, a voyage of twenty-nine hours' duration, with a rough beginning but a delightful ending. The people of Tasmania won all our hearts by their extreme cordiality and unbounded hospitality. Here we played Twenty-two of Tasmania, whom we defeated, after a somewhat uneventful match, by an innings and 32 runs. The only memorable feature of the game was the presence of Mr. J. C. Lord, who some years previously had played for Hants, and who on this occasion made 34 and 36 by dashing cricket. Off one over by Lillywhite he scored 14 runs. G. H. Bailey, who subsequently came to England in 1878 with Gregory's Australian team, was one of the Tasmanians, while the two Butlers (C. W. and E. H.), of Hobart Town, were also among our antagonists. It may be remembered, perhaps, that Mr. E. H. Butler, while on a visit to England, played on one occasion for the Gentlemen against the Players at Prince's Ground.

The drive by coach from Launceston to Hobart Town—a journey of a hundred and twenty-five miles—was a pleasant contrast to our coaching tours in the bush country. The road, which had been made in the old convict days, was in magnificent condition, and the scenery through which we passed realised all our expectations of the boasted beauties of the picturesque island. The coach left Launceston at five o'clock in the morning; but Bush, Gilbert, Mrs. Grace, and I stole a march upon it by travelling overnight to a place about forty miles on the road to Hobart Town, which we reached about ten o'clock at night. Our engagement at Hobart Town was a match against Twenty-two of Southern Tasmania, which was played on a splendid wicket, and proved enjoyable in every way. A very fine innings by G. F., who made 154, was the most notable feature of the game. This, besides being the record innings of our tour, was the highest score ever made in Tasmania, and the largest individual total reached by any English player who had up to that time visited Australia.

The Tasmanians did very well with the bat, and treated our bowlers with less respect than they had been accustomed to receive during our tour.

Lillywhite, who in his first over was hit for six, took his revenge by bowling Mr. Lord (who had done all the scoring at Launceston, and was expected to repeat his achievement at Hobart Town) for a duck. Another batsman made six fours off successive balls, while Mr. W. H. Walker hit me out of the ground twice in one over. Altogether, the Tasmanians made a very plucky fight, and though ultimately they were vanquished by eight wickets they gave us a lively game. The Governor of Tasmania, Sir Charles Du Cane, who was a member of the M.C.C., manifested keen interest in the game, watching nearly every ball that was bowled. At the luncheon one of the speakers remarked that fourteen years previously he had prophesied that an All England Eleven would be brought out to Australia, and that the results of their matches would be sent to England by telegraph. He seemed very proud to have seen the fulfilment of his prophecy.

On the way back to Launceston I had a couple of days' good shooting. To show how thoughtful the people were in everything that concerned our comfort, I may say that two gentlemen, prominent bankers in Australia, who were visiting Tasmania at this time, set themselves the task of lightening the burden of our journey by acting as our advance couriers. They travelled a few hours in front of us, and arranged that meals and rooms should be ready for us at the hotels on the route. We greatly enjoyed our sojourn in Tasmania, and particularly appreciated the splendid apples which are grown in the island, and which, though now to be seen in every good fruiterer's shop in England, were in those days a choice delicacy.

After returning from Tasmania we stayed in Melbourne just long enough to play the third match of our rubber against Victoria. As we had each won a match interest in this fixture was exceedingly keen, five thousand spectators surrounding the ground when play began. After our signal victory against the team of fifteen on our previous visit to Melbourne the authorities thought it wise to revert to the original order of things, and we consequently played a team of eighteen. I had an extraordinary run of bad luck in the toss in all the important matches, and in this case the spin of the coin went against me once more. The cricket was, on the whole, uneventful ; but it is curious to note that both G. F. and I were bowled by Midwinter, who afterwards came over to England and played for Gloucester under the birth qualification. I have vivid recollections of the tropical thunderstorm which broke over the ground on the last day of the match. In a few minutes the wicket was flooded, and though both sides were anxious to finish the rubber, further play was obviously impossible, and the match was drawn.

This was our last match in Victoria. The promoters of our tour had arranged for one match to be played in South Australia, and thither we turned our faces. Of course the match ought to have been played at Adelaide, but

in those days, though interest in cricket was keen
in the town, the Club was only a small one, and
was unable to make the promoters so good an
offer as the people of Kadina.   So for the sake of
few pounds we were sent up to that small copper
mining village in Yorke Peninsula.   We left
Melbourne by boat, and almost immediately
steamed into a terrific storm.   Sea-sickness and
all its consequent miseries overtook us all during
this journey, which instead of the usual forty-
eight was extended to seventy-four hours.   The
steamer pitched and rolled and tossed about in
an outrageous fashion, and when we reached
Port Adelaide we one and all struck against con-
tinuing the journey by sea.   We hired a coach at
Adelaide, and drove the remaining hundred miles,
of which seventy were over a bush track.   This
journey by coach was monotonous enough, but it
was heavenly by comparison with the coasting
voyages.

When we reached Kadina, we went out in
search of the cricket ground ; and a search
it really proved.   We came to an open space,
and then asked to be directed to the cricket
ground.   "This is it," some one said, and we
whistled in astonishment.   There was scarcely a
blade of grass to be seen, while the whole area
was covered with small stones.   On the morning
of the match a bushel of pebbles was swept up.
I fervently hope I shall never again have to play
cricket on such a ground.   Very naturally our
men funked batting on a wicket like that, and, in

consequence, no one was expected to make a big score. Our innings realised 64, a small enough total, but nevertheless quite sufficient to win for us a single innings victory. As to the Kadina Twenty-two, their wickets fell like ninepins, as may be imagined from the fact that they managed to make only 43 runs in their first innings, while in the second their aggregate was 13, of which only 8 were made from the bat. Eighteen out of the twenty-two utterly failed to score at all. Our bowlers enjoyed themselves, M'Intyre getting sixteen wickets for five runs, and Lillywhite thirteen for six. The match was a farce, and no one realised its ludicrous aspect more than we did.

Of course cricket like this cannot be taken seriously, and the match at Kadina is scarcely worth recording at all. One or two incidents which happened made it memorable. Mr. T. W. Wills, the old Rugbeian, had been coaching the Kadina team for over a month in view of the match, and as he had been instructing them in the game the Kadina people thought a good deal of his prowess, and expected him to do valiantly against us. He made a pair of spectacles—clean bowled in each innings—and after that the Kadina people were interested in him no more.

Another reminiscence of the match may be interesting. When Mr. Bush went in to bat he missed the first ball, and was clean bowled. As he was the last man in, the Kadina men began to move towards the tent, but Bush, in the coolest possible manner, picked up the stump, put it in the ground, and turning to the umpire said, "That was only my trial ball. I always insist on having a trial"; whereupon the umpire, no doubt thinking that Bush knew more about cricket than he did, said, "Certainly, sir," and gave him in. The decision, however, made no difference to the course of events, as Bush, after all the trouble he had taken to get another innings, failed to score—his partner being promptly dismissed in the next over.

A third incident is associated in my memory with the Kadina match. That great supporter of cricket in South Australia, Sir Edwin Smith, of Adelaide, offered a silver cup for the highest scorer against the English Eleven in this match. None of the Kadina men scored many runs, but two tied with totals of seven each, and after some discussion it was agreed that they should contest for the cup in a single wicket match, in which I was to bowl and two of the English team to field. One of the competitors for the cup was on friendly terms with us, and our sympathies lay with him. His antagonist batted first, and I disposed of him before he scored. Our friend then took his place at the wicket, and we hoped he would score, but he met with the same fate. Again each man batted, and again each man was dismissed for a duck. The contest was getting exciting, and the destiny of the cup hung in the balance, when for the third time I dismissed the first man for a duck. Then we had the satisfaction of seeing our friend make a single off a very flukey hit, and thus win the cup.

Our tour was now concluded, so far as our agreement with the promoters was concerned, but the Adelaide people, who considered they had been badly treated, sent up several of their leading cricketers to Kadina to invite us to play a supplementary match at Adelaide. As we had been sent at great inconvenience to Kadina, in the interests of the promoters' pockets, I sympathised with the Adelaide people and consented to play in their city. My acquiescence brought upon my head the wrath of the promoters, who had foolishly agreed with the people at Kadina that no other match should be played in South Australia, forgetting that my agreement with them was for fourteen matches only. They threatened all kinds of proceedings, but we carried out our intention to play at Adelaide, and I felt no compunction in the matter after the shabby treatment to which Adelaide had been subjected.

This addition to our original programme necessitated an all-night journey from Kadina, which in turn led to uncomfortable adventures. In the dark we lost the track, and began driving about in the bush, until at last, as we had taken seven hours to cover thirty-five miles, we thought it wiser to wait until daylight before proceeding on our journey. Consequently we did not reach Adelaide until the afternoon, and after our night's exposure were so stiff and tired that to play

cricket decently was almost beyond us. The
Twenty-two of South Australia, against whom we
played, did not, however, take full advantage of
our incapacity, as they lost eight wickets for ten
runs, and were finally disposed of for 66.
Eventually we won the match by seven wickets.
The lavish hospitality heaped upon us by the
Adelaide people made our last hours in the
Colony exceedingly pleasant.

On Saturday afternoon, March 28, we left
Adelaide by train for Glenelg, where we joined
the *Nubia*, homeward bound. Many of our
friends in Adelaide came with us to say good-bye
at the steamer's side. Our voyage to England
was an easy and delightful journey. We had a
rapid passage, through calm and placid seas, the
only untoward incident being a sand storm in the
Suez Canal. The latter half of the journey was
made in the steamship *Khedive*, which stopped
long enough at Alexandria to give us time to see
the races, in which I saw dromedaries competing
for the first and only time in my life. We landed
in England on May 18.

Our tour had, on the whole, been conspicuously
successful. We never lost a match after we got
into form, and our record for the tour ran : Fifteen
matches played, ten won, two drawn, and three
lost. Of course, in those days Australian cricket
had not reached the high standard to which it
has now attained. It was, however, steadily improving, and there is no doubt that the Colonial
cricketers had greatly benefited from the tours

made by the teams which had previously visited Australia under Stephenson and Parr. Caffyn and Lawrence, who had stayed out in Australia, had also done a great deal to develop interest and efficiency in the game. We met the pick of Australian cricketers at Melbourne and Sydney, though some of the men we played against in Tasmania were not to be despised. The bowling even at that date was very good indeed, especially that of Allan and Boyle, and the fielding was very fair. As we proved by experience, we could easily beat any team of fifteen that could be gathered together in Australia, but with eighteen or twenty-two against us victory was not so easy. The best cricketers we met were, as a rule, English University and Public School men, who had settled in the Colony, but some of the native-born showed considerable aptitude, especially in bowling.

What struck me most in Australia on this my first visit was the scanty attention that was given to the preparation of the wicket for cricket matches. Until I pointed out the fact that the cricket was always vastly improved by proper attention having been paid to the wickets several days before the match, they seemed to have no idea of the importance of good wickets. We had the satisfaction of knowing that in this matter, at any rate, we taught the Australians a thing or two. I have no doubt that this and the subsequent tours made by English teams had a most salutary influence on the development of

Australian cricket ; as, apart from the experience they gained by playing against the best cricketers we could send out, the vast interest taken in the various matches led to the adoption of cricket as the national game of the Colony.

On our return to England, we found that our doings in Australia had been followed by cricketers at home with the keenest possible interest, and that, for the first time, people in England had received the results of cricket matches played in Australia by means of the telegraph.

CHAPTER VI

CRICKET IN THE SEVENTIES

1870 IN the year 1870 the laws of cricket were altered in one important essential. Up to that time the bowler could only change ends once in an innings, but at a special general meeting of the M.C.C. the rule was amended, so that a bowler could be allowed to change ends twice. To prevent him bowling three successive overs, it was decreed that he should not bowl two overs in succession. The first time this new rule was brought into operation was in the match at Lord's between M.C.C. and Yorkshire on May 30 and 31. The amendment in the rules was an important addition to the freedom of bowlers, and removed a restriction under which many cricketers had chafed for a long time.

From a personal point of view the year 1870 is memorable to me, because it was one of my best all-round seasons. In both batting and bowling I met with remarkable success. I made nine individual scores of a hundred and upwards, and in thirty-three innings (among which were twelve for the M.C.C., four for Gloucester, and four for

the Gentlemen), I attained an average of over
54 runs. In 1870 the Gloucestershire County
Cricket Club was properly organised and constituted for the first time. The year was notable
in the annals of County Cricket generally, but
particularly for Gloucestershire, with which,
naturally, my ties were very close. At that
time Gloucester had no county cricket ground,
so we had to play our first match on Durdham
Down. We played Surrey twice in this season,
and beat them at Bristol by 51 runs, and at the
Oval by an innings and 129 runs.

On the occasion of the Surrey match on Durdham
Down a curious incident happened. The match
excited great interest, and a vast crowd assembled.
Our boundaries were marked by flags, but the
spectators encroached upon the ground. Pooley,
who was batting, hit the ball to leg, where it was
stopped by the spectators. He thereupon insisted
on the crowd being cleared back behind the
boundary flags. When this had been done,
Filgate, who was fielding at long leg, was able
to stand some yards farther back. I was bowling,
and by accident sent down a ball on the leg
side, which Pooley hit vigorously, with the result
that Filgate made a grand catch on the leg
boundary. It was assumed by the spectators that
I had laid a trap for Pooley, but nothing was
farther from my mind. Whenever I have bowled
a ball to leg (even by inadvertence) and the batsman has been dismissed off it, I have been given
the credit of having bowled a leg ball on pur-

pose. Indeed, the ball has often been called "W. G.'s trap." I may have been guilty of bowling these wily balls occasionally, but I have received much more credit than I ever deserved for securing wickets off leg balls. Besides the matches against Surrey, Gloucestershire also played the M.C.C. and Ground, and defeated them by an innings and 88 runs. The Gloucestershire Club thus entered on its County Cricket career with three signal successes in its first year of existence.

Something approaching a gloom was cast over the cricket season by the calamitous accident which happened at Lord's during the match between Notts and the M.C.C. on June 13, 14. At that time, as I have said, Lord's Ground was in a most unsatisfactory condition—so dangerous that some cricketers declined to play there. In this match Summers, a promising young professional player, who would have been a source of strength to Nottingham, lost his life through a blow on the head from a bumping ball. He had only just taken his place at the wicket in his second innings, when the bowler sent down a short-pitched ball, which bumped and hit Summers, knocking him down. When the accident happened no one imagined that it would end fatally, but the next day Summers unwisely appeared on the ground in the blazing sunshine, and afterwards travelled down to Nottingham. The heat of the sun, and the shaking up on the railway journey, aggravated the injury, with fatal results. The ball was certainly a short one, but it was the condition of the ground that made it bump. The bowler was not in the least to blame for the catastrophe, but he was terribly cut up, and I shall never forget his mental distraction. The blow was a hard one, but I firmly believe that the fatal consequence might have been obviated if Summers had been persuaded to rest awhile.

It may be interesting, as evidence of the comparative safety of cricket as a game, to note that in my thirty-five years' experience I have seen but two fatal accidents. The first was the case of Summers ; the second was that of a poor boy at Harrow. I was invited by Lord Bessborough to go down with him to Harrow to give the schoolboys some practice, and I always think that both he and I were indirectly the cause of this fatality, although it was one of a character that could not be foreseen. While another game was going on we were hitting catches to some of the boys, and the unfortunate boy who was killed was standing as umpire. I think he was looking round watching us, when a ball was hit to leg, and struck the poor boy behind the ear with such force that he gave one gasp and then expired. I am glad to say that in this case also, the players, who were the indirect cause of the boy's death, were in no way to blame.

Such catastrophes happen very infrequently, for the death-rate of cricket is exceedingly low, and the proportion of serious accidents very slight by comparison with casualties in other games. I am inclined to believe that the only real danger in cricket arises when spectators crowd round batsmen at practice. When I see the reckless way in which onlookers cluster round batsmen who are practising before big matches begin I am often surprised that there are not two or three severe accidents at every match. It is aston shing to me that the ball should so often go whizzing among the people without doing any more injury than bruising some one's shins.

This reference to accidents at cricket recalls an agonising mental experience I once had at Leicester. I was staying with a friend at a hospital, and one afternoon we went out on the grounds for a little cricket practice. After I had been batting a little while I hit a ball out of the hospital grounds into an adjacent street. We thought it was useless to go after the ball, so we abandoned play. A few minutes later the casualty-ward bell rang, and word was brought to us that a child had been struck on the head with a cricket ball, and was lying unconscious in the ward. We jumped to the conclusion that our ball had done the mischief, and with feelings easier imagined than described we hurried to attend the little patient. The injury was a severe one, and the case looked hopeless. I was greatly distressed, and felt very miserable, until some one inquired where the child had met with the accident. It then transpired that the injuries had been inflicted on a cricket ground a mile and a half away from

the hospital. I shall never forget my own feelings
while I was labouring under the delusion that I
was the cause of the child's injury, and in the
light of my own experience I can fully realise the
agony of mind of the bowler who was the un-
witting cause of poor Summer's death.

In this same year (1870) we played a very festive match at Beeston, near Nottingham, between
the Gentlemen of the South and the Gentlemen
of the North. My brother G. F. was in fine
fettle, and made a grand stand with Mr. I. D.
Walker, who was playing at this time in magnificent form. Fred scored 189, and Mr. Walker 179.
My own score of 77 was quite over-shadowed
by the brilliant displays of my brother and Mr.
Walker. Owing to the big scoring the match
was left drawn, but a little dispute which arose
during the Northern innings (in the course of
which Mr. A. N. Hornby played a fine innings of
103) makes me remember the event. The boundaries were marked, as was usual in those days,
by flags, and the line between the flags was
necessarily a matter of conjecture. One of the
Northern team skied a ball to the long fields,
where a fieldsman was standing close to the flag.
He caught the ball, and the batsman was walking
out, when some one shouted that the fieldsman
had overstepped the boundary line. The umpire,
of course, could not possibly see, and we adjourned to the out-field to take evidence, which
was very conflicting. Eventually one of the
leading men on the Northern side came running

out of the tent and said, "Oh yes, he was over the boundary," so the umpire promptly declared the batsman "not-out." We afterwards learnt that the gentleman, upon whose declaration the umpire's decision was founded, had been merely chaffing, and, as a matter of fact, had not seen the catch made. The dispute, however, was of a thoroughly friendly order, and added to, rather than retarded, the enjoyment of the match. In those days we worried less about securing victories—we were playing cricket for pleasure and not for records, of which we thought very little. Our first consideration was to have a good game, and we did not mind very much whether we won or lost, so long as the cricket was enjoyable.

I have noticed that batsmen who have to wait a long time with their pads on for their innings frequently fail to score. I attribute this very largely to the nervous strain of anticipation. In this match at Beeston, Mr. G. Strachan waited for about six hours for the dismissal of either G. F. or Mr. Walker, whom he was to succeed. When at last he did go in, he was dismissed with his second ball.

The North *v.* South match at Lord's this year (1870) was memorable for the fact that several of the Northern players, who, owing to the schism in the ranks of the professional cricketers, had not taken part in this encounter for some years, reappeared at Marylebone. Another interesting fact in connection with the match is that it was George Parr's last appearance at Lord's. Though forty-four years of age, he was then in good form, and secured 41 runs.

An incident in the M.C.C. *v.* Notts match this year (1870) corroborates my remark that cricket was not played in the seventies in the same strict spirit as it is at the present time, when everything seems to be sacrificed on the altar of records and championship honours. After the match had been in progress for a short time, Mr. Walker, who was fielding at point, dislocated his little finger in stopping a hard cut, and, in consequence, was unable to go on playing. After some little discussion Mr. Richardson was permitted by Daft, the captain of the Nottingham team, to take Mr. Walker's place. This was, technically, a breach of the rules, but really an act of chivalry, of a kind which I am afraid is not too common to-day. Daft's action evoked some strong feeling, and brought some unnecessary censures upon the M.C.C. for sanctioning such a course. The complaints were quite uncalled for, as it ought, in my opinion, to be the desire of every cricketer to play the game in a chivalrous spirit, irrespective of the consequence. Unfortunately the intensely partisan feeling which has developed out of the County Championship contests has, to some extent, destroyed the good-fellowship which prompted Daft to make his sportsmanlike concession. Still, I must mention a similar incident which happened in August, 1897. Lancashire won the toss against Sussex, and went in first. Bland, for Sussex, bowled three overs, and was then taken so ill that there was no chance of his taking any further part in the match. Mr. A. C. Maclaren most courteously allowed another man to take his place.

Though County Cricket was now being organised on a strict basis, questions of qualification, either birth or residential, did not give us much trouble in the early seventies, and during this season I played for Twenty-two of Worcestershire against the United North of England Eleven. The ground was not in the best order, and the twenty-two were all dismissed for 114, of which I made 74. I got out when the score stood 96 for seventeen wickets, my last nine partners having all failed to score a single run. We eventually won the match by thirteen wickets.

1871   The year 1871 was made remarkable by a succession of notable benefit matches. Willsher, H. H. Stephenson, and John Lillywhite were all given benefits, and as all three were players in the very front rank, a widespread interest was taken in the matches arranged on their behalf. For Willsher's benefit, which took place at Lord's on July 10, 11 and 12, a match between Married and Single was arranged. I played for the Single side, and made 189 (not out). Unfortunately for Willsher, rain set in, and on the second day not a single ball was bowled. Frequent showers interfered with the attendance on the third day, with the consequence that Willsher did not benefit very much. I was exceedingly sorry, and subsequently helped to arrange another match on his behalf. It was played at Mote Park, Maidstone, in September, between W. G. Grace's Eleven and Kent. I was fortunate enough to score 81 (not out) in the first innings, and 42 (not out) in the second, so that in the three innings of Willsher's benefit matches I scored 312 runs without being dismissed. I must not forget to mention a magnificent not-out innings of 126 by Mr. W. Yardley in the match at Maidstone.

H. H. Stephenson's benefit match took place— of course—at Kennington Oval, North v. South, on July 31, August 1 and 2. There was an immense crowd of spectators, and Stephenson benefited in consequence. Along with the spectators, I was disappointed with the way in which the match opened, as I was given out leg before wicket from the first ball bowled. The South scored 193, and then dismissed the North for 177. In our second innings I completely redeemed my failure in the first. At the end of the second day's play the South had scored 195 for two wickets, of which number 142 stood to my credit. The match was thus left in a crucial condition for the next day's play, and a grand crowd of spectators mustered for the finish. When the Southern score had reached 298 I had carried my overnight contribution to 200, and at luncheon time the score stood at 377 for four wickets, my share of the run-getting being now 246 (not out). When I had added 22 runs, and the total had reached 436, I was snapped at the wicket. My innings of 268 was the largest up to that time attained by me, and the greatest individual score ever made at the Oval. Needless to say, the match was a perfect success in every respect. H. H. Stephenson was delighted at my performance, and presented me with a ring, which I now have in my possession. In accordance with their custom, the Surrey Club presented me with a bat, bearing the following inscription on a gold plate :

PRESENTED TO

W. G. GRACE, Esq.,

BY THE SURREY COUNTY CRICKET CLUB,

FOR HIS MAGNIFICENT INNINGS OF

TWO HUNDRED AND SIXTY-EIGHT,

IN THE MATCH,

NORTH v. SOUTH,

AT KENNINGTON OVAL, 2ND AUGUST 1871.

I made my second, and last, appearance at the old Hove County Cricket Ground, at Brighton, at John Lillywhite's benefit, which took place on August 14, 15, and 16. The match was Gentlemen v. Players. This was the first year in which three of these matches were played, and Lillywhite, who was one of the most popular professional cricketers of his day, was favoured by splendid weather, and had a capital benefit. History repeated itself in my first innings, as J. C. Shaw, who had got my wicket with his first ball at H. H. Stephenson's benefit at the Oval, knocked my off stump out of the ground at Brighton before I had scored. But again I retrieved my misfortune by my second innings. At the end of the second day's play I was not out 200, and next morning I added 17 more before I was once again caught by the wicket-keeper, the catch in this case being off a ball to leg, which I skied. During this innings I had a long partnership with my brother G. F. Between us we put on 241 runs before we were separated. G. F.'s innings of 98 was the result of brilliant hitting. As one of the papers said : " It was a grand and faultless exhibition of superfine cricket from the first to last, his play being remarkable for some of the quickest and smartest hitting of the season, and noticeably for its absence of any-thing like a positive chance." After Lillywhite's match my brother and I were both made recipients of presentation bats.

After twenty-seven years of active participation in the game, the celebrated George Parr, of Nottingham, retired from cricket this year, playing for the last time for Notts against fourteen Gen-tlemen on May 29, 30, and 31, at Trent Bridge. He finished his brilliant career by making 32 (not out) and 53.

The first county match ever played by Glouces-tershire on an enclosed ground at home took place on August 3, 4, and 5, when, by per-mission of the Council of the College, who very kindly put the College Close at our disposal during the vacation, the match against Notting-ham took place on Clifton College Ground. This new epoch in the club's history aroused great enthusiasm. Several episodes made the match notable. My brother E. M. and I opened the Gloucestershire innings against the bowling of J. C. and Alfred Shaw, and made 134 runs before my dismissal dissolved the partnership. This was stated at the time to be the first occasion on which over a hundred runs had been made off the Nottingham bowling before a wicket fell. It is a fact worth mentioning, as an illustration of the way batsmen "get their eyes out" during the luncheon interval, that when we adjourned for lunch E. M. and I had made 129 for no wicket down, but that on resumption of play I was dismissed after five runs had been added to the score, while my brother lost his wicket with the total at 148. E. M.'s innings of 65 was a fine display of patient batting. Thanks to a splendid not-out innings of 51 by Richard Daft, Nottingham saved the match, which was left drawn just when Gloucestershire seemed within sight of victory.

A remarkable innings by Mr. T. G. Matthews for Gloucestershire against Surrey in a match played about a fortnight later should be chronicled as one of the historic events of the year. Mr. Matthews, who went in first, compiled 201 runs, which, in those days, was an extraordinary score. It is true that at that time Surrey was not quite so strong in bowling as the eleven is to-day; nevertheless, Mr. Matthews's innings was a grand performance.

This year was one of my best seasons. On

ten occasions I made upwards of a century in first-class matches. My highest total was 268 for South *v.* North, at Stephenson's match, and my other centuries were : 217 for Gentlemen *v.* Players, at Brighton (John Lillywhite's benefit match) ; .189 (not out) for Single *v.* Married, at Lord's (Edgar Willsher's benefit) ; 181 for M.C.C. *v.* Surrey, at Lord's ; 178 for South *v.* North, at Lord's ; 162 for Gentlemen of England *v.* Cambridge University, at Fenner's Ground ; 146 for M.C.C. *v.* Surrey, at the Oval ; 118 for Gentlemen of the South *v.* Gentlemen of the North, at Lillie Bridge, West Brompton ; 117 for M.C.C. *v.* Kent, at Canterbury ; and 116 for Gloucestershire *v.* Notts, at Nottingham (the first hundred ever scored on Nottingham ground). In these ten innings my combined scores reached 1692—an average of 188 ; my aggregate for the year in first-class matches was 2739 runs for thirty-five innings—an average of 78·9; and in all matches (first-class and otherwise) I made 3696 runs.

Just before the end of this year I lost my father. His death robbed Gloucestershire county cricket of one of its most ardent supporters. The work he did, first for the Mangotsfield Club, then for the West Gloucestershire, and finally for the Gloucestershire County Club, materially helped to popularise cricket in the West. Happily he lived to see the County Club, whose inception was in a large measure due to his initiative, on a firm and prosperous basis, and with a prominent place among the counties.

1872   The cricket season of 1872 was ushered in by
a period of rainy weather, with late frosts and
thunderstorms, with the result that until well on
in the season the bowlers had all the advantage.
Cricket opened early, with a match between the
North and South, at Liverpool, on April 29 and
30. Jupp and I, who went in first for the South,
scored 112 runs before we were separated, but
the rest of our side added only 22. One does not
expect to win a single innings victory with a score
of 134, but on this occasion that was achieved.
In their first innings the Northern team made
only 46, and on following on were all dismissed
for 64. Thus the aggregate of the Northern
team's two innings was two runs less than the
result of the stand made by Jupp and myself.

The most extraordinary match of the year was
one which took place at Lord's between the
M.C.C. and Surrey. Incessant rain, which fell
throughout Monday, May 13, delayed the start
until Tuesday, the 14th, when a wonderful succession of events was witnessed. The experiment of covering the wicket with tarpaulin to
protect it from the drenching rain had been tried,
but it turned out a dismal failure. When we
began to play the ground was very soft, and the
weather very cold. Jack Smith, of Cambridge,
and I went in to open the M.C.C. innings against
Southerton and Marten, and a most sensational
opening it proved. Almost immediately the
match began I was given out lbw by our own
umpire, Royston, and had to retire for a duck.

Smith soon followed, being caught by Jupp at long stop. Mr. Coote, the next batsman, was bowled in the same over, Shaw was sent back by the third ball he received, and Mr. D. R. Onslow was dismissed by his first ball. Mr. Brune and T. Hearne fell victims to successive balls by Southerton—which made seven wickets for no runs. We began to get very uneasy, and the crowd very excited. It seemed as if the whole team would be dismissed without a run. I can safely say that in my thirty-five years' experience I have never seen a more astonishing collapse. Fortunately the rot was stopped by Captain Beecher, who, amid great applause, gave the scorers their first work by hitting a leg ball for two, but the Captain lost his partner at this stage, and the score stood at eight wickets for two runs. When, six runs later, the Captain, who had done all the scoring, was dismissed, the telegraph board bore this extraordinary appearance :--

Total	8
Wickets	9
Last man	8

To our intense relief, the last wicket (Rylott and Howitt) put on 8 more runs. Then the sensational innings, which had occupied only forty-four minutes, came to its end for 16 runs. Though the Surrey men were very jubilant, their own innings was not much of a triumph, as we got them out for 49. Our second venture realised 71, and left the Surrey team 39 to get to win the match. The fact that they had difficulty in doing this speaks volumes for the condition of the ground. It was not until they had lost five wickets that they made the necessary runs. Thus the match, which was expected to go over three days, ended in one, no fewer than thirty-five wickets having fallen in a single day's play. Of course the bowlers had every conceivable advantage owing to the muddy state of the wicket, which was so bad that I do not think we should nowadays venture to begin a match on a ground in the condition Lord's was that day.

During this year two interesting experiments were tried, with a view to minimising the advantage which batsmen were supposed to have gained over bowlers. The first experiment was made at Lord's, in a match between the M.C.C. and the next Twenty, on May 9, when the wickets used were an inch higher and broader than usual—*i.e.*, they stood 29 inches by 9 inches. The experiment was a failure, and was never repeated. A month later (June 14 and 15), in a match between Birkenhead Park and Manchester, four wickets were used instead of three. This experiment was also a failure.

It has often been suggested that the height and width of the wickets should be enlarged, but in my opinion the suggestion is worthless. Its adoption would not sufficiently handicap the best batsmen, while it would seriously affect inferior players, who do occasionally make a few runs under present conditions, but would stand no chance against good bowling if the wickets were enlarged. Although it is often urged that the batsman has got the upper hand of the bowler—and, to a certain extent, I agree with this contention—I do not think any alteration in the size of the wickets would improve matters. We cannot control the weather, which is the most important factor in the success or failure of the batsmen. When wickets are dry and hard, the batsman has his day, but on bad wickets the bowler gets his turn, and on those occasions bowlers have no difficulty in dismissing batsmen cheaply—as, for instance, Southerton and Marten in the M.C.C. innings just recorded. The proposal to have four wickets is of no more value, as it would militate against second- and third-class players, leaving the first-class batsman unaffected.

After twenty-one years' service with the M.C.C., James Grundy resigned his duties at Lord's. At one time Grundy and Wootton were the mainstay of M.C.C. bowling, and in the sixties were for many years a formidable combination. Grundy was a fast medium pace, round-arm bowler. He always delivered the ball with his arm quite level with his shoulder. His bowling was very straight, but rather short pitched, which, however, helped rather than interfered with his success, owing to the roughness of the wickets at Lord's. I do not think he would have met with much success on our modern wickets.

This year saw great changes in the management of the Surrey Club. Mr. Wm. Burrup, who had

been honorary secretary for seventeen years, and
had piloted the Club through a difficult period in
its history, resigned his office.   He had rendered
signal service, not only to the Surrey Club, but to
cricket generally.   When he was first appointed
secretary, County Cricket was quite in its infancy,
and his office was almost a sinecure, as only
Surrey and Kent were playing inter - county
matches.   When he retired, Notts, Gloucester,
Middlesex, Yorkshire, Lancashire, and Sussex
could all boast of excellent county clubs, and
were all playing inter-county cricket.   This fact
alone indicates the rapidity with which cricket
leaped into popularity in the sixties and seventies.
Mr. Burrup did an immense amount of work
without any reward beyond the satisfaction he derived from promoting the interests of his county
and the game.   As a man he was the very essence
of geniality, and as an official was one of the
most popular secretaries of his time.   One of
my oldest friends, Mr. Charles W. Alcock, was
appointed to succeed him, with a salary of £250 a
year.   Mr. Alcock, who still retains the secretaryship, proved himself to be the right man in the
right place.   During his *régime* the Surrey Club
has enjoyed unbroken prosperity, and has held a
prominent—at times a pre-eminent—place among
the counties.   Moreover, improvements have been
repeatedly effected at Kennington Oval, the latest,
of course, being the erection of a magnificent
pavilion which was used for the first time last
season.

In the same year the Committee of the Gloucestershire County Club was reconstituted, and my brother E. M. was appointed secretary. Like Mr. Alcock, he still holds the office to the great advantage of the Club, and of cricket in the county.

An exciting finish to the match between Surrey and Gloucestershire at the Oval was one of the memorable events of the year. When the Surrey men began their second innings they wanted 110 runs to win the match. We had nine of them out for 108, when Southerton, who was not much of a batsman, came in, and managed to play out the rest of the over. I then had to bowl to Martin, and I gave him what Fitzgerald used to call a "high home and easy one," in the hope of a catch. Martin tried to hit the ball, but skied it to short leg. It was an exciting moment; if the catch was held Gloucestershire would win by one run; but it was missed, the batsmen made two more runs, and Gloucestershire lost by one wicket.

After this match Gloucestershire went on to Brighton to play Sussex. I then made my first acquaintance with the present Hove ground, which provides the easiest scoring wickets in the world, though it is no better than the old Hove ground in this respect.

Early in August of this year I left England for a cricketing tour in Canada. Gloucestershire had still two matches to play—against Notts and Sussex, who were at the head of the County

Championship table—and as it was feared that my absence would seriously weaken the Gloucestershire team, there were some talk of the matches being scratched. I am glad to say that nothing of the sort was found necessary, and that Gloucestershire avoided defeat in both matches. Indeed, thanks to my brothers E. M. and G. F., we won one outright, and had the best of the draw in the other. The scores in the Notts match, which was played at Clifton, August 22, 23, and 24, are worth recording: Gloucestershire first innings 317 (E. M. 108, G. F. 115 not out), Notts first innings 239; Gloucestershire second innings 167 for four wickets (E. M. 40, and G. F. not out 72). Scarcely less interesting are the scores in the Sussex match, which was also played at Clifton, August 26, 27, and 28: Gloucestershire first innings, 143 (E. M. 41); Sussex first innings, 244; Gloucestershire second innings, 253 (E. M. 32, G. F. 44). This left Sussex 153 to score to win, but G. F. bowled so well that they were dismissed for 92, and Gloucestershire won by 60. Seven wickets for 43 runs was the bowling average of G. F., who at this time was in the prime of his cricket career, and with both bat and ball was carrying all before him.

One of my brother G. F.'s best bowling feats was at Northampton, a few days later, when playing for the United South against the United North. His average on that occasion was four wickets for 11 runs in the first innings, and six

wickets for 13 runs in the second. When I mention that the United North team consisted of
J. Rowbotham, Hill, R. Iddison, Richard Daft,
Ephraim Lockwood, Bob Carpenter, Andrew
Greenwood, T. Hayward (who, by the way, got a
pair of spectacles), T. Plumb, Jack Smith, of
Cambridge, and J. C. Shaw, it will be seen that
the men against whom Fred's bowling proved so
destructive formed as good a team as could be
got together in the early seventies. As the result
of Fred's fine bowling, the United South were
victorious by eight wickets. The dismissal of
such men at an average cost of a little over two
runs per wicket affords conclusive evidence of
G. F.'s bowling ability.

One of our interesting Public School fixtures
—the annual match between Clifton College and
Cheltenham College—was instituted this year. It
was played at Clifton, and the home side, who
put their opponents in, won by six wickets,
F. Taylor, who afterwards played for Gloucestershire, making 98. Bob Thoms, the prince of
umpires, "stood" in this match; in 1898—
twenty-six years afterwards—I saw him again at
his post in the same match, encouraging batsmen
and bowlers with cheery words of counsel.

On several occasions during this year the
experiment of having five balls in a bowling
over, instead of the orthodox four, was tried,
and proved successful. It was little thought,
however, that the innovation would eventually
become the rule in first-class cricket, as it is

to-day. Many people objected to the change, but
it has stood the test of experience, and I do not
think any one would dream of reverting to the old
order of four balls to the over. It would be an
advantage, in the direction of saving time, if six
balls to the over became the order of the day.
The suggestion that it would fatigue the bowlers
to bowl six successive balls instead of five hardly
deserves serious consideration, as my experience
has taught me that it tires a man much less to
bowl two or three overs than to run after two or
three successive balls in fielding.

1873   During the preceding two or three seasons
County Cricket had been making rapid strides
into popularity, and was now exciting great
interest. With a view to promoting County
Cricket, and to bringing counties into contact,
which might otherwise have no opportunity of
competing with each other, and to establish an
interesting series of first-class matches on a
neutral ground, the Committee of the M.C.C.
decided at a meeting on January 24, 1873, to
offer a silver Challenge Cup for competition by
the Counties. The expenses of the matches were
to be borne by the M.C.C., and the winner of the
final tie was to hold the Cup for one year. The
Cup was to be kept in perpetuity by the County
team which won the final tie in three successive
years. Elaborate rules and regulations to govern
the contest were drafted and adopted, but the
whole arrangement collapsed, owing to the refusal
of several of the Counties to lend their co-opera-

tion. Only one match under the Championship
Cup Rules took place—between Kent and Sussex
at Lord's. The Marylebone Ground was in a
dangerous condition, and several of the Sussex
team were injured by the fast bowling of Mr.
G. E. Coles, who made his first appearance at
Lord's in this match. As no further contests
for the Cup could be arranged the project was
abandoned.

The vexed question of qualification for County
Cricket came up for serious consideration this
year. A conference of County delegates was held
in April, and a series of resolutions was submitted
to the M.C.C. for ratification. For this purpose a
special general meeting of the M.C.C. was held
on May 7, when the following suggested regulations were brought forward :—

" 1. That no cricketer, whether amateur or
professional, shall play for more than one
county during the same season.

" 2. Every cricketer, whether amateur or
professional, born in one county, and re-
siding in another, shall be free to choose at
the commencement of each season for which
of these counties he will play, and shall
during that season play for that county only.

" 3. A cricketer shall be qualified to play
for any county in which he resides, and has
resided, for the previous two years."

After a long discussion, these three resolutions
were adopted, and a fourth resolution, proposed

by Mr. C. Marsham, seconded by the Hon. C. G. Lyttelton (now Lord Cobham), was added :—

> " 4. An amateur shall be considered qualified by right of residence to play for any county in which he, or his parents, have property, or in which his parents did have property, at the time of their decease."

A meeting of county representatives was held on June 9, in the New Committee Room at Kennington Oval, to consider these rules, and more particularly the property qualification introduced in the fourth regulation, which had been added to the three submitted to the M.C.C. from the county delegates held in April. Representatives from Surrey, Middlesex, Sussex, Kent, Gloucestershire, Yorkshire, and Notts were present. Lancashire and Derbyshire were not represented. The first two rules were adopted without demur, but upon the third rule there was considerable difference of opinion. Ultimately on the suggestion of Captain Holden, seconded by myself, it was proposed that in place of Rules 3 and 4 the following should be substituted :—

> " 3. A cricketer shall be qualified to play for any county in which he is residing and has resided for the previous two years, or a cricketer may elect to play for the county in which his family home is, so long as it remains open to him as an occasional residence."

Another resolution was then carried as a suggestion to the M.C.C. as follows :—

> " 3. Should any question arise on the residential qualification the same shall be left to the decision of the Committee of the Marylebone Club."

These suggestions were forwarded to the M.C.C., and on their adoption by the premier Club became the rules of county qualification. Until 1888 they stood unamended, a modification being then made to enable a cricketer to play for his own county during the two years that he is qualifying for another. Now in 1899 further alterations are being made to deal with several matters about which there has been dissatisfaction.

Notts and Gloucestershire were at the top in the County Championship list this year, Notts winning five out of six matches, and drawing one, while Gloucestershire played six matches, winning four and drawing two. The Gloucestershire team consisted entirely of amateurs, while the Nottingham Eleven was composed of professionals.

In the course of this season Arthur Shrewsbury, the famous Notts batsman, came out as a cricketer, making his first appearance at Lord's on May 12 and 13 for the Colts of England v. M.C.C. Although he was only seventeen years of age, his form gave promise of great ability, though no one thought then that in a few years he would be at the top of the tree. Against the M.C.C. he scored 4 and 16 (not out). Prior to this appearance at Lord's, he had played for the Colts of Nottingham against the Notts County Eleven in the usual Easter Monday fixture. On that occasion he made 35 against the first-class bowling of the county team, which then included J. C. and A. Shaw, Morley, and Martin M'Intyre. Notwithstanding his promising *début*, Shrewsbury did not find a place in the Notts County Eleven until two years later. Like most of the Notts men, he was born in the county, his father being in business for many years in the borough of Nottingham.

Two great benefit matches took place this season. On Whit Monday, June 2 and 3, the annual match between the North and South at Lord's was given to the old popular bowler Wootton " as a recognition of his efficient service and exemplary conduct extending over twelve seasons." For the benefit of those to whom the name of Wootton may be unknown, I may say that he was a left-hand fast medium bowler—very straight, and with a good length. He bowled an over in quicker time than any bowler I ever played against. As soon as the ball was returned to him, he walked back about three paces, turned round sharply, and was at you again in a moment. If the batsman did not keep well on the look-out, Wootton would bowl before he was prepared with his defence. His success was for many years unsurpassed, especially in the early sixties, when he was associated with Grundy in all the M.C.C. matches. Between them this invincible pair did almost all the bowling for the Marylebone Club. I remember in a

Gentlemen *v.* Players match at Lord's I was in with my brother E. M., who played a ball towards mid-off and called me to run.   Wootton, who was wonderfully quick on his legs, fielded the ball with his left hand, and threw it in so smartly that I was run out by yards.   Wootton's benefit match was spoiled by the weather, and the cricket was slow.   Notwithstanding the rain, 6874 people passed through the turnstiles on the first day and 3206 on the second day.   These were considered very good attendances.   Martin M'Intyre, who was put on as a first change bowler, was in great form, taking eight wickets for 18 runs.

The second great benefit match was given to Joseph Rowbotham on July 28, 29, and 30, at Bramall Lane, Sheffield.   The contest was between Gloucestershire and Yorkshire, and an enormous number of spectators were present, 12,000, 7000, and 4000 paying for admission on the three days respctively.   The match, which provided very interesting cricket, ended in a six-wickets victory for Gloucestershire.   I made 79 and 15 (not out), thus keeping up my reputation for being in good form whenever I played in a benefit match.   On the first day the crowd was so great that the spectators encroached within thirty yards of the wicket.   Bramall Lane was a smaller ground then than it is now, and it only wanted a very small hit to send the ball among the onlookers.

In this year we played a match at Prince's Ground between North and South for that deserving institution, the Cricketers' Fund. With their usual generosity, Messrs. Prince, the proprietors, granted free use of their ground for the purpose. Notwithstanding inclement weather there were large attendances each day, and the Fund benefited to the extent of £159. I think it is a great pity that a match of this kind is not included in each season's fixtures, as the object is beyond praise.

I was extremely fortunate in each of the Gentlemen *v.* Players matches this year. We played three, viz., one at Lord's, one at the Oval, and one at Prince's. At Lord's I scored 163, at the Oval 158, and at Prince's 70, making an aggregate of 391 in three innings. In this season I had also a wonderful spell of luck at the Oval, where I played seven innings which gave an average of 151 runs for each time out—my scores being 83, 8 (not out), 134, 158, 192 (not out), 24 and 5 (not out), a total of 604.

Mr. W. W. Read, the great Surrey batsman, first played for his county this season. Like Shrewsbury, he was seventeen years of age when he came out as a first-class cricketer. By his scores of 3 and 30 he made a favourable impression, though his sudden leap into prominence was not expected. Two years later he stood at the top of the Surrey batting averages.

There was at this time keen rivalry between the M.C.C. and Ground and the Surrey Club and Ground, and the annual match between them, which has long since dropped out of the cricket

calendar, aroused widespread interest. It is
scarcely necessary to say that the Marylebone
Club generally had the best of the encounters.
My brother G. F. was made a member of the
Surrey Club, so that he might play for them
against the M.C.C. this year. The match proved
an extraordinary one. Surrey in their first innings
made 105, to which we replied with 204. Then
a severe thunderstorm interrupted play, and of
course damaged the wicket. Thanks to G. F.'s
fine hitting, the Surrey innings realised 153, to
which G. F. contributed 60. He was stumped off
my bowling, which he had been knocking about
pretty freely.

This left the M.C.C. with 55 runs to get to
win the match. Thinking that I should not be
wanted, I put myself sixth in the order of going
in. Mr. Duncan and Rylott, who started our
innings, took the score up to 26, when Rylott was
run out. As half the runs had been scored for
the loss of one wicket, an easy victory seemed in
sight, but "there's many a slip 'twixt cup and lip,"
and cricket is full of uncertainties. My brother
G. F. bowled Mr. Duncan and Captain Young in
one over. The score crept up to 39, and then
stood still while Mr. Udall, Mr. Herbert, Mr.
Tomkinson, and Alfred Shaw were all disposed
of. At 41 Mr. Anstruther was dismissed, and five
runs later Biddulph was bowled. Nine wickets
were down, and still nine runs were required.
I had gone in at the fall of the sixth wicket, but
I had lost my partners so rapidly that I had had

no opportunity of scoring. At last I was joined
by Clayton, the eleventh batsman, and between
us we scored eight more runs, which made a tie.
Southerton was bowling, and from his last over
Clayton was missed at mid-off, and then from
the following ball he was missed by G. F., who
failed to effect a hard catch in the long field.

This providential escape gave us the victory, as
we scored a run off the last-named hit, and so
won this most exciting match for the old Club.
It was a good thing for Surrey that G. F. did
play for them, otherwise the match would have
been a one-sided affair. Fred's batting helped
up their total, while his bowling captured five
wickets for 24 runs. If he had caught Clayton
in the long field he would have saved them from
defeat. As it was, he helped them to escape a
severe drubbing.

At the end of this season I paid my first visit to
Australia, taking out the team to whose achievements a chapter of these reminiscences is devoted.

We came back to England from Australia just
in time for the cricket season, reaching home on
May 17. E. M. had a match at Thornbury v.
Clifton on May 21, and G. F. and I played for
him. Clifton went in first and made 122. Then
came our turn, and, much to everybody's surprise,
G. F. made 123, and I 259. The total of the
innings was 429 for four wickets. As we had only
been in England four days, it was clear we had
not lost our form on the voyage.

1874   About this time several of the cricketers whose

names are now almost household words were making their first appearances in first - class cricket. In the previous year (1873) we recorded the *débûts* of Mr. W. W. Read and Arthur Shrewsbury. The year 1874 saw the first appearances of two more well-known amateurs—Mr. A. G. Steel and Mr. A. P. Lucas. Mr. Steel played for the first time at Lord's for Marlborough *v.* Rugby in their annual match. He was then a schoolboy of fifteen, but he did well in his first big match, as in the first innings he carried out his bat for 41 runs. It is interesting to note that he was described by a contemporary writer as "a very promising bat, if he chooses to take the trouble to improve, and a useful change bowler, but there is room for improvement in his fielding." Whether he deserved these half-hearted remarks I do not know, but I do know that he not only improved, but very soon was good enough an all-round cricketer to deserve a place in any team. Mr. A. P. Lucas, who made his first appearance in the Surrey team, is now playing for Essex County Cricket Club, and bats as well as ever, although, like myself, he does not get faster in the field.

Once again I scored well in a benefit match this season. Luke Greenwood was given a benefit at Sheffield, when Gloucestershire played Yorkshire. After scoring 163, I took four wickets in the first innings and seven in the second. Gloucestershire won easily by an innings and 94 runs, rain having spoiled the wicket for the

Yorkshiremen. Tom Emmett, who had a bowling engagement for a local club in Yorkshire,
did not play in this match, as the local club
refused to let him off to play for the county.
Such an action is bad enough at any time, but,
considering that this was a benefit match for one
of Yorkshire's most valuable players, it was a
discreditable proceeding. Some of the cricket
leagues of the present time do not free professionals for county engagements as readily as
they ought, but this is sometimes the fault of
the professionals themselves, who, in taking the
engagements, should take care that their agree-
ments do not debar them from playing for their
counties when wanted. Between us, G. F. and
I took every wicket in both the Yorkshire innings.
Mr. F. Townsend, who was at that time one of
Gloucestershire's most reliable men, and whose
son, C. L. Townsend, is an invaluable member
of the present team, played a fine hitting innings
of 66.

"Gentlemen of England who had not been
educated at the Universities" v. "Gentlemen of
England who had been educated at the Universities." This was the unusual title given to a match
which was played for the first and, I believe, the
last time in this season. Among the non-Univer-
sity men were Messrs. V. E. and I. D. Walker,
A. N. Hornby, A. Appleby, G. F., and myself; the
University team included Messrs. D. Buchanan,
C. A. Absalom, F. E. R. Fryer, and W. S. Patterson, but was not at full strength.

A very curious and amusing incident happened in one of the Thornbury matches this season. My brothers G. F. and E. M. and my cousin W. R. Gilbert played for Thornbury *v.* Sneyd Park, Clifton, in a match on Durdham Down. E. M. won the toss (as usual) for Thornbury. My brother G. F. and W. R. Gilbert opened the innings, which had been in progress for a few minutes, when a ball was bowled rather wide on the off-side. The umpire promptly called "Wide," but, simultaneously, Gilbert, who made a practice of running after wide balls and tipping them past short slip, just touched this ball, and was caught. This is the only time I have ever known this occur in my cricket career, although I have occasionally heard an umpire call " Wide " when the batsman has subsequently hit the ball. In this case the umpire, on being appealed to for the catch, replied, "I have already given my decision, ' Wide,' " so Gilbert continued his innings, much to the amusement of everybody. Even his opponents regarded the decision as a great joke. But when 150 runs went up, and G. F. and Gilbert were still batting, the fieldsmen looked at the decision in another light, and began to think the umpire was a bit of a duffer for not having given Gilbert out. When they had got rid of G. F. and the batsman who followed him Gilbert was joined by Mr. J. W. Fletcher, the well-known runner, and the pair kept possession of the wickets until the drawing of stumps. E. M. little dreamt, when he put himself down fifth on the list, that his services would not be required. The feelings of the Sneyd Park team (which included three members of the Gloucestershire County Eleven) heightened in intensity as Gilbert's score went upwards, and their remarks when he finally walked out with 254 (not out) to his credit can hardly be repeated. As to the umpire—well, he, like a modern football referee, left the ground with an escort.

For the first time the Canterbury Week this year was opened with a match between Kent and Gloucestershire Combined *v*. England, and the county combination won by 54 runs. I just missed bringing off a feat of scoring 100 in each innings — my scores being 94 and 121. Edgar Willsher, who was included in the combined counties team, had, it was noted at the time, taken part in the Canterbury Week twenty-three years before.

Towards the end of this season England was visited by a team of twenty-two American baseball players, who came over here to give English people some insight into the American national game. Besides their exhibitions of baseball, in which game, of course, they excelled, they included in their programme a few cricket matches, and did very creditably. The visitors consisted of eleven members of the Boston Athletic Club and eleven of the Philadelphian Athletes—the two leading baseball clubs in the United States. They landed in Liverpool at the end of July, and began their tour by giving an exhibition of baseball at

Edgehill, which was then the ground of the Liverpool Cricket Club, now at Aigburth. The Americans were a fine body of men, and their brilliant catching and fielding and throwing-in excited great admiration. They gave similar exhibitions at different centres, but the baseball game did not find much favour amongst English spectators. Their first appearance at a cricket match was at Lord's on August 3 and 4, when twelve of the M.C.C. were pitted against eighteen of the American baseball players. During their tour they played seven cricket matches, winning four, drawing three, and losing none. It should, however, be said that they met only very inferior teams.

Owing to the soft and sticky wickets, 1875 **1875** was pre-eminently a bowlers' year—the batting averages were low, while the bowlers achieved some extraordinary successes. Throughout the season Alfred Shaw was simply irresistible. I shall never forget his brilliant success in the M.C.C. *v.* Notts match at Lord's on June 14 and 15. In their second innings the M.C.C. scored 98 runs, but Shaw, though he bowled throughout the innings, had the following analysis :

Overs 41.2   Maidens 36   Runs 7   Wickets 7

This would have been a wonderful performance against any team, but when it is recollected that his opponents were W. G. Grace, I. D. Walker, W. H. Hadow, A. W. Ridley, C. F. Buller, A. J. Webbe, Lord Harris, H. W. Renny-Tailyour,

A. S. Duncan, A. W. Herbert, and R. Clayton, and that six out of the seven batsmen he dismissed were bowled, Shaw's achievement is simply marvellous.   In my long career I have never seen this feat equalled, when consideration is given to the length of the innings and the calibre of the batsmen.   I ought to add that, as a recognition of his triumph, Shaw was afterwards presented with a valuable silver teapot.

During this season Mr. G. Strachan (who represented Gloucestershire by birth qualification before he became captain of the Surrey Eleven, for whom he played by residential qualification) also did a great bowling feat.   The occasion was the Gentlemen *v.* Players match at the Oval. When five wickets had fallen Mr. Strachan was put on to bowl.   His analysis at the end of the innings stood :—

Overs 8.3   Maidens 8   Runs 0   Wickets 5

I saw an almost identical feat at Lord's in 1896— M.C.C. and Ground *v.* The Ninth Australian Team. On this occasion the Australians were got rid of for 18 runs, the smallest score ever made by an Australian team in this country.   When the total stood at 18 for three wickets, I put on Pougher, and not another run was scored, Pougher doing this extraordinary feat of bowling :—

Overs 3   Maidens 3   Runs 0   Wickets 5

Almost all the most interesting cricket of this season took place in the Gentlemen *v.* Players

matches. In the first, Alfred Shaw achieved the
wonderful record just mentioned. The second
match, which took place at Lord's on July 5, 6,
and 7, was played in fine weather on a perfect
wicket, and the first half of the game was very
even. The Gentlemen scored 153, of which
number Mr. G. H. Longman contributed 70.
The Players responded with 169. I took seven
wickets for 64. To open the Gentlemen's second
innings, Mr. A. J. Webbe and I faced the bowling
of Alfred Shaw and Morley. At this time the now
well-known Middlesex amateur (who had played
for Harrow in the previous year) was an undergraduate at Oxford, where, playing for Trinity
College v. Exeter College, he made the highest
score of the season, 299 not out. This was his first
year in first-class cricket, and he did conspicuously
well, especially in this match. I was in my best
form, and when the score stood at 38 I had made
33. At 55 M'Intyre went on for Alfred Shaw,
who had hurt his foot, and did not bowl again in
this match. At the luncheon adjournment I had
scored 45 out of 60. After the interval, Mr. Webbe
and I got well set, and carried the score on to
203, for which we had been batting two hours
and a half. My partner was then caught at the
wicket. His 65 was a fine display for one so
young (he was only twenty at the time), and one
of the papers remarked that there had not been
a better innings for a long time. Since that
memorable day, Mr. Webbe and I have had many
a long partnership, but I do not think that either

of us will ever forget our association in this match of 1875. Later in the same season Webbe, playing for Middlesex against Notts, added lustre to his reputation by another brilliant innings of 97. In the Players' second innings I got five wickets for 61 runs, so that altogether with bat and ball the match was one of my best all-round performances.

Another of the notable achievements of this great bowlers' year took place at Tunbridge Wells on August 19 and 20, when Allen Hill, bowling for the North *v.* South, captured the wickets of myself, Charlwood, and my brother G. F. with the first, second, and fourth balls of his first over.

Sussex and Notts divided the County Championship honours this year. Middlesex, although Mr. Webbe was now playing for them, had an exceptionally unlucky season, being the only county that did not win a single match. Justice compels me to add that rain, and rain alone, robbed them of a victory over Nottingham.

Although I once exceeded 200, and six times topped the century this season, it was a bowling rather than a batting year with me. In fifty innings I captured 192 wickets for an average of 12 runs apiece—the largest number I ever obtained in any single year.

1876 If 1875 was a bowlers' year, the season of 1876 gave the batsman the fullest possible opportunity for revenge. It was incomparably my most productive batting season, and it was a year of record-scores all over the country. As the weather remained perfect throughout most of the season, wickets were hard and dry, and the bat gained a most unusual mastery over the ball.

Three Gentlemen *v.* Players matches were played this year. The first, at Kennington Oval, was remarkable for the high average totals in all the innings. The Players made 237 and 257, and the Gentlemen 229 and 201 for four wickets—an aggregate of 924 runs for thirty-four wickets. I was dismissed for a duck in the first innings, but in the second I knocked up 90 in my speediest fashion. The match, however, remained unfinished. In the second match, at Lord's, I made 169, an innings which I remember well, because I re-collect hitting Emmett twice in one over for a six and a seven—all run out. The average of scoring was again very high, 800 runs being made at the expense of thirty wickets. Ultimately the Gentle-men won by an innings and 98 runs.

The practice of bowling five balls to the over became pretty general in this season, and though some of the old fogies, who dislike changes even when they are improvements, protested against the innovation, it found ready favour.

In recognition of the valuable services he had rendered for many years, the M.C.C. set aside the Whit-Monday match at Lord's (North *v.* South) as Tom Hearne's benefit. Notwithstanding the weather was unpropitious, the old cricketer had a very good bonus as the result of the match.

The largest score I ever reached in a single

innings was made at Grimsby, when the United South of England Eleven played Twenty-two of Grimsby. Before the match began some of the Twenty-two frankly expressed their opinion that we had brought rather a weak team, but before the match was over they had changed their mind. I went in first with Tom Humphrey, the old Surrey favourite. Some of our players were late in arriving, and when they reached the field, just before lunch, and saw that Humphrey and I were in, they imagined that we must be the last men, and rushed to the pavilion to get ready to bat. Then they learned that we were the first.

At the end of the day I made 140 (not out), and our score was 213 for two wickets. Throughout the whole of the next day I kept possession of the wickets, and at the close of play 314 (not out) stood to my credit. All things have their end, and our innings came to a conclusion late in the third day, for a total of 681, of which my contribution was 400. Up to 350 I did not give a chance, and it was estimated that I was thirteen and a half hours at the wicket. During that time I had faced fifteen different bowlers. What made the innings remarkable was the presence of twenty-two fieldsmen in the field. My not-out innings of 400 was then the second highest score ever made by a batsman in one innings, Mr. Tylecote's 404 at Clifton College being its only superior.

This score at Grimsby was the forerunner of a succession of batting triumphs in August; in fact

1876 was the most extraordinary batting year I had until 1895.

The first match in the Canterbury Week was, as in the previous year, between Kent and Gloucestershire v. The Rest of England. This was another high-scoring match, and the finish was very exciting. For the Kent and Gloucestershire combination, Mr. W. R. Gilbert played a very fine innings of 143 in the first innings, and in the second I made 91, while, for the Rest of England, Mr. A. J. Webbe made 109. Over 1100 runs were scored in the match, which was drawn when the Counties still wanted 30 runs with two wickets to fall.

For the first time the names of the batsmen were in this match arranged in the order of going in, and printed in large letters on the telegraph board, so that they could be read from all parts of the field. At this time the telegraph board had been in use for thirty years. A comical reminiscence comes to my mind as I write. When Lord Harris joined Gilbert, the attendant at the telegraph board left out the H, and put up "'Arris." The mistake was not rectified for a few minutes, during which the crowd cheered lustily. As may be imagined, such an incident led to much merriment.

The second match of the Canterbury Week— M.C.C. v. Kent—was a memorable event of the year. Kent, who went in first, gave us a long outing in the field, scoring 473, to which Lord Harris contributed 154 in his finest style. This

was the highest score he had made up to that
time.   The only other batsman to reach 50 was
G. G. Hearne.   The M.C.C. team, which consisted
entirely of amateurs, made 144, or 329 behind
the Kent total.   When we went in a second time,
I played a rather freer game than usual.   As I
had to play at Bristol on the following Monday,
and did not think we could save the match, I
meant to get home as soon as possible.   Consequently I opened my shoulders to the bowling
—so much so that I made 20 runs off two successive overs from Hearne.   The first hundred
was on the telegraph board after forty-five
minutes' play, and when stumps were drawn the
score stood at 217 for four wickets, of which my
share was 133 (not out).   As I had only been
batting for an hour and fifty minutes, I had
scored at the rate of about seventy an hour.
Resuming my innings next morning, with Mr.
Crutchley as partner, the score was carried to
430, the partnership having realised 227 runs.
Eventually I was dismissed, having made 344 out
of 546 in the course of six hours and twenty
minutes.   *Bell's Life*, in referring to this innings,
said : " He scored 344 runs without positively
giving a chance, and his hits consisted of fifty-one
4's, eight 3's, twenty 2's, and seventy-six singles."
Up to that time the record score in a first-class
match was William Ward's 278, which was made
in 1820 ; my 344 was not surpassed until Mr. A. C.
Maclaren made his 424 against Somerset nineteen
years later.

Mr. C. A. Absolon, and Mr. Foord-Kelcey, who did most of the bowling for Kent in the seventies, were keen competitors as to who should go on first at the beginning of the innings, each hoping to get my wicket, but towards Saturday afternoon their ardour had cooled down, and instead of volunteering to bowl, Lord Harris had great trouble in making them take the ball at all. Altogether ten different bowlers had a shot at me in this innings. It goes without saying that there was no third match in the Canterbury Week this year.

I was rather tired when I reached Bristol on Sunday night after travelling from Canterbury, but a good night's rest refreshed me, and when we began the Gloucester v. Notts match at Clifton on the Monday I ran up another score of 177 in three hours. In those days we ran out most of the hits on the Clifton College Ground. My score was made up of one 7, two 6's, one 5, twenty-three 4's, four 3's, nine 2's, and twenty-one singles.

In the very next match played at Cheltenham on the Thursday, Friday, and Saturday of the same week, I again found myself in form, and made the highest score I ever reached in a County match. At the end of the first day's play I was not out 216, with the score at 353. Mr. W. O. Moberly, who was my partner when stumps were drawn, had made 73 (not out). Heavy rain delayed the start next morning, but Moberly and I raised the total to 429, when I lost my partner, who had played a fine consistent innings of 108, while our partnership had realised 261 runs. The remaining wickets fell rapidly, until the last man, Mr. J. A. Bush, joined me, the score standing at 466. I still needed a few runs to complete my 300, and on coming in Bush, with his usual good humour, remarked, " All right, old man, I'll stay in until you get your runs." He was as good as his word, for he kept up his wicket until I had made 318, when Ulyett bowled him out. As this score was made against the first-rate bowling of Yorkshire, I consider it the best innings of my career.

About this time, when I was scoring freely in almost every match I played, bowlers did not conceal their reluctance to keep on bowling when I was batting. In this match, as in the last two or three in which I played, the bowlers were quite tired before the innings was half over, and being desirous if possible to avoid having their averages spoilt, were not at all anxious to take the ball. Lockwood, who was captain of Yorkshire this season, never had his team under firm control, and he found it difficult to get any one to bowl. All sorts of excuses were made by the bowlers when they were requested to go on. Hill was pressed to take a few overs, but he tried to excuse himself. While Lockwood was persuading him to bowl, Tom Emmett joined in the conversation, and turning to Lockwood said, " Why don't you make him ? you are captain !" Then some one suggested that Tom should have a go himself. Tom, however, showed no anxiety, and some one

remarked, " You're frightened to go on yourself !"
Nettled by this remark, Emmett took the ball, and
began to bowl, but he was so angry that he could
not get near the wicket. During his first over
most of his balls went anywhere but in the
direction of the batsman's wicket. At all times
Emmett was erratic, but on this occasion he
excelled himself.

This incident affords an opportunity for saying
that Tom Emmett bowled more wides, which
were not called by the umpire, than any man I
have ever played with. He invariably bowled
on the off-side for catches, but in his first over
he never seemed to know where he was going to
send the ball. Sometimes his first two or three
deliveries would be yards wide of the wicket,
but every now and then he put in a ball which
was absolutely unplayable. I am not sure that
this erratic tendency was not the secret of his
success, as the batsman never knew when a good
ball was coming. Umpires were always lenient
to Tom, and let many a " wide " go uncalled when
he was bowling.

I have already said that August in this year was
the most productive batting month of my career.
I was in exceptional form, and seemed to have
unbroken success wherever I went. A list of my
journeys and innings for the month may be interesting. On July 31, August 1 and 2, I played at
Keighley for the United South against a local
twenty-two, and scored 20 and 73. From Keighley
we went to Hull, where on August 3, 4, and 5

I played for the United South against the United North, and made 126 and 82. Then came the Canterbury Week, and my scores of 9 and 91, and 344, followed by 177 at Clifton on the 14th, 15th, and 16th, and 318 at Cheltenham on the 17th, 18th, and 19th. I went next to Birmingham, where, playing for the United South against Twenty-two of Birmingham, I made 18. Returning to Bristol I made 78 and 7 for Gloucestershire against Sussex, and 29 for Gloucestershire against Surrey.

Altogether in August 1876 I made 1389 runs, a total which I may be forgiven for mentioning was greater than any other batsman made in the whole year in first-class cricket. In the forty-two innings which I had in the course of the season I made 2622 runs—an average of 62.18—while in the whole year in all matches I scored 3908. Until May in 1895 I never surpassed my success in this August, which still is the highest run-getting month of my thirty-five years' first-class cricket. In some respects, of course, my success in May 1895, when I scored 1000 runs, is more notable, as high scores are easier to attain on the dry wickets of August than on the soft wickets of May. Moreover, I was only twenty-eight years of age in 1876, while I was forty-seven in 1895.

Gloucestershire did extremely well this season, playing eight matches, winning five, and losing none, thereby taking premier place in the County Championship.

At the close of the season James Lillywhite's team—the fourth to go out from England—visited

Australia. It was a professional team, consisting of Lillywhite, Charlwood, Greenwood, Armytage, Emmett, Hill, Ulyett, Jupp, Southerton, Pooley, A. Shaw, and J. Selby. They played twenty-three matches, winning eleven, drawing four, and losing eight. One of the principal features of this trip was that an Australian Eleven for the first time beat an Eleven of England, thus demonstrating that the previous visit of English teams had had a beneficial effect upon Australian cricket. It should be added that one man (C. Bannerman, who scored 165, and then had to retire hurt) was the principal factor in securing this defeat of the English team; but it is an acknowledged fact that two or three men almost invariably do everything in most matches. The match in which the English team were beaten took place at Melbourne on March 15, 16, and 17, 1877, but a fortnight later the English Eleven had their revenge by defeating their former victors by four wickets. The rubber remained undecided, as the other match was drawn. Spofforth, who declined to play in the first match, played in the second and bowled successfully.

In the autumn of 1876 Mr. R. A. Fitzgerald, **1877** the Secretary of the M.C.C., resigned his office on the ground of ill-health. He had held his post to the great advantage of the Club and of cricket generally for a term of thirteen years, during which period the membership of the Club had increased threefold, while the whole conditions of cricket at Lord's had undergone a great change

for the better. Mr. H. Perkins was elected
Secretary *pro tem.*, but in the beginning of the
1877 season, when it was found that Mr. Fitzgerald could not resume his duties, Mr. Perkins
entered on the permanent secretaryship. This
appointment was a case of one good Secretary
being followed by another, as for twenty-one
years Mr. Perkins discharged his duties with the
utmost efficiency. At the beginning of 1898
Mr. Perkins resigned, and was succeeded by Mr.
F. E. Lacey, the old Cambridge and Hampshire
cricketer.

For the first time Middlesex played all their
home matches this season at Lord's, which has
now been their headquarters for twenty-two
years. For some years previously Middlesex had
played their home matches at Prince's Ground,
and then for a short period at Lillie Bridge.
The removal of Middlesex proved to be the
beginning of the decline of cricket at Prince's,
and the ground was soon to disappear altogether.
First one corner, and then another piece of the
picturesque ground at Hans Place, Sloane Square,
was cut off by the builders, and though two or
three important matches were played there in the
following year, Prince's Cricket Ground soon
ceased to exist. The first appearance of Middlesex at Lord's was against Yorkshire, when Bates,
who afterwards became one of the best men of
the Yorkshire team, made his *début* at Marylebone.

This was a great year for Gloucestershire

County Cricket, the team doing better than in any previous year. They went through the season unbeaten, and were victorious in seven out of their eight matches. For the second time they were at the top of the County averages. One engagement in their season's programme was a match against England at the Oval, which the Gloucestershire men won by five wickets. It is an interesting fact that up to this year the Gloucestershire team had been composed entirely of amateurs. This season, however, Midwinter, who had played against the team I took to Australia in 1873, returned to England, and as he was a Gloucestershire man by birth, we played him in the County Eleven. He was an addition to the strength of the team in both batting and bowling. The match, which was played at Lord's this season between a combined team of Gloucestershire and Yorkshire v. The Rest of England was remarkable for the success of the Gloucester shire men, who carried everything before them. Of the score of 199 made by the combined counties in their first innings, the Gloucestershire members of the team made 126, while in the second innings they contributed 151 out of the total of 231. I made 110, which included one big hit out of the ground into Dark's garden. This was Midwinter's first match at Lord's.

The rapid growth of interest in County Cricket, and the multiplication of inter-county matches, destroyed almost all interest in other fixtures, except, of course, the Gentlemen v. Players, the

Inter-'Varsity, and the North *v*. South matches. In consequence of this the All England Eleven and the United South team, which for many years had travelled up and down the country playing local combinations, found their popularity waning. The All England Eleven dropped out of the running this season, and, although the United South Eleven continued to exist for three or four years longer, its fortunes declined rapidly. During this season the Eleven played about ten matches. I remember playing in one at the end of September on Colonel Buchanan's grounds at Coatbridge, when we were beaten by twenty-two of Drumpelier. This was the first occasion on which I met Alec Watson, who afterwards became well known as the Lancashire bowler, and who in this match got us all out. The match was played for the benefit of John Sands, who had been coach for upwards of fourteen years to the Drumpelier Club. Sands is still living near Hastings, and never fails to attend the Cricket Week, where he is a familiar figure to those who frequent the Hastings Cricket Ground.

I succeeded better with the ball than with the bat this year, and in bowling for Gloucestershire against Notts I performed one feat worth noting. My analysis for the match was :—

Overs 76   Maidens 36   Runs 89   Wickets 17

The last seven wickets were secured without a single run being made. We had two fieldsmen at long leg, and batsman after batsman sent

catches in their direction. The captain of the
Nottingham team reproved his men for their
folly, but, much to their amusement, fell himself
a victim in exactly the same way.

This year marks a distinct epoch in English **1878**
cricket, as it was in 1878 we had our first visit
from an Australian team. The team, which was
captained by Mr. D. W. Gregory, consisted of
Messrs. W. L. Murdoch, C. Bannerman, Alec
Bannerman, T. Horan, T. W. Garrett, G. H.
Bailey, F. R. Spofforth, H. F. Boyle, F. E. Allan,
and J. M. C. Blackham. W. Midwinter, who was
resident in England, joined the team on its arrival,
and Mr. Conway acted as its manager. Of the
twelve cricketers constituting the team, six hailed
from New South Wales, five were Victorians, and
one came from Tasmania. Before sailing for
England the team had had a preliminary canter
in New Zealand, from which colony they returned
to Australia for a short tour, which they finished
up at Melbourne with a match against eighteen
of Victoria.

The prospect of the Australians' visit excited
keen interest in England; their arrival was
eagerly anticipated, and their welcome was
thoroughly hearty. Their first match was an
intense disappointment, as they were badly
beaten on a wet wicket by Notts, who, thanks to
a fine innings by Selby and the wonderful
bowling of A. Shaw and Morley, won by an
innings and 14 runs. From Nottingham the
Australians came to London, and on May 27

made their first appearance at Lord's, where the turf had been severely damaged by the heavy and persistent rain which fell throughout May.

The match was between the M.C.C. and the Australians, and was played under somewhat depressing conditions. Owing to the wet morning there were not five hundred persons present when the Australians arrived on the ground. The match, however, proved one of the most remarkable and sensational ever played at Lord's, as may be judged from the fact that play was all over in the course of six hours. The hot sunshine, which followed the soaking showers, baked the surface of the ground, and made the wicket almost unplayable. The M.C.C., who batted first, made a disastrous start. The first wicket (my own) fell with the score at 4, and the second when but a single had been added. Eighteen overs produced 25 runs, and then Spofforth took the ball. The "demon" bowler's fast deliveries met with immediate and wonderful success, as in six overs he took six wickets (five of them bowled, and three in one over) for 4 runs.

In sixty-five minutes the M.C.C. innings was over for 33 runs. The excitement now ran high, but it grew even intenser when the Australians had lost eight wickets for 23 runs. Alfred Shaw and Morley shared the bowling, and the condition of the wicket may be gathered from the fact that Shaw bowled forty-six balls before a run was scored off him. Eventually the Australian innings ended for 41. But cricket of an even more sensa-

tional character was in store, and the spectators
sat in a fever of excitement while the whole ten
wickets of the M.C.C. fell for 19 runs. The Australians, left with only 12 runs to score to win, gained
the victory by nine wickets, and this remarkable
match ended after four and a half hours of actual
cricket. It was, no doubt, a glorious victory for
Australia, although the condition of the ground
accounted for the phenomenally small scores.
The defeat of the old club by the colonials led
Punch to perpetrate the familiar rhyme :—

> The Australians came down like a wolf on a fold,
> The Marylebone Club for a trifle were bowled,
> Our Grace before dinner was very soon done,
> And Grace after dinner did not get a run.

Their brilliant success in this match removed
the doubts which had been entertained in some
quarters as to the calibre of the Australian
cricketers, whose failure at Nottingham had led
people to discount their powers. The visit of the
Cornstalks was memorable in many respects, for,
apart from it being the first visit of an Australian
team, their first sensational victory at Lord's will
never be forgotten. Moreover, their subsequent
record was sufficiently good to inspire confidence
and maintain interest in their doings. Altogether they played thirty-seven matches, winning
eighteen, drawing twelve, and losing only seven.
Most of the counties suffered defeat at their
hands ; their principal defeats being in their
matches with Notts, Gentlemen of England,

Yorkshire, and Cambridge University. They
proved themselves antagonists worthy of our
steel, and before their tour ended we recognised
that they were a good all-round team. Spofforth's bowling and Blackham's wicket-keeping
made a deep impression upon all who saw them
play, and, considering the small number of first-
class Australian cricketers from whom they had
to make their selection, their bowlers generally
showed great proficiency. This visit was the
forerunner of an unbroken series of visits and
return visits to and from Australia, and as I write
these recollections of our first visitors we are
having the pleasure of witnessing the highly
creditable performances of the tenth team which
has visited England since 1878.

In connection with the visit of the Australians
this year, I may mention one curious incident.
Although Midwinter joined the Australian team
on its arrival, he promised to play for Gloucestershire in all our matches. On June 20, when the
Gloucestershire men arrived at the Oval to play
Surrey, I received a message to the effect that
Midwinter would be absent, as he was playing
for the Australians at Lord's. In consequence of
his defection, Gloucestershire mustered only ten
men. I immediately started off for Lord's, where
I found Midwinter with his pads on, waiting to
bat. After some persuasion he returned with me
to the Oval to play for Gloucestershire.

Apart from the visit of the Australian team, the
greatest interest this season was centred in the

achievements of the Cambridge University team, which went through the season without suffering defeat. The Eleven, which was captained by E. (now Canon) Lyttelton, now master of Hailey-bury College, was probably the finest combination either University has ever put into the field. The names of the men it included speak for themselves —A. P. Lucas, A. Lyttelton, E. Lyttelton, H. Whit-field, D. Q. Steel, L. K. Jarvis, A. G. Steel, F. W. Kingston, Ivo Bligh, P. H. Morton, and A. F. J. Ford. The Inter-'Varsity match this year was made remarkable by a succession of incidents, the most remarkable being that while Cambridge opened their second innings by scoring 117 runs before a wicket fell, Oxford concluded theirs for 32 runs. It is almost unnecessary to remind cricketers that Cambridge won the match by 238 runs. In A. G. Steel and P. H. Morton the Cantabs had two brilliant bowlers, while A. P. Lucas, the two Lytteltons, A. G. Steel, and A. F. J. Ford were scarcely less successful with the bat.

An unfortunate dispute makes the match be-tween the Australians and the Players at Kenning-ton Oval worthy of notice. As the Australians refused to pay the English professionals what they asked, some of our best Players declined to parti-cipate in the match. Consequently the Players' team was by no means representative, and the Australians had an easy victory. Barratt achieved the feat of getting all ten wickets in the first Australian innings, though curiously he did not bowl down a single wicket. There were seven

ducks in one Australian innings, and six in the
first innings of the Players. I devoutly hope that
these unfortunate disputes as to what professionals
are to be paid for their services in representative
matches are now at an end, as a committee has
been formed to govern the test matches of the
present season. It is to be hoped that the committee will not be dissolved, but will remain in
existence to settle such financial details in the
future, both as to the teams playing in test matches
at home and those visiting Australia.

While the Australians were in England the
Melbourne Club invited the brothers Walker to
take out an amateur team for the winter of 1878–79.
Owing, however, to the death of his brother, Mr.
I. D. Walker was unable to undertake the tour,
but Lord Harris came to the rescue. As it was
found impossible to secure the requisite number
of amateurs, two professionals — Ulyett and
Emmett — were included. The amateurs who
made up the team consisted of Lord Harris,
C. Absolon, L. Hone, A. N. Hornby, A. P. Lucas,
F. A. Mackinnon, H. C. Maul, F. Penn, V. Royle,
S. S. Schultz, and A. J. Webbe. They left Southampton on October 17, 1878, and between the
day they arrived in Australia and the end of March
played thirteen matches, winning six, losing three,
and drawing four. They were the fifth English
team to visit Australia, and their welcome was
enthusiastic, and the interest they aroused was as
keen as ever.

The harmony of the tour was destroyed by

a disturbance which took place at Sydney. Murdoch, who had been batting brilliantly, was given "run out" by the umpire, whereupon the crowd shouted, " Not out !" "Go bac'., Murdoch !" "Another umpire !" and so on. At the same time the spectators rushed to the wickets, and in the words of the *Australasian*, "rowdyism became rampant." "The English team," said the *Sydney Mail*, "soon found themselves in the centre of a surging, gesticulating, and shouting mob, and one rowdy struck Lord Harris across the body with a whip or stick." Further cricket was impossible that day, and a deputation subsequently waited upon Lord Harris to express the extreme regret of the cricketers of Sydney at the disgraceful scene which had taken place. Throughout Australia the discreditable affair was deeply deplored, and all the papers condemned the outrage. Lord Harris, in a letter to England, stated that the disturbance was started by professional betting-men in the pavilion, and reproached the committee and officers of the Association for permitting betting on the ground. In reply to Lord Harris' letter, Mr. G. M. Gibbon, writing on behalf of the New South Wales Cricket Association, denied that betting was sanctioned, and insisted that the demonstration was entirely against the umpire, and, bad though it was, sprang from no mercenary motive. This unfortunate episode, however, marred the pleasure which the tour might otherwise have afforded to the English cricketers.

County Cricket, in spite of the visit of the Australians, maintained and even increased its hold on popular interest this season. Gloucestershire, who for two seasons had headed the Championship table, took second place, as Middlesex went to the top, playing only six matches, of which they won three and drew three ; while Gloucester, who played ten, won four, lost two, and drew four. Surrey, who in 1877 had raised themselves from the eighth to the second position in the Counties, fell back to the seventh place.

This was one of my " off " seasons, as with neither bat nor ball did I quite maintain my reputation. For the first time in ten years my aggregate for the season was exceeded by another batsman. It is a curious fact that the names of E. M., G. F., and myself did not appear this year in the list of batsmen who made individual innings of 200 or over during the season. A compiler of cricket statistics remarked at the time that during the previous.ten years his annual list of the hitters of two hundreds had invariably contained the contributions of one, sometimes two, and more frequently of all three of us.

1879 The exceptionally severe, and almost unprecedentedly prolonged winter of 1878 and 1879 (which began in October and continued until May), played havoc with the wickets in the early part of this season. It is worth while mentioning that quite a number of cricket matches on the ice were played during this winter, the most notable, perhaps, being one played by moonlight on the ice in Windsor Home Park. In another match played at Grantchester, near Cambridge, no fewer than 600 runs were made for fifteen wickets. During this cricket on the ice season of 1878–79 one batsman made 105 (not out) — a record, I should think, for the game played in this manner.

The severe winter was followed by a wet summer, and the cricket season of 1879 will be remembered for the cold, wind, and rain, which made cricket uncomfortable for the players and unpleasant for the spectators. On no less than eleven days, when important matches should have been in progress, cricket was quite impossible at Lord's. In consequence, attendances were generally small, and an unusual number of matches were left unfinished.

The Whit Week match between North and South at Lord's was set apart by the M.C.C. authorities for the benefit of Alfred Shaw, and as the Notts bowler was deservedly popular among all cricketers, the match was regarded as one of the great events of the season. But Whit Monday turned out the most dismal, dreary, and depressing day of that rainy summer, and Shaw was robbed of what should have been the most remunerative day of his benefit. Shaw, however, distinguished himself by a magnificent bowling feat, his analysis for the second innings of the South being :

Overs 43   Maidens 30   Runs 21   Wickets 8

It had been arranged that a complimentary
match in my honour between " Over Thirty" and
" Under Thirty" should be played at Lord's on
July 21, 22, 23, but as the unfavourable weather
had interfered with Shaw's benefit, the M.C.C.
sanctioned my suggestion that the proceeds of this
complimentary match, less the expenses, should
be added as a subscription to Alfred Shaw's list.
Unfortunately, the weather was again disastrous,
and Shaw reaped all too little from the proceeds
of this event. Eventually the " Over Thirty"
team, which consisted of W. G. Grace, E. M.
Grace, F. Townsend, J. Selby, William Oscroft,
T. Emmett, F. Wyld, Alfred Shaw, E. Pooley and
W. Mycroft, defeated the " Under Thirty" team,
which was composed of the Hon. A. Lyttelton,
F. Penn, G. F. Grace, V. Royle, Hon. Ivo Bligh,
W. Bates,W. Barnes, G. G. Hearne, George Ulyett,
F. Morley, and R. G. Barlow, by seven wickets.

After this match I was made the recipient of a
national testimonial, consisting of a cheque, a
clock, and obelisks, made of marble and bronze.
The presentation took place in front of the pavilion
at Lord's, and Lord Fitzhardinge, who, with the
Duke of Beaufort, had been the initiators of the
movement, made the presentation.   Lord Charles
Russell in a speech, which I can never forget,
expressed his delight at the increasing popularity
of cricket as the sport of the people, from prince
to peasant, and in alluding to the fact that the
Prince of Wales was one of those who had sub-
scribed, hazarded the opinion that the Prince had

done so to show his respect for the one great game
of the people, requiring in those who play it the
national essentials—patience, fortitude, pluck, and
fostering the respect for law and love of fair play,
which are characteristic of the English people.
The demonstration of good wishes which accompanied the presentation made a deep impression on my mind, and I need scarcely say that the
congratulations of friends and comrades, as well
as those of thousands of people to whom I was
unknown personally, deepened my attachment to
the game, which has been the delight of my life.

After the English cricket season Richard Daft
took out a professional team to Canada and
America. The team, which consisted of R. Daft,
A. Shaw, J. Selby, A. Shrewsbury, W. Oscroft,
W. Barnes, F. Morley, T. Emmett, G. Ulyett,
E. Lockwood, W. Bates, and G. Pinder, returned
with an unbroken record, having played twelve
matches, in nine of which they were victorious,
while three were drawn. The success of the tour
equalled that of Mr. R. A. Fitzgerald in 1872,
which was composed entirely of amateurs, and
played eight matches, winning seven and leaving
one unfinished. Daft's team had a very pleasant
trip, and the tour was a financial as well as a
cricketing success.

CHAPTER VII

CRICKET IN THE EIGHTIES

IN turning from a survey of the progress of cricket in the seventies to a brief summary of the outstanding features of cricket in the eighties, it may be interesting to glance back and in a few sentences compare the position of County Cricket held in 1870 with the place it had secured in the mind of the public in 1880. In 1870 County Cricket was hardly organised at all. With the exception of Surrey, no county played more than six inter-county matches in 1870, while three, Gloucestershire, Lancashire, and Middlesex, played but two matches each. In 1880 nearly every county played home and return matches with each of the other seven counties. In 1870 there were only twenty-two county matches played; in 1880 there were thirty-eight inter-county matches played. During the intervening decade popular interest in County Cricket had advanced with striking rapidity, to the detriment, it must even be said, of such a time-honoured fixture as North *v.* South. Where hundreds attended as spectators at cricket matches in 1870, thousands assembled for County Cricket matches in 1880.

Early in the season (May 17 and 18) Richard **1880** Daft's Canadian team played an Eleven of England at Lord's for the benefit of the Cricketers' Fund. As the match took place in Whit Week there was a capital attendance of spectators, and although the weather was cold the wicket was dry and fast. Unfortunately, the match only lasted two days, but I am glad to say that the Fund received a substantial cheque. Daft's team were ultimately defeated by 109 runs.

As I was now entering upon my professional career I did not take part in first-class County Cricket until somewhat late in the season, although in May and June I played in some local matches in Gloucestershire and scored heavily. For the second time I failed to reach a thousand runs in first-class cricket this season. Nottingham, which had been creeping up in the County Championship tables during the previous two or three years, took first place this season. Until August the Nottingham Eleven had an unbroken record of success, their only defeat of the season being at the hands of Yorkshire. Gloucester had the distinction of being the only county team which was not vanquished by Notts. This was William Barnes' great year. Throughout the season he was in fine form, and at its close he was the only batsman whose aggregate exceeded a thousand runs.

A second Australian team—the first to be brought over by Mr. W. L. Murdoch—visited England this year, and played thirty-seven matches, of which they won twenty-one, lost four, and drew twelve — a slightly better record than that of Gregory's team two years earlier. The second team consisted of W. L. Murdoch, F. R. Spofforth, A. C. Bannerman, J. M. Blackham, H. F. Boyle, W. H. Moule, J. Slight, G. J. Bonnor, T. U. Groube, P. S. M'Donnell, G. E. Palmer, G. Alexander, A. H. Jarvis. Nine out of the thirteen were Victorians, three came from New South Wales, and one from South Australia.

Another visit from an Australian team, following as it then seemed so rapidly after the first, was considered a doubtful experiment, especially as there was a growing prejudice in England against speculating and travelling teams. Moreover, the M.C.C. and the counties had all made their fixtures before it was definitely announced that the Australians were actually coming. In consequence very few first-class fixtures could be secured for the visitors, who did not make a single appearance at Lord's. I made an attempt to arrange a match at Marylebone in July, but though the M.C.C. granted the use of the ground, it was found impossible. Quite towards the end of their tour it was arranged, through the exertions of Lord Harris, Mr. Alcock, and myself, that a match against England should take place on September 6, 7, and 8 at Kennington Oval. It

was admitted that this one match converted the
trip from a comparative failure into a financial
success. The match proved remarkable in every
way ; it was, perhaps, one of the most famous of
the contests between England and Australia. A
week before the encounter took place I was on a
visit to Mr. Porter at Kingsclere, where we had
a cricket match and a few days' shooting. I
came straight up to London for the test match,
and as I had not been playing in first-class cricket
for some little time, I did not expect any conspicuous personal success. Nevertheless, I scored
152 out of the 420 made by England in the first
innings.

The English team was as good an Eleven as
could have been got together, and the bowling of
A. G. Steel, Shaw, and Morley made havoc of the
Australians in their first innings, which realised
only 149 runs. Facing a huge deficit, the
Australians began their second innings, when
Murdoch distinguished himself by a brilliant and
faultless contribution of 153. It was expected
that England would gain a single innings victory,
but so gallantly did the Australians face the odds
against them that the match had to be fought out
to the bitter end. Eventually England won by
five wickets, after a most exciting finish. My
brother, G. F., who was playing in this match—it
was the last big match in which he did play—
atoned for a pair of spectacles by dismissing
Bonnor with a catch which is remembered to

this day. Bonnor got hold of a ball from Shaw, and sent a tremendous skier into the long field, which G. F. judged in a wonderful way. Mr. Frederick Gale, who chained the distance himself, with two of the Oval Ground men, stated that the hit measured 115 yards as a minimum. When at its greatest height the ball seemed to hang in the air, and two runs were finished before it dropped into G. F.'s hands. Throughout the tour the batting of Murdoch, the wicket - keeping of Blackham, and the wonderfully accurate throwing in of the fieldsmen impressed the spectators greatly ; while Spofforth's remarkable bowling was the subject of general conversation in all cricket circles.

Within a fortnight of the victory over Australia my brother G. F. died. The premature death of a young man in the pride of his strength and the prime of his life came as a shock to all his countless friends. I need scarcely enlarge on the brilliance of his career. He was one of the finest all-round cricketers I have ever seen, and a first-rate sportsman in every sense. As a batsman he was an invaluable run-getter; as a bowler he always rendered his side timely assistance ; while as a fieldsman he was unsurpassed. He loved the game, and threw himself heart and soul into his play, whether it was batting, bowling, or fielding. The news of his death was everywhere received with feelings of sincere regret, and in the match which was being played at the Crystal Palace between the Australians and the Players of

England each cricketer wore a bow or band of black crape. When the Australians were entertained at a banquet at the Mansion House, the Lord Mayor made a short and touching reference to G. F. amid silence which told better than words how deeply his death had touched the hearts of his comrades in the cricket field. He had played in the Canterbury Week before he was sixteen ; for Gloucestershire before he was seventeen ; for the Gentlemen of England before he was twenty ; and from that time onward was regarded as indispensable in any of the great representative matches.

The most notable feature of this season's cricket **1881** was the extraordinary form displayed by the Lancashire Eleven, which took the first place in the Championship table after a season of almost unparalleled brilliancy. Its record of an unbroken series of decisive victories was almost unique. Its claim to be the premier county could not be challenged. In batting and bowling the team was remarkably strong, while in its fielding there was not a weak spot. With Mr. Hornby as captain, Mr. A. G. Steel, Barlow, Briggs, and Mr. Lancashire as mainstays in batting, and Mr. A. G. Steel, Barlow, Watson, Nash, Crossland, and Briggs as bowlers; and with Pilling as wicket-keeper, the team this year was impregnable in its strength, and it was not surprising that Yorkshire, Kent, and Surrey were each twice defeated, and that no county was able to inflict a reverse on the Lancastrians.

Gloucestershire had an unfortunate season, losing as many matches as it won, and taking third place in the Championship table, down which she gradually sank to the sixth and eighth place in the next two years. I was not playing much this season, and my aggregate for the year fell to 792, which I think is the low-water mark of my batting career. The calls made upon my time by my profession reduced my opportunities for first-class cricket, and throughout the season I played in only twenty-one innings.

At the close of the year Alfred Shaw, who again headed the bowling averages, took out a professional team to Australia, consisting of A. Shaw, Shrewsbury, Selby, Scotton, Bates, Peate, Emmett, Ulyett, Barlow, Pilling, Midwinter, Lillywhite. The team played five matches in America, seven in New Zealand, and eighteen in Australia ; they were fifteen times victorious, and on three occasions only were defeated, twelve matches being drawn. During the tour, which I must say was a great financial success, Ulyett, Bates, and Barlow scored over a thousand runs each, while Peate captured no fewer than 264 wickets. Some of the principal Lancastrians in the colonies made a special presentation to Barlow and Pilling, who made themselves very popular on the other side of the world.

1882   During this season public interest centred in the doings of the third Australian team to visit England. The team, which consisted of W. L. Murdoch, T. W. Garrett, S. P. Jones, H. H.

Massie, F. R. Spofforth, A. C. Bannerman, J. M. Blackham, G. J. Bonnor, H. F. Boyle, T. Horan, P. S. M'Donnell, G. E. Palmer, and G. Giffen, was, in my opinion, the best Australia has ever sent over to the mother country. So brilliant were their achievements, and so completely did they captivate the British public, that the ordinary inter-county matches suffered eclipse. They were foemen thoroughly worthy of our steel, plucky, resolute, and resourceful, and they proved their ability to meet, and in most cases to beat, the best teams we could set against them. Besides winning two out of the three matches played against representative English Elevens, they defeated every one of our principal counties, and inflicted a single innings defeat on the Gentlemen. Their record of twenty-four victories against four defeats was a series of successes aptly described as a "triumphal march through England." In spite of our slow wickets, they scored freely, and whenever the wicket helped the bowlers Spofforth, Boyle, Garrett, and Giffen proved too much for most of our batsmen, while their fielding was conspicuously good.

Notwithstanding the wet season, the standard of scoring reached a high level. Six batsmen obtained an aggregate of a thousand runs each, Ulyett, with 1542, heading the aggregates. I was handicapped a little by illness at the beginning of the season, and just failed to reach my 1000 runs. The most successful batsman of the year was Mr. C. T. Studd, who was in magnificent form, and with both bat and ball took first place among the amateurs. Peate was an easy first in the bowling averages, as, notwithstanding a sprained ankle, he was the only first-class bowler who took over two hundred wickets in the season. Crossland, the Lancashire fast bowler, who came to the front about this time, was remarkably successful. Of all the bowlers I have ever played against, Crossland had the most doubtful action, and I am inclined to think that he ought to have been no-balled in every over. His pace was terrific, and his yorkers exceedingly difficult to play.

There are many good stories about Crossland, and one of the best may well be repeated here. While playing in a small match he bowled one of his fast yorkers, which hit the unfortunate batsman on the leg. The batsman walked away from his wicket, and the umpire called, " You're not out." " No," he replied, " but I'm going," and he went. Apparently he had had quite enough of it, and I don't blame him, for with Crossland on the war-path a batsman who stood up to his bowling had a good chance of being hurt. During this season Robert Peel made his appearance for Yorkshire, and was regarded as the only young bowler who showed any real promise.

Crossland was about the last fast bowler to come into prominence for some years, as at this time fast bowling was rapidly on the decline. In the sixties and early seventies, when I first began to play cricket, fast bowling was quite the vogue, but towards the end of the seventies a rage for slow bowling set in. It is a little curious to note that the fashion has changed, and that at the present time fast bowling has again come to the front.

During this season cricket lost a zealous supporter by the death of James Lillywhite, founder of "Lillywhite's Cricketers' Annual," and a first-rate player in his day.

The County Championship honours were divided between Lancashire and Notts, who each lost but one match during the season. Lancashire, as they have a reputation for doing, began badly, but ended up brilliantly ; Nottingham opened the season auspiciously, and closed it unfortunately. The success of Nottingham was all the more gratifying because in the previous year they had lost status, owing to a "strike" of their leading professionals, with whom, however, friendly relations had been restored. This was Nottingham's first season without the services of Richard Daft, who closed his career in the previous year. The Midland County had, however, received a valuable addition to their strength in Attewell and Flowers, who at this time began to play for the county. Gloucestershire had an unfortunate season, winning only two matches out of ten.

The seventh English team to visit Australia left England at the close of this season, with the Hon. Ivo Bligh as captain. For the first time the Committee of the Melbourne Cricket

Club undertook the management of the tour on their own responsibility. The team consisted of Mr. A. G. Steel, Mr. E. T. Studd, W. W. Read, E. F. S. Tylecote, Hon. Ivo Bligh, G. F. H. Leslie. G. B. Studd, G. F. Vernon, Bates, Barlow, Barnes, and Morley. Unfortunately, the steamer in which they embarked collided with a sailing ship, and in the accident Morley, the only fast bowler of the team, sustained a broken rib. The injury, which was not discovered for some time, deprived the team of his services. Moreover, the delay which resulted from the accident upset the programme of the tour, as the team were ten days late in reaching Australia. Their record was a trifle disappointing, as they won only nine of their eighteen matches, and were three times beaten. Mr. A. G. Steel was an easy first in both the batting and bowling averages.

1883　Two important amendments of the laws of cricket came into operation during this season, and gave universal satisfaction. Acceding to the unanimous wish of the leading counties, the M.C.C. introduced a law by which the batting side was given the option of having the wicket rolled for ten minutes before play commenced on the second and third mornings of a match. Up to this time it had been the rule that the wicket should only be rolled between the innings of the competing sides—a regulation which inflicted an injustice upon a team which began their innings late in one day, after their opponents had monopolised the wicket all day. Before this new rule came into operation the side winning the toss secured an altogether unfair advantage over their opponents, who, in many cases, lost the chance of having the wicket rolled in the morning through getting a few minutes' play overnight. If rain had fallen in the night, or a heavy dew had damped the ground, the batting side often found the wicket detrimental to their chances. The new rule swept away this grievance.

The second amendment of the laws changed the system of appointing umpires, by making it unlawful for an umpire to stand in a match in which his own county was engaged.

The questionable bowling of Crossland and two or three other prominent bowlers led to some unpleasantness, as umpires at this time, as now, seemed peculiarly loath to enforce the penalties by no-balling. Lord Harris gave notice of his intention to move an addition to the law enforcing an umpire to call "No ball" if he was not of opinion that the bowler's delivery was absolutely fair—a proposition which was ultimately adopted.

County cricket excited especially keen interest this year, the close competition between Notts and Yorks engaging public attention. Nottingham, in spite of Morley's illness, Oscroft's collapse, and Selby's injury, earned the Championship of the year, being beaten only once, though Yorkshire won more matches. Surrey, who had had a succession of unlucky seasons, had a successful year, principally due to the batting of Mr. W. W.

Read, who was at his very best this season, topping the averages with an aggregate of 1573, and
an average of 47.   Mr. Key came into prominence this year, while in Henderson the county
found an excellent all-round player.   Pooley's
retirement robbed the Surrey team of an invaluable wicket-keeper.   Gloucestershire was again
unfortunate, Midwinter's return to Australia
weakening the bowling.   Mr. C. T. Studd had
a brilliant season, both as batsman and bowler.

For the first time for many years I was an
absentee from the Gentlemen v. Players match at
the Oval.   Both of these matches proved exceptionally interesting this season.   The match at
Lord's was remarkable for the fact that 1066 runs
were scored for the loss of thirty-three wickets,
the Gentlemen winning by seven wickets,
while the encounter at the Oval was unique,
because for the first and only time in the history
of these matches the result was a tie.

1884   By this time it had almost become the general
rule for an Australian team to visit us every
alternate year.   The movements of the fourth
Australian team which came to England this
season were watched with a specially keen interest, and indeed almost monopolised the attention of the public.   The team consisted of :
P. S. M'Donnell, G. Alexander, G. Giffen, G. E.
Palmer, F. R. Spofforth, W. L. Murdoch,
W. Midwinter, H. F. Boyle, J. Mc. Blackham,
G. J. Bonnor, A. C. Bannerman, W. H. Cooper,
and H. J. H. Scott, and undertook a programme

of thirty-five engagements. The Marylebone Club
and the principal counties gave the visitors every
facility, and a larger number of really important
matches figured in their list than had been the
case in the three previous teams. They played
on the whole against strong elevens, but of the
thirty-two matches in which they took part they
managed to win eighteen and lose only seven.
They were favoured by fine weather and hard
wickets, but hampered by the failure of their
slow bowler, W. H. Cooper, who had to stand
out from most of their matches. As the team
consisted of only twelve players and the manager
(who did not play), the whole burden of their
programme fell upon eleven men. Three test
matches were played—viz., at Manchester, Lord's,
and the Oval. The match at Old Trafford on
July 10, 11, and 12 was utterly spoilt by the rain,
which prevented any play on the first day, and,
in consequence, the match was left unfinished.
England won the second match at Lord's on
July 22, 23, and 24, by an innings and 5 runs,
Mr. A. G. Steel playing a brilliant innings of 148.
The third test match—at the Oval—August 11, 12,
and 13, was remarkable for the large score of 551
made by the Australians, three of whom headed
the century. Murdoch made 211, M'Donnell
103, and H. J. H. Scott 112. I particularly
remember this match, because I fielded in every
position in the field. Towards the end of the
Australian innings, when Alfred Lyttelton went
on to bowl, I even took the gloves, and caught

Midwinter at the wicket off Lyttelton's lobs.
Every man on the English side bowled. Lyttelton, who went on last, was the most successful,
securing four wickets for nineteen runs.

Another curious fact is that Scotton, who went
in first with me, and played a patient innings of
90, was the last man to be dismissed, whilst
W. W. Read, who went in tenth man, scored
117. When Mr. Read joined Scotton, the
Nottingham stonewaller was 53 (not out), and
when Mr. Read had got his hundred Scotton was
still in his eighties. It is obvious that Mr. Read
did all the run-getting—in 2½ hours he made 117,
whilst Scotton in 5¾ hours only made 90. It was
due to these batsmen that the match was saved
for England. It ended, like the Manchester fixture, in a draw. It was very unsatisfactory to the
Australians that they should have been beaten in
the only match finished, when they had certainly
the best of the two matches which were drawn ;
in the first case the weather robbed them of a
probable victory, and in the second their own
enormous score made it impossible to conclude
the match.

Though Murdoch headed the averages, and
M'Donnell scored consistently, Giffen proved
himself the best all-round man of the team. The
laurels were, however, accorded to Spofforth,
whose extraordinary bowling was the principal
cause of the Australian successes. During the
tour he bowled 1561 overs, and captured 211
wickets at a cost of 12.76 runs apiece. The

tour was in all senses a success, and increased our appreciation of the cricketing abilities of the Australians.

Simultaneously with the visit of the Australians, England was for the first time visited by an American team of cricketers. I say for the first time, because, though the baseball team which visited England ten years previously played a few cricket matches, their object in coming was to give exhibitions of the American national game of baseball. The Philadelphian team received a very hearty welcome and seemed well satisfied with the results of their tour. In arranging their fixtures they modestly requested that all their opponents should be amateurs. They made a very fair show against some of the English County amateur teams, and out of their eighteen matches won eight and lost five. Interest in their doings was eclipsed by the excitement which attended the Australian tour.

I have often thought that the power of cricket to bring peoples of different countries into friendly relationships has never been properly recognised. I believe that the interchanging of visits by cricketing teams has helped to deepen British interest in our colonies and to bind us in closer harmony with other nations. English cricketers have met and fought in friendly rivalry Australian aborigines, Canadians, Americans, Australians, South Africans, and Parsees, and I am disposed to think that the good fellowship born on the cricket-field has done more than is recognised to knit together the various sections of the British Empire and to advance the cause of civilisation.

By the right of unquestionable superiority Nottingham was awarded the County Championship this season. Their record was the feature of the year's cricket, and was indeed almost without a parallel. Of their ten matches they won nine and drew the tenth in their favour. No other county placed so fine a combination in the field, and their extraordinary series of triumphs was the result of splendid all-round excellence. Throughout the season they were without the services of Fred. Morley, whose injuries in the collision on his outward voyage to Australia in 1882 kept him out of the cricket-field, and finally led to his death at the close of this season. Attewell came to the fore, and with Alfred Shaw contributed materially to the success of the county. Gloucestershire had a disastrous season, scoring only one success, and that by only seven runs. Although I suffered from an injured hand, and severely strained my leg, I made 572 runs for the county and 1361 runs in all matches.

Cricket lost some ardent supporters during 1884. Among them I must include my mother, who died in July. She had always taken a deep interest in the game, and scarcely ever missed a Gloucestershire match. To the score-books and records which she kept with her own hands I have already acknowledged my indebtedness. Another ardent supporter of cricket who died this year was the Hon. Robert Grimston, who played first for Harrow and then for Oxford, and was President of the M.C.C. The Rev. A. R. Ward, who died in September, was another liberal friend of cricket. He played for Cambridge in 1853 and 1854, and was a staunch supporter of the Cambridge University Club. The death of George Frederick Pardon, better known as " Captain Crawley," robbed cricket of one of its best friends on the Press. He was one of the Pardon family, who have brought cricket reporting to its highest degree of efficiency. John Wisden, who was one of the best all-round cricketers in the fifties, and who in 1850 bowled down all ten wickets for the South against the North at Lord's ; and E. B. Fawcett, whose throw of 126 yards when he was eighteen held the record for many years as the longest throw of the cricket-ball, also died during this year.

At the close of this season Alfred Shaw took out a team to Australia. It consisted of A. Shaw, Barnes, Scotton, Attewell, Flowers, Shrewsbury, Peel, Hunter, Ulyett, Bates, Lillywhite, M. Read, and Briggs. Thirty-three matches were played, of which sixteen were won, two lost, and no fewer than fifteen drawn. Five test matches were played. The first, which took place at Adelaide, was won by England by eight wickets. The Australian Eleven were thoroughly representative, and the feature of the match was the batting of M'Donnell, who played two fine innings of 124 and 83. Barnes, who throughout the tour was remarkably successful with both bat and ball, heading the averages in both, did nearly as well, scoring 134 and 28 (not out). Through some unfortunate misunderstanding Murdoch's team, which had just returned from its tour in England, refused to play in the next test match, which took place at Melbourne, and which was won by Shaw's Eleven by ten wickets ; Briggs, with an innings of 121, being the chief scorer for England.

At Sydney another thoroughly representative Australian team was put into the field, although Murdoch, who had had quite enough cricket for a time, did not take part. After a very exciting match Australia gained the victory by six runs. Spofforth was on the spot, and though he was knocked about by Read and Flowers, who made the stand of the English innings, he took ten wickets for 144 runs, and practically won the match for Australia. Rain spoiled the wicket for the Englishmen in the fourth match, which was played at Sydney, and the Australians, who had a strong eleven, won by eight wickets. The fifth match of the series was played at Melbourne, and again England won, this time by an innings and 98 runs. In justice to Australia, it should be said that the eleven in this match was not representative of Colonial cricket, as several of the best players, who had refused to play in the first test match at Melbourne, were barred from playing in this encounter. Moreover, rain spoilt the wicket for the Australian second innings, and made victory comparatively easy for Shaw's Eleven. The

Englishmen received the heartiest possible reception, and the trip was equally pleasant and profitable.

This year we had a season of strictly English sport, interesting from first to last, but without sensations. In the absence of an Australian team County Cricket again assumed its paramount place with the cricketing public. Nottingham were hardly expected to maintain the standard of extraordinary brilliance which gave them the premiership in the previous year ; nevertheless, they retained their proud position at the top of the Championship table, though Yorkshire were close rivals. Lancashire and Surrey did extremely well, the former receiving magnificent assistance from Briggs, who was now one of the best all-round cricketers of the day, while Mr. W. W. Read's phenomenal achievements with the bat contributed in no small measure to the success of his county. Mr. A. G. Steel, who had been called to the Bar, found his professional engagements multiplying so rapidly that he was only able to play in two matches. Lancashire, in fact, lost some of its mainstays this year. Crossland, the fast bowler, was disqualified, owing to a breach in the residential rules ; and Pilling, the prince of wicketkeepers, owing to ill-health, was unable to keep wicket regularly. Kent lost the services of E. F. S. Tylecote, and Lord Harris retired from the captaincy of the Eleven.

Warm, dry weather kept the wickets hard and

fast throughout the season, and large scores were frequent. The professionals had perhaps the best of the year's cricket—Shrewsbury, Gunn, Maurice Read batting exceptionally well. Briggs, who had been played as a batsman, showed wonderful form as a bowler, and headed the bowling averages, while Lohmann, who was played for his bowling, rendered his county valuable service with the bat. For the first time for eleven years the professionals won the Gentlemen v. Players match at Lord's. Mr. W. W. Read was the highest scorer of the year, with an aggregate of 1880 runs in 42 completed innings ; his average in Surrey County matches being 59 per innings. Gloucestershire, which had been passing through a period of tribulation, took the sixth place among the counties. I was in my best form, and in twenty-six innings for my county scored 1004 runs, my biggest innings being 221 (not out) against Middlesex.

Mr. A. J. Webbe succeeded Mr. I. D. Walker in the captaincy of the Middlesex team this year, a post which he filled with credit to himself and advantage to his county till the end of last year. The departure of Mr. T. C. Studd on missionary service in China robbed the ranks of our amateurs of one of our most brilliant young players. Mr. A. P. Lucas could not play owing to ill-health, and the Hon. Alfred Lyttelton only took part in one match. As some compensation for these heavy losses the Middlesex team received an accession of strength in Mr. A. E. Stoddart, who for fourteen

years continued to do the Metropolitan county
yeoman service.

Benefit matches were given to Humphrey and
Watson this season, and another match was
arranged for the benefit of the widow and children
of F. Morley.

Briggs and Pilling broke all previous records
for a last wicket stand by putting on 173 runs for
Lancashire against Surrey at Liverpool on July 16.

On returning from Australia, Alfred Shaw's
Eleven played three matches : (1) against Lord
Sheffield's Eleven, which ended in a draw ;
(2) against an Eleven of England at Harrogate,
which was abandoned owing to the rain ; and
(3) against Louis Hall's Eleven at Bradford.
Both of the last-named matches are notable for
curious incidents. I played for the Eleven of
England, and when I got out, 53 runs were on
the telegraph board, towards which my contribution was 51, including two drives out of the
ground for six. In the match against Hall's
Eleven, Shaw's team went in first and scored 230.
When the last man in Hall's Eleven came in,
23 runs were needed to save the follow on, and
Shaw's team, not being anxious to make their
opponents follow on, bowled and fielded care-
lessly, but, just when it appeared as if they had
succeeded in this endeavour, Peate intentionally
knocked his wicket down. As he did not hit his
wicket until the ball had gone by, a dispute arose
as to whether he was out, and the discussion on
the point extended over twenty minutes, during

which play was suspended. These little deviations from the strict order of cricket are always to be regretted, and, although the rules do not prohibit batsmen from knocking down their wicket to secure a follow on, or penalise bowlers and fieldsmen for deliberately throwing away runs in order to prevent the follow on, the adoption of these tactics almost invariably leads to unpleasantness.

The obituary of this year included Martin M'Intyre, who was one of my Australian team of 1873–74, and a first-rate all-round cricketer ; John Walker, the eldest of the famous Walker family, and one of the finest amateur cricketers of the fifties or sixties ; William D. Baker, who was instrumental in the acquisition of Kennington Oval, which had previously been a market-garden ; and Edgar Willsher, the old Kent bowler, who was for many years the manager of Prince's Cricket Ground.

Two curious incidents which excited considerable interest occurred this year. While practising at Loretto on July 1, a batsman hit the ball along the ground at a fast pace. A large rat, which was coming out of a hole at the edge of the turf, was struck by the ball and killed on the spot. While a match between Caius and Trinity Hall was in progress at Cambridge on August 12, a ball, bowled by Mr. Cordeaux, hit a swallow which was flying across the wicket and killed it.

1886 Another, the fifth, Australian team, visited England this year, but, though they came with a flourish of trumpets as the strongest Eleven that

Australia had ever sent us, their tour was something of a disappointment; the team, which came
under the auspices of the Melbourne C.C. (which
took the management as well as the risk of the
tour), consisting of H. J. H. Scott, G. J. Bonnor,
G. E. Palmer, J. Mc. Blackham, W. Bruce, J.
McIlwraith, J. W. Trumble, E. Evans, S. P. Jones,
T. W. Garrett, F. R. Spofforth, A. H. Jarvis, and
G. Giffen. Their programme was too long for
all practical purposes, extending over an almost
unbroken series of 130 consecutive days. Towards the end of their thirty-nine matches public
interest in their doings somewhat dwindled away.
Twenty-two of their matches were left unfinished,
and of the seventeen which were brought to a
definite issue the Australians won nine.

The three test matches were won by England.
The first test match, at Manchester, was won by
the Englishmen with four wickets to spare after
an exciting finish, but at Kennington Oval the
Australians were defeated by an innings and 217
runs. It should be admitted that the heavy rain
which fell after England had scored 434 in their
first innings, to which I contributed 170, robbed
the Australians of any possible chance of avoid-
ing defeat. In the match at Lord's, where
Shrewsbury made 164 and Barnes 58, England
won by an innings and 106 runs, Briggs taking
eleven wickets for 74 runs. Perhaps it is only
fair to say that the Australians were very unfortunate, as Spofforth, who had done so much for
them on previous occasions, met with an accident,

which took the sting out of his bowling, while Bonnor, whose tremendous hitting had often served the Australians in good stead, was incapacitated from play during August and September by an injured foot. In their hour of need George Giffen rose to the occasion, and performed the extraordinary feat of endurance of bowling 7000 balls and obtaining 1450 runs during the tour.

For the third time in succession Nottingham won the County Championship. Out of fourteen matches they won seven and drew the remainder. Shrewsbury, with an average of 46 runs per innings — the highest County average of the season—served his county splendidly. Surrey, with ten victories and three defeats, were Nottingham's principal rivals. Abel established a reputation by a season of consistent scoring, which realised 1164 runs, while Lohmann's double triumph with bat and ball was one of the features of the county's season. Middlesex improved its position in the Championship, but Gloucestershire, with six defeats and two victories, sank again to the bottom of the table. I was the top scorer of the season, with 1846 runs in fifty-two innings, but Mr. W. W. Read, with 1825 runs and forty-three innings, headed the averages. Though Watson preceded him in the bowling averages, Tom Emmett was the most successful bowler of the year.

During this season a team of Parsee cricketers paid us a visit, but met with very little success, even against second- and third-rate clubs.

Mr. E. J. Sanders, who had taken a team of amateurs to America in 1885, repeated the experiment this season, and had a very pleasant tour, marred, however, by the illness and subsequent death of Mr. A. R. Cobb, who at one time kept wicket for Oxford. Mr. Sanders' team again proved too strong for American cricketers, and returned with an unbeaten record.

The ninth English Team to visit Australia went out at the close of this season, under the captaincy of Shrewsbury. It consisted of Shrewsbury, Barnes, Gunn, Scotton, Alfred Shaw, Flowers, Sherwin, Lohmann, Maurice Read, Briggs, Barlow, Lillywhite, and Bates, and was one of the strongest teams that ever went out to Australia. Their record of twenty-nine matches, twelve victories, two defeats, and fifteen drawn games was extremely creditable. Two test matches were played, and both were won by the English Eleven. A match between the Smokers and Non-smokers, played on the East Melbourne Ground, proved remarkable on account of the extraordinarily high scoring. The Non-Smokers, who went in first, made 803, the highest total obtained in a high-class match up to that time. Shrewsbury headed the score with 236, while Gunn made 150, and W. Bruce 131. The Smokers scored 356, Palmer with a fine innings of 118, Briggs with 86, and Flowers with 69 being the chief contributors. In the second innings the Smokers made 135 for five wickets, but the last wicket fell, if one could call it falling, by a curious incident. Scotton, who was batting when the time came for close of play, wanted to secure the ball as a memento of the occasion, and, when the last ball was bowled, he blocked it very gently, picked up the ball and put it into his pocket. For this transgression of the strict letter of the rules he was given out.

1887   The tide of fortune turned against Nottingham this season, and the Midland County, which had three times headed the county tables, fell back to the third place, Surrey, with ten wins and two losses, securing the premiership for the first time in fourteen years, while Lancashire, with eight victories and three defeats, made a good second. Shrewsbury was far and away the best average run-getter of the season, as in twenty-one innings he scored 1653 runs, making his average 78.15. Six times he scored over the century, and against Middlesex he batted for ten hours and a quarter without giving a chance for 267 runs. Wickets were good and dry, and large individual innings were unusually frequent. In this season the Players, who were now in great batting form, defeated the Gentlemen with an innings to spare in both matches. In the absence of visitors from abroad, County Cricket excited very keen interest, although public attention was in some measure distracted from cricket by the national celebration of the Queen's Jubilee.

By far the most important event of the season was the formation of the County Cricket Council. The questions of birth and residential qualification had vexed the minds of cricketers for some years past, and, as I have already recorded in these Reminiscences, a code of rules bearing on qualification came into operation in 1873. The question was reopened in 1881, but it was not until July 1887 that County Cricket was organised on a thoroughly representative basis. On that date, at a meeting of county delegates, it was agreed :

(1) "That a County Cricket Council be formed.

(2) "That the Council consist of one representative each from the counties of Nottinghamshire, Yorkshire, Surrey, Kent, Lancashire, Sussex, Gloucestershire, Middlesex, Derbyshire, Essex, Warwickshire, Norfolk, Leicestershire, Staffordshire, Somersetshire, Northamptonshire, Hampshire, Durham, Hertfordshire, and Cheshire.

(3) "That it shall be competent for the Council to alter or amend the rules of County Cricket Qualification.

(4) "That upon all questions raised under the rules of County Cricket Qualification the Committee of the M.C.C. shall adjudicate."

Among the notable events of the year was a first wicket score of 266 by Shrewsbury and Mr. Stoddart, made for England v. M.C.C. in the Centenary Festival at Lord's on June 13.

Gloucestershire had another bad season, as, out of fourteen county matches, we only gained one solitary victory against Sussex, though three of the draws were certainly in our favour. Notwithstanding that we were so low down, I personally did extremely well, and for the second time in my career performed the feat of scoring 100 in both innings of one match. Nineteen years previously I achieved this feat in the Canterbury Week ; this year I repeated the achievement against Kent on our own ground on August 25, 26, and 27. In the fourteen matches in which I played for Gloucestershire I had twenty-seven innings, and scored 1405 runs, making my county average 63. We had great difficulty in getting a good team to represent Gloucestershire in the early part of the season, and, though Woof bowled admirably, our bowling was the source of our weakness.

I remember the match against Kent, not only because I made 100 in each innings, but because my brother E. M. and I scored 127, before we were parted. E. M. had a very narrow escape early in his innings. He gave a very easy chance—in fact, it was two chances in one, as, after skying the ball to short slip, he ran down the wickets. The catch was missed, but by this time E. M. was down at my end, I, thinking he was sure to be caught, having kept in my ground. The captain and the other fieldsmen shouted to short-slip to throw the ball in and run E. M. out, but the fieldsman was flustered at missing the catch, and threw the ball to the wrong end, with the result that E. M., who was very nimble in getting across the wicket, got back to his ground, and showed his appreciation of the blunder by knocking the bowling about for some time. It is

hardly necessary to say that the Kent captain
was extremely annoyed—so much so that he
expressed the wish that short-slip had never been
born.

Two English teams went out to Australia for
the winter of 1887–88, and toured simultaneously
in the colony. One, which went out under the
auspices of the Melbourne Club, was captained
by Lord Hawke (then the Hon. M. B. Hawke),
until the death of his father summoned him home.
It consisted of the Hon. M. B. Hawke, Bates,
Peel, Rawlin, Attewell, Mr. A. E. Newton, Mr.
G. F. Vernon (who captained the team on Lord
Hawke's return home), Mr. A. E. Stoddart,
Mr. T. C. O'Brien, Mr. W. W. Read, Mr. M. P.
Bowden, Beaumont, and Abel. The second
team, which was managed by Shrewsbury and
James Lillywhite, consisted of Mr. C. A. Smith,
(captain), Mr. W. Newham, Mr. G. Brann, Mr.
L. C. Docker, J. Lillywhite, Lohmann, J. M.
Read, Briggs, Pilling, Ulyett, Preston, Shrews-
bury, and Pougher. Both in Australia and in
England some ill-feeling sprang from this dupli-
cation of teams, and the inevitable result was
that, from the financial point of view, both tours
were failures. It was said that the Melbourne
Club lost a large sum upon the tour of Mr.
Vernon's team, while Shrewsbury's and Lillywhite's losses, though smaller, must have been
considerable. Mr. Vernon's team had a slightly
better record than that of Shrewsbury and Lillywhite, though the latter achieved some brilliant

feats. Mr. Vernon's team played twenty-six matches, won eleven, drew fourteen, and lost one, while Shrewsbury and Lillywhite's team played twenty-five matches, won fourteen, drew nine, and lost two. Mr. W. W. Read headed the batting averages of Mr. Vernon's team by scoring 592 runs in nine completed innings. Peel and Attewell bowled amazingly well, each bowling over 5000 balls, and securing 213 and 135 wickets respectively for about the same average— viz., 7.5. Shrewsbury's batting was quite the feature of the tour of his team, his average being 58.9. Lohmann and Briggs shared the bowling honours, the Surrey bowler doing exceptionally well. The match between Shrewsbury's Team and Victoria, played at Melbourne in December 1887, was productive of three distinct records in international matches. The Englishmen won by an innings and 456 runs, which was the most decisive victory ever gained in a match between an English and an Australian team. The English score of 624 runs was at that time the highest total in any match between English and Colonial cricketers, while Shrewsbury's innings of 232 was the highest individual score made up to that date by an English batsman in Australia. Shrewsbury created another record by topping the second century twice during the tour.

1888   The weather, always a most important factor in cricket, played us falsely throughout this season. Rain fell pitilessly throughout June and July, and again in September, with the result that drawn matches were monotonously frequent and depressing experiences the order of the day. The sixth Australian team, which was in England during this season, had a somewhat melancholy time. They were without George Giffen, who had been the mainstay of the previous teams, while H. Moses, who was to have been included, disappointed English cricketers who had heard so much of his achievements, by failing to come. The team, which was composed of P. S. M'Donnell (captain), C. T. B. Turner, J. J. Ferris, A. C. Bannerman, S. P. Jones, J. D. Edwards, G. J. Bonnor, H. Trott, J. Mc. Blackham, H. F. Boyle, J. Worrall, J. J. Lyons, A. H. Jarvis, did not claim to be thoroughly representative of Australian cricket at its best, and they left Australia amid gloomy prognostications of failure and collapse. On the whole, however, they played extremely well, and their record of nineteen victories against fourteen losses was better than was expected. They were without the services of Spofforth, who had expressed his inability to make any further trips —a resolution to which, as is well known, he did not adhere — but they had the assistance of Mr. S. M. J. Woods, who was then at Cambridge University, and, of course, Mr. Murdoch, who had retired for a period from first-class cricket. On the other hand, they brought with them the most formidable pair of bowlers Australia could ever boast—Mr. C. T. B. Turner and Mr. J. J. Ferris. What would have been the result of

their programme of forty matches if these two
formidable bowlers had not been in the team it
would be idle to speculate, but there is absolutely
no doubt that from beginning to end of the tour
they were the mainstays of the team.   The exertions they made were remarkable even as feats of
endurance, for day after day they bowled with
almost constant success.   It may be interesting
to set forth the averages of these two bowlers, as
figures speak more eloquently than words in re-
vealing the services they rendered :—

	Overs.	Maidens.	Runs.	Wickets.	Average.
Ferris	2222.2	998	3103	220	14.23
Turner	2589.3	1222	3492	313	11.38

The fact that throughout the tour the other
Australian bowlers did not bowl 1500 overs
between them, and in all captured less than 120
wickets, demonstrates how completely Ferris and
Turner monopolised the bowling. On slow wickets
this pair of bowlers showed their extraordinary
power, and it is not too much to say that their
bowling falsified the prophecies of ill-fortune with
which the team left Australia.   The batting of the
team was somewhat uncertain, and the victories
they won were triumphs of the ball rather than
of the bat. Bonnor and Lyons hit out with
vigour, and H. Trott was a consistent run-getter.
Neither with bat nor ball did Mr. S. M. J. Woods
give promise of the sterling qualities of which he
proved himself the possessor as years went on.
In the three test matches England won the

rubber, the Australians being victorious at Lord's by 61 runs, but suffering defeat by an innings and 137 runs at Kennington Oval, and by an innings and 21 runs at Old Trafford. It should, however, be said that, though the victory of the Australians at Lord's was very creditable, they were considerably helped by the bad light in which the Englishmen had to play their second innings.

By another brilliant season, and a record of twelve victories and only one defeat, Surrey maintained the Championship this year. The success of the team was to a great degree due to the captaincy of Mr. John Shuter, who inspired in his men the enthusiasm he himself possessed. Their victories were due to consistent play in all departments, and to the pluck with which they fought out their matches and triumphed over adverse conditions, either of weather or wicket. Up to the end of August they had an absolutely unbroken record of wins, and during the season they inflicted defeat upon five of the leading counties—Kent, Yorkshire, Nottingham, Middlesex, and Sussex—in both the home and return matches. Lancashire alone succeeded in beating them. During this season Lohmann, although he had had two years of continuous cricket, played up to his very best form, and established a reputation as one of the best all-round cricketers of his day. Mr. W. W. Read and Abel batted with remarkable consistency, and on many a critical occasion rendered invaluable service.

Kent, which had for many years been in the background, got into the second place in the Championship, thanks in the main to the bowling of Walter Wright, Alec Hearne, and Martin. Gloucestershire looked up a little, and went to the fourth place, while Sussex sank back to the bottom of the counties, and for some years continued to hold the wooden spoon of cricket.

Another team of Parsee cricketers paid us a visit this year, and had a successful tour from a cricket point of view, but came to grief financially. They showed a conspicuous improvement upon the team which came over two years previously, but their record of eleven defeats and eight victories proved that they were not equal to our second- and third-rate clubs. Their object in visiting England was educational rather than mercenary, and as they succeeded, in spite of a programme of thirty-one matches, in seeing some cricket played by the best exponents of the game, they returned to India well satisfied with the results of their tour. The measure of ability they displayed was satisfactory proof that the native races of India, though hitherto unaccustomed to sport which demanded much physical exertion or endurance, were capable of assimilating the national game of the English people.

It is interesting to note that Mr. A. C. MacLaren, one of our most brilliant amateur bats, was one of the mainstays of the Harrow team this season. Mr. E. C. Streatfeild, who afterwards played for Cambridge, and then for Surrey, was one of the

most promising youngsters of Public School
cricket at this time. Mr. W. W. Read headed
the batting averages, though I had the highest
aggregate, and in August, against Yorkshire, for
the third time in my career, scored a century
twice in one match. Abel was the only other
batsman who scored more than a thousand runs
this season. The bowling honours of the year
were shared by Briggs, Lohmann, and Peel,
though Alec Hearne and Martin did yeoman
service for Kent.

A new epoch in cricket history was opened at
the end of this season by a visit which was paid
by an English team of cricketers to South Africa.
With the growth of English population in Cape
Colony, cricket began to take its place in South
African life, and at the request of a number of
Colonials interested in cricket, Major Warton
undertook the formation of an English team. He
had the hearty co-operation of Mr. C. A. Smith,
the Sussex captain, and Sir Donald Currie, the
founder of the Castle Line. Major Warton, who
acted as honorary secretary of the team, managed
to secure the services of thirteen cricketers, who,
though not all of the first rank, proved a combination sufficiently strong to test the quality of
South African cricket and to stimulate its development by a series of friendly matches. The party
consisted of Mr. C. A. Smith (captain),
Mr. M. P. Bowden, the Hon. C. Coventry,
Mr. E. M. Master, Mr. J. H. Roberts, Mr. B. A. F.
Grieve, Mr. A. G. Skinner, Wood, Maurice Read,

Abel, Briggs, Fothergill, and F. Hearne. Unfortunately Mr. J. H. Roberts lost his father in the early days of the tour, and had to return home, Ulyett being summoned to South Africa to take his place. The success of the tour—which had been regarded as a rash experiment—exceeded the anticipations of all concerned, and the members of the team were everywhere greeted with the utmost kindness and open-handed hospitality. Travelling in South Africa in those days was primitive and uncomfortable, and as seven hundred and fifty miles had to be traversed in coaches and carts a good deal of time was occupied in getting from place to place. Of the hundred and forty-six days covered by the tour, only fifty-seven were devoted to cricket, while twenty-five were spent in coaches, carts, and railway trains. Of the matches, it is only necessary to say that nineteen were played, thirteen won, and four lost.

1889   The visit and tour of a team of Philadelphian amateur cricketers added to the interest of English cricket this season. The Philadelphians came over with the most unselfish motives to test their strength by contests with English clubs, and to see English cricket played at its best for educational purposes. As they handed their share of all gate receipts to the Cricketers' Fund, their tour commended itself to all lovers of the game, and was a complete success in every respect. Though the team were admittedly not thoroughly representative of Philadelphian

cricket, their record was very creditable, as of
twelve matches played they won four, lost three,
and drew five.   They were weak in bowling,
but they batted well, making 4360 runs for 173
wickets, an average of over 25, and fielded fairly
well.   In all respects they clearly demonstrated
that cricket had gone ahead in Philadelphia since
last an American team had visited England.

The rules of cricket underwent some changes
this season.   At its annual meeting in May, the
M.C.C. adopted three new laws, which were
embodied in the rules as follows :—

" 1. That the over in future shall consist of
five balls instead of four.

" 2. That the bowler may change ends as
often as he pleases, but may not bowl two overs
in succession.

" 3. That the captain of the batting side may
declare the innings at an end in a one-day
match, whenever he chooses to do so ; but only
on the last day of a match arranged for more
than one day."

These amendments were all in the direction of
extending the liberty of cricketers, and though
they met with some hostility in certain quarters,
they have proved valuable, and no one would
now think of repealing them.   The law permitting
captains to declare their innings closed has helped
to reduce the number of drawn matches, which
are nearly always unsatisfactory, and often
exasperating.   Moreover, it has obviated the unpleasantness which arises when a batting team,

having scored enough runs to bring victory within their grasp, want to get out and deliberately sacrifice wickets.

The County Cricket Council also made two important alterations in the rules governing County Cricket. In December 1888 they added a clause to the effect :—

"That a man can play for his old county during the two years that he is qualifying for another."

A clause was also introduced decreeing that, for the purposes of County Cricket, county boundaries are not affected by the Local Government Act, 1888.

At its next meeting in the following December, resolutions were passed thus :—

"1. In the interests of County Cricket it is desirable that an official classification of counties should be made annually by this Council, and that a committee of the County Council, consisting of the President, with three representatives from first-class and three from second-class counties, be appointed to recommend a scheme for this purpose ; such scheme to include a scheme of promotion by merit, under which a county may rise from one class to another.

"2. That all three-day matches shall begin at twelve o'clock the first day, and not later than 11.30 following days."

All these reforms were preceded by agitation on the one hand and opposition on the other, but their adoption cleared the atmosphere for a time, and was ultimately conducive to greater harmony in cricket circles.

Nottingham forced themselves once more to the front this season, and by a continuous series of decisive victories concentrated public attention upon themselves, and finally secured the first position among the counties. Until they met Surrey in the August Bank Holiday match at the Oval they had seemed invincible, but once defeated their form deteriorated. At the close of the season their record was nine wins, two losses, three draws. Lancashire and Surrey tied for the second place, with the identical record of ten victories, three defeats, and one draw each. Gloucestershire had a somewhat better season and Middlesex, who were well served by Stoddart's all-round play, Mr. Nepean's effective leg-break bowling, and Mr. O'Brien's hard hitting, moved up two places in the Championship, while Yorkshire, who lost ten matches and only won two, descended to the seventh place. By this time Cheshire, Derbyshire, Leicestershire, Warwickshire, Somersetshire, and Essex were steadily forcing themselves to the front.

CHAPTER VIII

CRICKET IN THE NINETIES

1890 In the autumn of 1889 a team of English cricketers, with Mr. G. F. Vernon at their head, visited India. The team was composed entirely of amateurs. They played thirteen matches, eleven in India and two in Ceylon, and returned with a record of ten wins, two draws, and one defeat—at the hands of the Parsees. They had a very pleasurable trip, and were delighted with the hospitality with which they were received throughout the Great Dependency.

The tour of the seventh Australian team, who came to England in 1890, was not so successful as some of the previous ones. The team consisted of: W. L. Murdoch (captain), C. T. B. Turner, J. J. Ferris, P. C. Charlton, S. E. Gregory, S. P. Jones, J. E. Barrett, H. Trott, J. Mc. Blackham, F. H. Walters, H. Trumble, J. J. Lyons, and K. E. Burn, and was regarded as fairly representative, but their record of thirteen victories and sixteen defeats in the thirty-eight matches showed they were below the standard of previous teams. In bowling they were un-

questionably strong, as, in addition to Turner
and Ferris, they had a brilliant recruit in
Hugh Trumble ; but in batting they were weak.
Walters, from whom much was expected, did
not come up to expectations, but Barrett, a left-
handed batsman, did well (though his style was
not prepossessing), and achieved the feat, never
before accomplished in a test match, of going in
first and carrying his bat through the innings.
Murdoch did not have the best of luck,
though once or twice he scored freely, but, whatever may be said about this team, the fact
remains that they were disappointed with their
own record quite as much as the English
cricketers were.

Surrey once more secured the County Championship by the right of unquestionable supremacy. The presence of the Australian team did
not seriously interfere with public interest in
County Cricket. Lancashire took second place,
and Kent and Yorkshire tied for third. Surrey's
success was due in a considerable measure to
Lohmann, who for the third season in succession
took over 200 wickets. He was splendidly supported by Sharpe, who shared most of the
bowling with him. The Eleven, however, batted
with remarkable consistency, and fielded brilliantly from beginning to end of the season.
Lancashire, for the first time, had the services
this season of Mr. A. C. MacLaren, who made his
first appearance for his county memorable by a
brilliant innings of 108 at Brighton. Mold met

with conspicuous success as a fast bowler, though his delivery was certainly open to suspicion. Albert Ward, who had also joined the team the previous year, established a reputation as a reliable bat, but Sugg, whose hard hitting had materially assisted the county in the previous year, was extremely erratic, and scored inconsistently. This year Mr. A. G. Steel did not represent his county in a single match, and though he made a few subsequent appearances he let it be understood that he regarded his cricketing days as over. Mr. F. S. Jackson was Yorkshire's principal recruit this season, during which Ulyett returned to his old form, and Robert Peel had a brilliant season—he never bowled better. Gloucestershire looked up a little this year, though in the early part of the season, when they had not their strongest team at command, they suffered a series of discouraging defeats. E. M., who was now the oldest first-class cricketer playing regular County Cricket, recovered some of his old form. I headed the county averages, although I succeeded in getting into three figures on only one occasion. Mr. James Cranston batted brilliantly, and was by far the best left-handed batsman of the day. Twice against Yorkshire he scored the century. Woof, who was coach at Cheltenham College, could give us no assistance until the season was well advanced, but when he did play he bowled magnificently. During this season J. T. Hearne made his first appearance for Middlesex, and from the outset gave evidence of the marked ability which he has displayed ever since.

Three records were made during this season. Playing for Notts against Sussex in May, Gunn and Shrewsbury compiled 398 runs before they were separated, which was then the most productive partnership in a first-class match. The highest aggregate ever made in a first-class match in England was the total of 1339 runs scored in June on the Hove Ground in a match between Cambridge University and Sussex. In June, William Gunn made 288 for the Players against the Australians at Lord's, which was the highest individual score against an Australian team in England. Cambridge introduced three good men into first-class cricket this season— Mr. E. C. Streatfeild and Mr. R. N. Douglas, both of whom played for Surrey, and Mr. G. McGregor, who played for Middlesex, and proved himself the best amateur wicket-keeper since Alfred Lyttelton. His selection to play for England in the test match against Australia while he was still at Cambridge was an early recognition of his extraordinary capacity as a wicket-keeper.

An important scheme of County Cricket classification was formulated at the close of this season by the County Cricket Council. It had been a grievance, and a just grievance, among the second- and third-class counties that they had no opportunity of raising themselves into the first-class. As one or two of the best second-class counties were showing form quite equal to that of one or two of the weaker first-class, it was manifestly unfair that they should be debarred from the possibility of promotion. The Cricket Council set itself to legislate upon the issue, and appointed a sub-committee to draft a scheme. This committee reported to a special meeting of the Council, held at Kennington Oval on August 11, under the presidency of Mr. John Shuter, captain of the Surrey Club. The following delegates were present : Hon. Ivo Bligh (Kent), W. G. Grace (Gloucestershire), Mr. J. B. Wostinholm (Yorkshire), Mr. W. Newham (Sussex), Mr. H. W. Bainbridge (Warwickshire), Mr. A. Wilson (Derbyshire), Mr. T. Burdett (Leicestershire), Mr. H. K. Grierson (Hampshire), Mr. C. E. Green (Essex), Mr. T. A. Vialls (Northamptonshire) and the Norfolk representative.

After discussion, which extended over two hours, the following scheme was drafted :—

" 1. That for the season 1891 the counties be divided into three classes, namely—

" First-class : Notts, Lancashire, Surrey, Kent, Middlesex, Gloucestershire, Yorkshire, Sussex.

" Second - class : Warwickshire, Derbyshire, Leicestershire, Somersetshire, Hampshire, Essex, Staffordshire, Cheshire.

" Third - class : Hertfordshire, Northampton-shire, Norfolk, Lincolnshire, Northumberland, Devonshire, Durham, Glamorganshire.

" 2. As to the number of matches required to be played by each county :—

(*a*) That each of the first-class counties be required to play two matches with at least six other first-class counties. These six to include two matches with the Champion County of the previous year.

(*b*) That each second-class county play two matches with at least three other third-class counties.

" 3. That in each of the three classes an order of merit be drawn up from the results of the season's play of 1891 and future years, and that this order be determined by the same method as that by which the Championship of the first-class counties is at present decided—viz., by subtracting losses from wins and not counting drawn games.

" 4. That in 1892 the lowest county in the first-class and the highest in the second-class play each other home and home matches, these constituting a series which shall be termed 'the qualifying series.' The same arrangement to apply to the lowest of the second-class and the highest of the third-class.

" 5. That if a county be by these means reduced in class it shall for the following season be considered the highest in the class to which it has descended, and shall follow the course of procedure set forth in 4.

" That, on the other hand, if a county, after playing in a qualifying series as the highest of an inferior class, shall have to remain in the same class, it shall not be considered the highest for the next season, unless it shall obtain such a position by virtue of its performance in that season."

The second-class counties were not, however, satisfied with this scheme, which was discussed at a meeting of their representatives held at Lord's on October 25, under the chairmanship of Dr. Russell Bencraft. All the second-class counties had delegates present, with the exception of Somerset and Leicestershire, both of which, however, sent letters disapproving of the scheme. The complaint was that the promotion under the scheme would be too slow. Various suggestions were made, such as the abolition of classification and the institution of a system of all-round equality. Ultimately a series of suggested amendments of the scheme was agreed to, and it was arranged that they should be presented to the County Cricket Council for consideration.

The meeting of the Cricket Council to consider these points was held at Lord's on December 8, and was largely attended. The amendments advocated by the second-class counties were duly presented as follows :—

In Rule II. (*b*) to omit the clause : "These three to include the Champion County in the second-class for the previous year."

To strike out IV. and V. and substitute the following :—

" IV. That at the end of each season, in the month of August or September, the lowest

county in the first-class shall play the highest
of the second-class for the right of place. One
game only shall be played, and upon neutral
ground, to a finish, the winner being placed in
the superior class and the loser in the class
below for the following year.

" Note.—(a) In the event of two counties
being equal at the top or bottom of either
class, the question of their superiority shall
first be decided on neutral ground, played to
a finish, and followed immediately by the
match for right of place in the superior class
for the next year.

" Note.—(b) In the event of three counties
being equal, either at the bottom of the first
or top of the second-class, the matter shall
remain in abeyance for that year.

" V. Should the trial matches fail to define
the positions of competing counties, the Cricket
Council itself shall undertake the classification
for the following year.

" Note.—(c) This scheme shall apply also
to the lowest of the second and the highest
of the third-class counties."

The first amendment proved acceptable to the
meeting, and the two rules were struck out ; but
upon the subsequent proposals there was a hopeless conflict of opinion, and eventually a resolution suspending the Council *sine die* was carried
by the casting vote of the chairman (Mr. M. J.
Ellison). Thus the County Cricket Council

abruptly terminated its career after an existence of scarcely more than three years. It has never been revived, and probably never will be resuscitated, as the experience of the three years of its existence showed that its authority was not recognised as it should have been, and that any hard-and-fast system which curtailed the liberty of any county in making its fixtures for the season was impracticable and prejudicial to the interests of cricket.

The English team of amateurs which left England for America, with Lord Hawke as captain, in the middle of September had a thoroughly enjoyable tour. The team consisted of Lord Hawke, Lord Throwley, Messrs. C. W. Wright, H. T. Hewett, S. M. J. Woods, C. Wreford-Brown, K. J. Key, J. H. J. Hornsby, G. W. Ricketts, Hon. H. Milles, G. W. Hillyard, K. M'Alpine. Their programme, which was arranged by the Germantown Club, consisted of eight matches in Philadelphia, New York, Baltimore, Boston, Chicago, Toronto, and Ottawa, and their record was six victories (four single innings wins), one defeat (by the Gentlemen of Philadelphia), and one draw (in favour of the Englishmen). Mr. S. M. J. Woods was the hero of the tour, his fast bowling being especially destructive.

1891 The Somersetshire team assumed its place among the first-class counties for the first time this season, and, thanks mainly to Mr. L. C. H. Palairet's batting and Mr. S. M. J. Woods's bowling, was bracketed with Kent for the fifth place in the

County Championship table.   County Cricket, in
the absence of an Australian team, retained the
sole interest of the public throughout the season.
Unfortunately we had another rainy summer, and
of the sixty-eight inter-county matches no fewer
than fourteen were drawn, while one, between
Lancashire and Kent, was abandoned without
wickets being pitched owing to incessant rain.

Surrey asserted their unquestionable superiority
over all their rivals by winning twelve out of
sixteen matches and losing only twice.   How
infinitely inferior to Surrey were all the other
counties may be judged from the fact that
Lancashire, which took second place in the table,
won only eight and lost four out of fifteen matches.
Surrey owed a very great deal to the skill of
George Lohmann, who surpassed all his previous
records, and with bat and ball proved a tower of
strength to his county.   A bowling average of
132 wickets at a cost of 10.87 runs, and a batting
average of 26.7 runs in sixteen innings are
certainly notable.   Lockwood came out as a
bowler, and materially assisted Sharpe and
Lohmann in leading the attack.   Abel had a
brilliant batting record, and in spite of the fact
that the weather was detrimental to high scoring,
his average at the end of the season was 43.

The Lancashire Eleven kept up their reputation
for finishing their season with a flourish.   In spite
of the loss they suffered by the partial retirement
of Mr. A. N. Hornby, their indefatigable captain,
and R. G. Barlow, their stubborn stonewaller, the

Lancashire men pulled themselves together, and when, towards the end of the season, Mr. A. C. Maclaren, who had made so distinguished a *début* in the previous year, placed his services at their command, they fought their battles with indomitable pluck, and were almost irresistible.

Gloucestershire fared badly this season, mainly through weak batting. Mr. J. Cranston, who had rejoined the team in 1889, and played with all his wonted brilliance for two seasons, was, owing to ill-health, omitted from the team. By spraining my knee early in the season I was kept out of the cricket-field for a good part of the summer, and consequently had the worst season in my whole career. For my county I played twenty-two innings for 440 runs. Throughout the summer I did not score a century in first-class cricket.

Richard Pilling, the world-renowned wicket-keeper, fell a victim to consumption this year. The Lancashire County Club had sent him abroad for an extended tour in the hope that climatic change would recruit his health, but the famous cricketer returned home merely to die. He was a great loss to cricket, for at that time first-rate wicket-keepers were as rare as they are now. Pilling was a man who had always commanded respect, and his untimely death was mourned by all lovers of cricket.

A new chapter—and a short one—was added to the annals of cricket by the appearance this season of two Elevens of " Lady Cricketers," who travelled about the country and played exhibition matches. They claimed that they did play, and not burlesque, the game, but interest in their doings did not survive long. Cricket is not a game for women, and although the fair sex occasionally join in a picnic game, they are not constitutionally adapted for the sport. If the lady cricketers expected to popularise the game among women they failed dismally. At all events, they had their day and ceased to be.

At the end of 1891 I paid my second visit to Australia, when I captained the team organised and taken out to the Colony by Lord Sheffield. As this was the first occasion on which the sole responsibility for the visit of an English team to Australia had been undertaken by one individual, the tour was in some senses unique. It was certainly a pleasant experience for every member of the team, as the arrangements were all made on a scale of great generosity. Financially, the tour was only a partial success, but Lord Sheffield had no desire for pecuniary benefit, and the results of the visit was to his complete satisfaction, with the exception of our losing two of the three test matches. The team consisted of Messrs. W. G. Grace (captain), A. E. Stoddart, G. McGregor, O. G. Radcliffe, H. Philipson, Lohmann, Abel, Maurice Read, Sharpe, Attewell, Briggs, Bean, Peel. Alfred Shaw, who had gained experience during his previous visits to Australia, served the team as its manager, and served it admirably.

As eighteen years had intervened since my

previous visit to the Colony, and, as I was in my forty-fourth year, some of my friends thought I was making a mistake in paying another visit. I met, however, with great success with the bat, and headed the batting averages in both the eleven-a-side matches and in those against odds. I played in twenty-six out of the twenty-seven matches which composed our tour, and in thirty-one innings made 921 runs. Mr. Stoddart, however, exceeded my aggregate by 39 runs, but as he had played in every match his average was smaller. Though as a team we scarcely realised all that was expected of us, we won twelve and lost only two matches, but thirteen were drawn. Three test matches were played — one each at Melbourne, Sydney, and Adelaide. In the two former we lost, but in the last named we scored 499 runs, and won a single-innings victory, with 230 runs to spare, rain having spoilt the wicket.

Naturally, I found many things had changed in Australia since my first visit. The quality of Colonial cricket had vastly improved. Wickets were now as perfect and true as at Lord's or Kennington Oval, and locomotion was infinitely easier and far more pleasant. Railway extension enabled us to dispense with the tedious coach drives through the bush and the uncomfortable coasting voyages which had been the bugbears of our tour in the seventies. One thing remained unchanged—the hospitable spirit of the Australian people, who heaped kindnesses upon us, and gave us a hearty welcome wherever we went.

PHOTO BY] [MIDWINTER, BRISTOL.

MRS. GRACE.
(Mother of W. G. Grace.)

DR. H. M. GRACE.

(*Father of W. G. Grace.*)

THE CHESTNUTS, DOWNEND, BRISTOL.

From an old photograph.

THE AUSTRALIAN ABORIGINES TEAM, 1868.

(With CHARLIE LAWRENCE, Manager.)

ALFRED LUBBOCK.   W. G. GRACE.   J. C. PATTISON.   C. J. OTTAWAY.

EDGAR LUBBOCK.   R. A. FITZGERALD.   A. APPLEBY.

C. K. FRANCIS.

W. M. ROSE.

F. P. U. PICKERING.   HON. G. (NOW LORD) HARRIS.   A. N. HORNBY.

R. A. FITZGERALD'S CANADIAN TEAM, 1872.

J. C. PATTISON.   EDGAR LUBBOCK.

A. N. HORNBY.   HON. G. (NOW LORD) HARRIS.

C. K. FRANCIS.   W. G. GRACE.

A GROUP TAKEN AT NIAGARA FALLS, 1872.

[*Reproduced from an old photograph.*]

G. F. GRACE.

(*Died* 1880.)

E. M. GRACE,

W. G. GRACE.

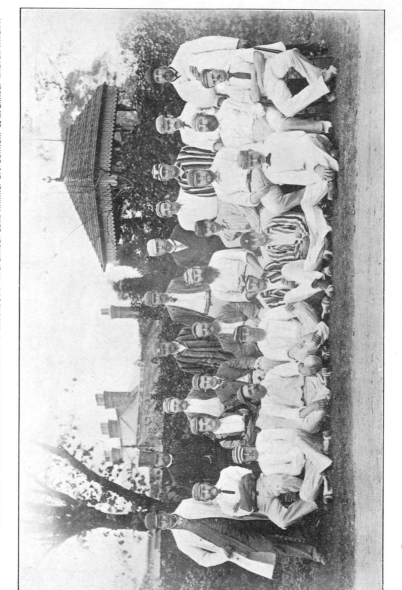

T HEARNE.

A. BANNERMAN. T. C. O'BRIEN. C. I. THORNTON. GEORGE GIFFEN. G. E. PALMER. R. PILLING. W. OSCROFT.

R. G. BARLOW. S. CHRISTOPHERSON. H. J. H. SCOTT W. L. MURDOCH. W. G. GRACE. LORD HARRIS. G. J. BONNOR. E. M. GRACE. WALTER WRIGHT.

W. GUNN. E. PEATE. C. O. CLARKE. P. S. McDONNELL. M. P. BOWDEN. T. EMMETT.

SMOKERS v. NON-SMOKERS (1884).

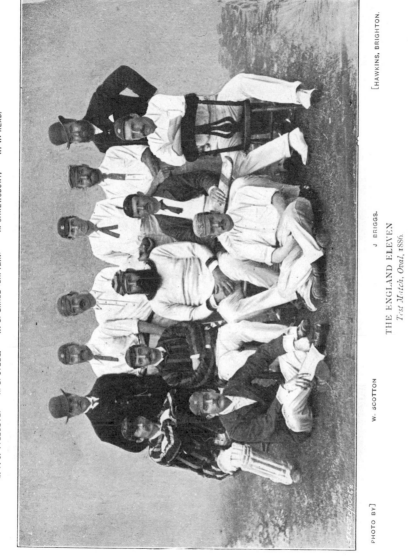

F. FARRANDS (UMPIRE). GEO. ULYETT. W. BARNES. GEORGE LOHMANN. R. G. BARLOW. G. K. PULLEN (UMPIRE).

E. F. S. TYLECOTE. A. G. STEE—. W. G. GRACE (CAPTAIN) A. SHREWSBURY. W. W. READ.

W. SCOTTON J BRIGGS.

PHOTO BY] [HAWKINS, BRIGHTON.

THE ENGLAND ELEVEN

Test Match, Oval, 1886.

A. E. STODDART.   M. READ.   H. P. PHILIPSON.   O. G. RADCLIFFE.

ABEL.   LOHMANN.   G. MACGREGOR.   BRIGGS.   PEEL.   W. G. GRACE.   ATTEWELL.   BEAN.   SHARPE.

LORD SHEFFIELD'S AUSTRALIAN TEAM, 1891-2.

[Photograph taken in the Botanical Gardens, Adelaide.]

H. B. STEEL.   C. L. TOWNSEND.   E. C. HORNBY.

This Photograph was taken after a Match at Clifton, between Clifton College and Liverpool and District, when C. L. Townsend (then a school-boy) bowled both Mr. H. B. Steel and Mr. E. C. Hornby before a run was scored.

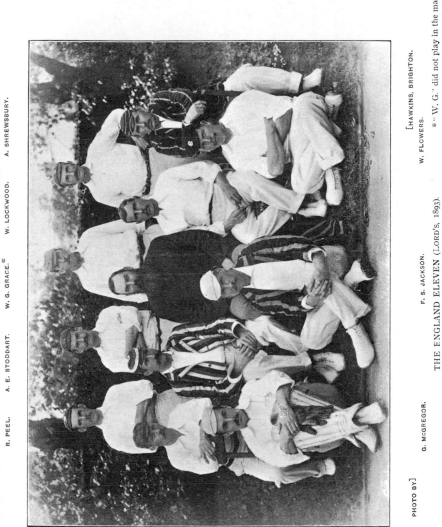

R. PEEL. A. E. STODDART. W. G. GRACE.* W. LOCKWOOD. A. SHREWSBURY.

W. FLOWERS.

G. McGREGOR. F. S. JACKSON.

PHOTO BY]

[HAWKINS, BRIGHTON.

THE ENGLAND ELEVEN (LORD'S, 1893).

* "W. G." did not play in the match.

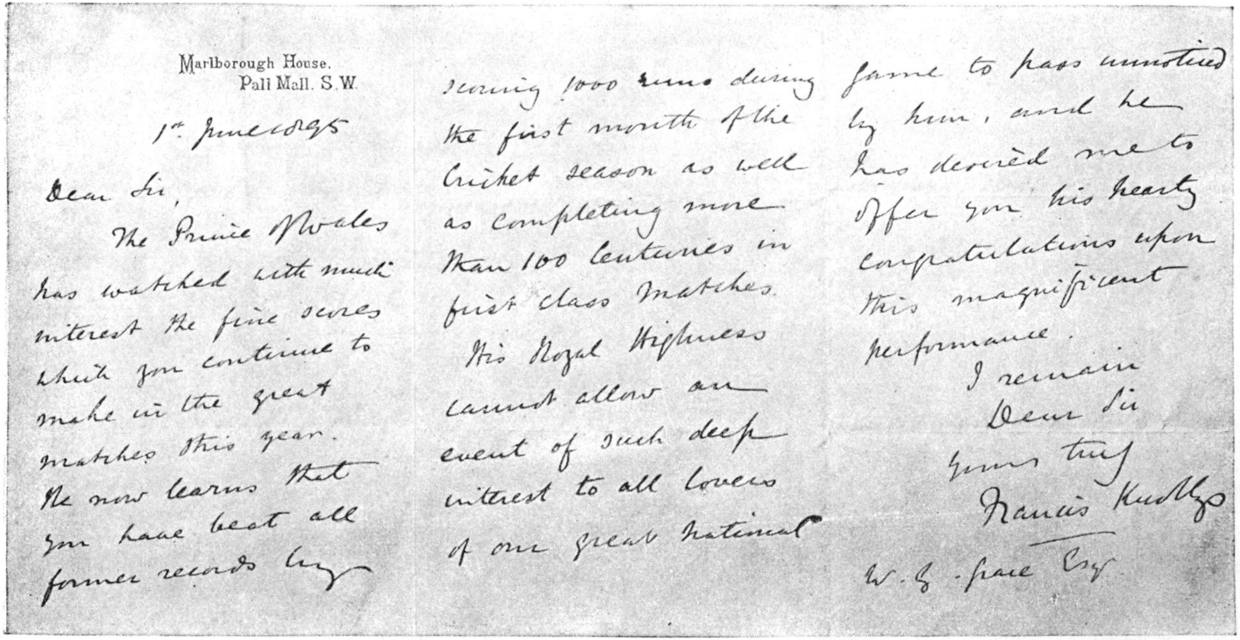

Marlborough House.
Pall Mall. S.W

1st June 1895

Dear Sir,

The Prince of Wales has watched with much interest the fine series which you continue to make in the great matches this year. He was learns that you have beat all former records by scoring 1000 runs during the first month the cricket season so well so completing your having 100 centuries in first class matches. His Royal Highness cannot allow an event of such deep interest to all lovers of our great national game to pass unnoticed by him, and he has desired me to offer you his hearty congratulations upon this magnificent performance.

I remain
Dear Sir
Yours truly
Francis Knollys

W. G. Grace Esq

FACSIMILE OF LETTER FROM THE PRINCE OF WALES TO W. G. GRACE, CONGRATULATING HIM ON HIS THOUSAND RUNS. IN MAY. 1895.

We were entertained regally all over the Colony, and fêted in every city we visited. Interest in our tour was keen from first to last, and I think I can safely say that we aroused the enthusiasm of spectators in Australia, who just before our visit only went in hundreds to see an inter-colonial match. They came in thousands to see us, and ever since the interest in cricket has been as keen as it is in England.

Simultaneously with the tour of Lord Sheffield's team in Australia, a team of fifteen English cricketers, with Mr. W. W. Read at their head, was touring in South Africa. The team, which was composed of Messrs. W. W. Read (captain), W. L. Murdoch, J. J. Ferris (who had settled in England, and was qualifying to play for Gloucestershire), G. Brann, Chatterton, Wood, A. Hearne, Barton, Leaney, Pougher, G. G. Hearne, J. T. Hearne, Ayres, Martin, Brockwell, played twenty matches (nineteen against odds), and returned without suffering defeat, with thirteen victories gained. Though the tour was not a financial success, the members of the team had an enjoyable trip. Chatterton was far and away the most conspicuous success as a batsman, with an average of 41 runs per innings, but it was in the marked supremacy of their bowling that the Englishmen triumphed, Mr. Ferris especially overwhelming the South Africans. His record of 235 wickets for 5.9 runs was remarkable—even for Ferris. Mr. W. W. Read was not in his best form, his twenty-three innings realising only 371 runs.

1892   Favoured by dry wickets, the batsmen had a glorious time this season, and high scoring was general rather than exceptional. Six amateurs and three professionals exceeded a thousand runs during the season, and forty-one individual scores of a century and upwards were made in first-class cricket. Perhaps the most notable successes of the year were Mr. L. C. H. Palairet and Mr. H. T. Hewett, two Oxford Blues, who played for Somerset, and batted brilliantly throughout the season.

County cricket, having again no rival in popular interest, was followed with intense zest, and was all the more interesting this season, because each of the nine first-class counties played home and away matches with each other. Surrey and Notts made a desperate fight for the premier position. Until the middle of August Nottingham had an unbroken series of triumphs, but just when the Championship seemed within their grasp their form declined, and they ultimately had to rest satisfied with second place. The August Bank Holiday match between these old rivals attracted to Kennington Oval an attendance which far exceeded all previous English records, as no fewer than 63,763 spectators paid for admission. To the dismay of the Surrey crowd, Nottingham scored a signal victory. It must be said that the secret of Nottingham's subsequent deterioration this season was not far to seek. Some of the members of the team obviously thought more of their own averages than of the interests of their

side. The possibility of victory in two or three
of their matches was thrown away by the slow
play of the Notts batsmen. Surrey's position at
the top of the Championship table was due to
splendid all-round cricket, to the return to form
of Mr. W. W. Read, and to the brilliant bowling
of Lohmann and Lockwood, the latter of whom
was now a good all-round cricketer. It was
during this season that Surrey made a fine discovery in Tom Richardson, the fast bowler, who
during the last seven years has done them magnificent service, and who in his first season took
101 wickets at a cost of 13½ runs apiece.

Gloucestershire having secured the services of
Mr. J. J. Ferris (by residential qualification,) entered on this season with great hopes of retrieving
the failures of the last few years, but these hopes
were not realised. For some inexplicable reason,
Mr. Ferris was not successful with the ball. His
bowling, which had been the surprise and admiration of all cricketers when he was playing
for the Australian teams, proved terribly expensive to Gloucestershire. Moreover, his collapse
seemed to discourage the other bowlers, and the
team, weak in this department, spent many a long
day in the field. The Gloucestershire batting
showed a marked improvement on the previous
year's form, but the ineffectual bowling crippled
the Eleven, which won one victory over Kent
in the early days of the season, and was then
subjected to a disheartening series of defeats.
Yorkshire found two valuable recruits in Hirst

and Tunnicliffe, now among the county's main-stays.

1893   The eighth team of Australians came this summer, but disappointed the hopes of their fellow-countrymen and failed to realise the anticipations of English cricketers. Before their arrival they were considered a team absolutely representative of Australian cricket, but they signally failed to hold their own against our best County Elevens, and though two out of the test matches were drawn they lost the third (at Kennington Oval) by an innings and 43 runs. The team consisted of Messrs. J. Mc. Blackham (captain), H. Graham, J. J. Lyons, G. H. S. Trott, A. C. Bannerman, G. Giffen, W. Bruce, S. E. Gregory, H. Trumble, R. W. McLeod, W. F. Giffen, C. T. B. Turner, A. Coningham, and A. H. Jarvis. Mr. Murdoch, who had settled in England, and was qualifying to play for Sussex, was not included in the Australian team, and H. Moses, whose fame as an all-round cricketer made all English lovers of the game anxious to see him among the visitors, was a conspicuous absentee. Blackham captained the team, who began their tour early in May, and played two matches a week for eighteen weeks. Of the thirty-six matches which their tour comprised, they won eighteen, lost ten, and drew eight, but in the twelve really representative matches in which they met picked Elevens of English players they won only two—viz., the Players and the North; and lost six, viz., England, Shrewsbury's Eleven, Lord Sheffield's Eleven, the

M.C.C., and both matches against the South of England.

On two or three occasions they showed remarkable pluck in fighting uphill battles. The magnificent display of hitting given by Lyons in the match against M.C.C. at Lord's on Friday, May 19, will always be memorable, as more dashing batting has never perhaps been seen at Lord's. The South Australian forced the play to such an extent that 100 runs were made in fifty minutes, and the big hitter had completed his century in one hour. In the match against the past and present of Oxford and Cambridge Universities, the Australians surpassed all previous records of the highest innings in first-class cricket, by compiling a mammoth score of 843 runs. Though the team against which this feat was achieved was far from the best the Universities might have put into the field, such a total clearly showed the batting strength of Australia. Indeed, if batting alone could win matches, Blackham's team would have had a very different record. Their weakness was in bowling, which failed to meet with success owing to the hard, dry wickets. Even the redoubtable Turner was ineffective on rain-damaged wickets. Giffen was more successful, but overwork led to staleness, while Trumble showed great improvement as a bowler. The fielding, which had hitherto been a feature of the play of Australian teams, was throughout the tour unequal, and on several occasions distinctly poor.

At the close of their English tour in September,

the Australian team (minus Turner) crossed the Atlantic for a short series of matches in America, but they met with scanty success, being severely beaten on their arrival in Philadelphia, and winning only four out of their six engagements.

The presence of the Australian team in England did not in the least diminish interest in County Cricket, which has now too firm a hold on popular favour to be prejudiced by any extraneous events. Again each county team met every other county in home and home matches, and of seventy-two encounters fifty-nine were decided—a fact which speaks well for the weather this summer. The Championship tables were completely turned, Surrey, who had led in 1892, falling to fifth place, while Yorkshire, which had been sixth in the previous year, and had had a long succession of unfortunate seasons, leaped into the premiership, with Lancashire, Middlesex and Kent following in the order named. Yorkshire thoroughly deserved the honours. They were earned by twelve victories out of sixteen inter-county matches. The Championship had not been held by a Northern team for years, and as almost every man in the Yorkshire team was a native of the county the triumph of the Eleven gave great satisfaction. The credit for the success of Yorkshire rested on batsmen and bowlers alike. Brown, who topped the county batting averages, rendered brilliant service, while Tunnicliffe also distinguished himself. Lancashire, who twice defeated the champion county, proved a good second to Yorkshire, but the need for a good bowler to take the place of Alec Watson was keenly felt.

For Middlesex, Mr. Stoddart had a brilliant season, performing the feat of scoring two centuries in one match.   Sussex, with Mr. W. L. Murdoch as captain, looked up a little, the feature of their play being Walter Humphreys' success with his lob-bowling ; but Gloucestershire dropped to the last place in the Championship table. Though I was not so successful as in the previous year, I headed the county batting averages, and in first-class cricket scored 1609 runs, with an average of 35.34.   I had a curious run of ill-luck in the toss this year, as in ten out of our sixteen county matches the spin of the coin, upon which so much sometimes depends in cricket, went against me.

An incident which occurred in the Oxford and Cambridge match this season caused much immediate excitement and afterwards led to prolonged controversy.   Up to this time the side with a deficit of 80 runs had to follow their innings.   The Cambridge Eleven had scored 182.   The Dark Blues then made 95 for the loss of nine wickets, when Mr. W. H. Brain and Mr. T. S. B. Wilson were the last men in. Eight runs were wanted to save the follow-on, and when three more were added the batsmen were seen to consult together between the wickets.   It was at once assumed by all who realised the situation that Oxford meant to throw away a wicket so that the Dark Blues might bat again.   Cambridge, however, had everything to lose by a compulsory follow-on, and Mr. C. M. Wells, who was bowling, took measures to frustrate it. First he passed the bowling crease and bowled a wide to the boundary, then tried to bowl another wide, and bowled his third ball to the boundary, thus giving Oxford eight runs and preventing the follow-on. A scene of excitement followed, and the episode became the nine days' wonder of the cricket world. Too much, I think, was made of the incident, and a lot of breath was wasted on unnecessary abuse of the Cambridge bowler. The situation was a curious one. Apparently both sides were determined to take advantage of an unavoidable flaw in the rules, for if the Cambridge bowler had not thrown away eight runs, the Oxford batsmen would have thrown away the tenth wicket. Between the two transgressions of the spirit in which sportsmanlike cricket should be played there was practically nothing to choose. It was, to use a common phrase, six of one and half a dozen of the other. Personally, if I believed a batsman meant to sacrifice his wicket in order to secure a follow-on for his side, I should throw away runs to frustrate his purpose ; but, on the other hand, if I saw that a bowler was bent on preventing a follow-on innings by sending down wides and no-balls, I should knock my wicket down without hesitation. It passes the wit of man to frame rules which would prevent such episodes occurring, and the lawgivers of cricket are compelled to throw themselves upon the chivalrous instincts of cricketers and appeal to them to play out the game in the spirit of sportsmen and not in the temper of men at enmity.

As an outcome of this incident, and the agitation to which it gave rise, the law concerning follow-on innings was amended by the M.C.C., so that a compulsory follow-on innings is occasioned by a deficit of 120. The question whether the law should be further amended, if not, indeed, abolished altogether, is still discussed in cricket circles. Some experienced cricketers hold that the leading side should have the option of doing what they think best, while others advocate the abolition of any rule involving a follow-on innings. The question is an open one, capable of being viewed from several standpoints. Sometimes the compulsory follow-on innings confers a distinct advantage upon the batting side, who have an opportunity of repeating their innings against exhausted bowlers and tired fieldsmen. On the other hand, the follow-on innings inevitably leads to many matches being definitely concluded which would otherwise be drawn. The whole issue often turns on the condition of the wicket and the prospects of the weather, and I am not indisposed to believe that the optional principle advocated by my brother E. M. would be the best solution of the problem.

There are one or two other vexed questions in cricket which are frequent bones of contention in minor matches. Disputes sometimes arise and bad feeling is engendered by a bowler putting down the wicket of a batsman whose excess of zeal in backing up tempts him to leave his ground before the ball has left the bowler's hand. Some people argue that to put a batsman out in this way is sharp practice on the bowler's part, but I take the opposite view very strongly. If there is any sharp practice in the matter, I think it is on the part of the batsman who tries to gain an unfair advantage by leaving his crease before the ball is bowled. When a batsman is run out in this way I always think he has got his deserts. This does not often happen in first-class cricket. The only instance I remember was, I think, in a match between Yorkshire and Cambridge University. When Harrison, the Yorkshire fast bowler, was bowling, he remarked to Tom Emmett that one of the Cambridge batsmen got out of his ground before each ball was bowled. "I shall put him out if he goes on doing it," said Harrison. After an over or two Emmett, who had been watching the player, advised Harrison to put him out, which the bowler did—much to the disgust of the batsman.

Sometimes batsmen are put out for leaving their ground to pick up a straw or pat down a bump before the ball is dead. I have seen R. G. Barlow, the Lancashire stonewaller, play a ball to mid-off and then, before the fieldsman picked it up, begin patting the wicket a yard or two beyond his crease. On one occasion a fieldsman flung the ball in, and had the wicket down before Barlow could recover his ground. In cases of this kind also my sympathies go against the batsmen, who deserve to lose their wickets for being so stupid as to leave their ground while the ball is still in play. On the other hand, if a batsman is deceived into believing himself out by the wicket-keeper tossing up the ball and saying, "You're out, sir" (as has happened several times within my recollection), and is then put out, I am strongly of opinion that an umpire ought to give a verdict in the batsman's favour. To delude a batsman out of his ground by conveying the idea that he has been caught at the wicket or in the slips is taking a manifestly unfair advantage over an adversary, and a batsman dismissed by such a subterfuge has a distinct grievance. Under the rule governing fair and unfair play, of which he is left sole judge, the umpire has full power to give a decision in favour of the batsman, though technically he may have been stumped or run out. Cases of this kind always give rise to disputes and destroy the perfect harmony without which cricket is shorn of half its delights.

Apart from the stupendous total made by the Australians in their match with the Past and Present Universities team, this season would have been remarkable for high individual and collective scoring. One of the most noteworthy of the events of the summer was the tremendous score made by Notts against Sussex at Brighton on June 8, 9, and 10. The Sussex bowling was

weak and the Hove Ground was in its fastest
run-getting condition, with the result that Notts
scored 674, which was then the second highest
total in the history of County Cricket, Surrey's
698, also against Sussex, at the Oval in 1888, being
its only superior.   The Notts innings at Brighton
was all the more remarkable because three batsmen topped the century, Shrewsbury making
164, Gunn 156, and Barnes 102.   The Notts huge
score, however, enabled Sussex to escape defeat,
as the Notts men had retained possession of the
wickets until all chance of dismissing Sussex
twice was lost.   There was no necessity for
monopolising the wickets until late in the second
day, as a month before Nottingham had found
that just about half their Brighton score (to be
exact, 386 runs) was sufficient to beat Sussex,
with an innings to spare.   Playing for averages,
and averages alone, was the curse of Nottingham
cricket about this time, and I have less hesitation in saying so because the Notts men themselves realised the truth and have mended their
ways.

1894   At the annual gathering of county secretaries—
who meet towards the close of each year for the
arrangement of fixtures for the next year—the
question of county classification, which had not
ceased to be a grievance since the collapse of the
Cricket Council, was reopened.   Yorkshire and
Derbyshire were the prime movers in a proposal
to abolish the distinction between first and second
class counties, but the meeting decided that they

had no legislative authority, and the question was adjourned to a special meeting of county secretaries convened by Yorkshire and held at Lord's on May 1. Delegates were present from Yorkshire, Notts, Middlesex, Kent, Surrey, Sussex, Somerset, Warwickshire, Derbyshire, Leicestershire, Hampshire, and Essex. Mr. M. J. Ellison, President of Yorkshire C.C., advanced the proposition, "That for the purposes of classification there should be no distinction drawn between counties who play out and home three-day matches with not less than six other counties," but after some discussion this resolution was withdrawn, and the meeting unanimously agreed to a proposal to request the M.C.C to consider and advise upon the whole question of classification of counties. So the premier club, which for a century had been the lawgiver of cricket generally, became the lawgiver of County Cricket. The fact that the counties, after failing through their own organisations, and even through the specially established but short-lived County Cricket Council, should unanimously agree to make the Marylebone Club their High Court of Appeal is eloquent testimony to the M.C.C.

Though I am slightly anticipating the sequence of events, I may as well add here that the Marylebone Club cheerfully accepted the responsibility, and, at the request of leading counties, prepared a scheme for regulating the County Championship. Their scheme (which was made public on October 20, 1894) met with the hearty

concurrence of the counties, and since that date
the contest for the Championship has been regu-
lated by it.   The scheme as finally adopted is as
follows :—

"Cricketing counties shall be considered
as belonging to the first class or not.   There
is no necessity for further subdivision.

" First-class   counties   are   those   whose
matches with one another, with the M.C.C.
and Ground, with the Universities, with the
Australians, and such other Elevens as shall
be adjudged 'first-class matches' by the
M.C.C. Committee, are used in compilation
of first-class batting and bowling averages.

" There shall be no limit to the number of
first-class counties.   The M.C.C. Committee
may bring new counties into the list, may
remove existing ones from it, or may do
both.   The list for 1895 is as follows :—

" Derbyshire.	Middlesex.
Essex.	Nottinghamshire.
Gloucestershire.	Somersetshire.
Hampshire.	Surrey.
Kent.	Sussex.
Lancashire.	Warwickshire.
Leicestershire.	Yorkshire.

"After the close of each cricket season
the Committee of the M.C.C. shall decide the
County Championship.

" It shall be competed for by first-class
counties.   No county shall be eligible unless

it shall have played at least eight out-and-home matches with other counties ; provided that, if no play can take place owing to weather or other unavoidable causes, such match shall be reckoned as unfinished.

" One point shall be reckoned for each win, one deducted for each loss ; unfinished games shall not be reckoned.

" The county which, during the season, shall have, in finished matches, obtained the greatest proportionate number of points shall be reckoned the Champion county."

These rules became the charter of County Cricket classification, and, coming into operation in the following season, have never been amended, nor have they given cause for grievance or dissatisfaction.

Though this rearrangement of counties was not made public until October, it was agreed at the beginning of this season (1894) that Derbyshire, Warwickshire, Leicestershire, and Essex should be promoted to first-class rank, and the matches played by these counties should be regarded as first-class. Thus, in anticipation of the drastic changes which subsequently became law, a silent revolution was wrought. The new first-class counties did not, however, compete for the Championship, as the fixtures for the season had been made prior to their promotion in the previous December. The competition accordingly followed the old lines, the nine original first-class counties playing out and home matches with each other. Of the seventy-two inter-county matches, sixty-one were brought to a definite issue and nine were unfinished. One, Surrey *v.* Leicester, resulted in a tie, and another, Yorkshire *v.* Kent, was abandoned without play owing to rain.

The contests for the County Cricket Championship excited intense interest. Yorkshire, the premier county of 1893, finding her position assailed by Surrey, fought desperately hard for the laurels, but the Southern county brought the honours back to the South of the Thames once more. It was a neck-and-neck race for points between the two counties, but Surrey, by thirteen victories, two defeats, and one tie, had a point's advantage over Yorkshire, who won twelve, lost two, and drew one out of their fifteen engagements. Yorkshire had ill-luck, as on their form they should have beaten Kent, if rain had not led to the abandonment of the match, and they were robbed of victory over Somerset by the same enemy of cricket.

Surrey owed a vast deal to Brockwell, whose batting was at once brilliant and consistent, and to the bowling of Richardson (by now the best fast bowler in England), who during this season captured 120 wickets at an average of 11.38 runs, in Surrey matches.

Mr. John Shuter, to the regret of all who knew how devotedly he had served the county, resigned his captaincy, and was succeeded by Mr. K. J.

Key, who still retains the office.   Brown, who was the only Yorkshire batsman to score a thousand runs this season, gave his county invaluable assistance, while Mr. F. S. Jackson's inclusion in all important matches strengthened the team.   This season saw the withdrawal from active participation in cricket of George Ulyett, a professional whose name will figure often in the annals of the game.

Gloucestershire, which had again the unenviable distinction of being at the bottom instead of the top of the tree, had another disastrous year. During the season Mr. G. L. Jessop, of Cheltenham and Cambridge, joined the team, and has proved an exceedingly valuable acquisition.   My record in inter-county matches was disappointing, my average for sixteen innings being only 18.9, though in first-class cricket I scored 1293 runs, with an average of just under 30.   Ferris failed to meet with any conspicuous success, but F. G. Roberts bowled consistently.   Mr. C. L. Townsend, who had made a most promising *début* in the previous year, added to his reputation as a bowler.

The presence of a team of South African cricketers in England did not interfere with County Cricket.   They came, they saw, but they emphatically did not conquer.   On the contrary, they had a poor time of it, for, though they played creditably, winning twelve and losing five out of twenty-four engagements, their tour failed to excite interest, and was not a financial

success. They brought with them a brilliant
young batsman, Mr. C. O. H. Sewell, son of
Mr. J. J. Sewell, who in the sixties was a distinguished member of the Gloucestershire Eleven.
A team of Dutch gentlemen who came over here
in August for a brief tour also failed to command
interest, and, after playing a few minor clubs, and
losing seven out of ten matches, they returned to
Holland, sadder but perhaps wiser cricketers.

The team of amateurs taken out by Lord
Hawke for a short tour in Canada and America
in the autumn of 1894 made no pretence to being
representative of our best amateur cricketers, but
they proved far too good for our Transatlantic
cousins, and returned with an unbroken record.

Brilliant success attended the tour of the
English cricketers who went out to Australia
under Mr. A. E. Stoddart at the close of this
season. The team itself was a very strong one,
consisting of Mr. A. E. Stoddart, Mr. A. C. Mac-
Laren, Mr. F. G. J. Ford, Mr. H. Philipson,
Mr. L. H. Gay, Richardson, Brockwell, Lockwood, Albert Ward, Briggs, Peel, J. T. Brown,
and Walter Humphreys, and its record of twenty-
three matches—nine victories, four defeats, and
ten draws — was thoroughly satisfactory. The
responsibility for the tour, which was a splendid
financial success, was undertaken by the Melbourne Cricket Club and the trustees of the
Sydney Ground. The five test matches excited
tremendous interest both in England and Australia ; record crowds watched the games at

Melbourne, Adelaide, and Sydney, while news of the progress of the games, which was telegraphed every few minutes, was awaited with extraordinary interest in England. When the fifth match of the rubber began at Melbourne the honours were divided and excitement ran high. At last tidings came that Mr. Stoddart's team had won a brilliant victory, and the jubilation in English cricket circles was unbounded. The first test match was quite an historic event, as Mr. Stoddart's Team gained a victory by ten runs, after the Australians had compiled the enormous total of 586. Altogether no fewer than 1514 runs were scored in the match—an aggregate which still holds the record in first-class cricket. Though the Englishmen were helped by rain damaging the wicket before the Australian innings closed, the fact that they pulled off the match proved the calibre of Mr. Stoddart's Eleven. Mr. Gay and Humphreys turned out failures, but Mr. Stoddart, who headed the batting averages, Mr. MacLaren, Albert Ward, and J. T. Brown gave the Colonials a splendid display of batting.

The year 1895 proved the crowning point of **1895** my cricketing career. I was in great form at the very beginning of the season, and eclipsed all my own records by scoring a thousand runs in the month of May. The feat had never been achieved before, and it was naturally a matter of supreme satisfaction to me that I should, in my forty-seventh year, be enabled to surpass all the achievements of my youth. Moreover, I completed my "century of centuries" in first-class cricket. I was particularly glad that my hundredth century was made on the ground of the Gloucestershire County Club, with which I had been so long associated. Until the end of the summer I went through a period of lionising, which, though gratifying, was distinctly embarrassing. For the second time I was made the recipient of a national testimonial through the Gloucestershire County Cricket Club and the M.C.C., while through the proprietors of the *Daily Telegraph* I received a handsome cheque, the product of a "shilling" testimonial, contributed by thousands of known and unknown friends. I was honoured by a letter of congratulation from the Prince of Wales, the receipt of which, I need hardly say, gave me profound pleasure.

Not for nine years had I had such a batting season, for, after scoring a thousand runs between the 9th and 30th of May, I continued in form until wet weather spoiled the wickets. Altogether I scored 2346 runs in first-class cricket, an aggregate quite equal, I think, to my 2739 in the season of 1871, and my 2622 in 1876. Nine times I scored a century—on two occasions passed the second hundred.

I have been asked by a student of psychology if I can give any explanation of the mental processes involved in "playing into form," or "getting set," or "getting one's eye in." I am not a psychologist, but if a plain statement of the facts as they present themselves to my mind is of any use to theorists I shall be glad to give them here. The first element in the process of getting set is a little luck at the beginning of one's innings. Every cricketer knows that in the early stages of a batsman's innings—*i.e.*, before he gets his eye in—luck plays an important part. A batsman, for instance, hits a ball which by fortune rather than design goes safely past a fieldsman, when a few feet in another direction might have meant being caught out. Often enough a matter of a few inches converts a chance into a boundary hit, and when the spectators are clapping him for a fine stroke, a batsman is frequently conscious that the hit was a lucky one, as he might have been caught. But when the batsman has got through this stage of his innings, a change comes over him. The ball seems to expand until it appears to him to be the size of a football. He can watch its career through the air after it has left the bowler's hand with perfect ease, and time it with precision. Indeed he feels incapable of missing it. Whether this is a mental or optical illusion I cannot decide, but it is the experience of all cricketers when "set." It is certainly not a matter of confidence, as a batsman may play a most brilliant innings when he feels far from confident. Once thoroughly "set" the apparent expansion of the size of the ball continues almost indefinitely. It remains unbroken by intervals, say for luncheon or adjournments for the night, and a batsman may go from one ground to another and still find his "eye in."

A change in the weather, with its consequent effect on the wicket, almost invariably breaks the spell. During the early part of this season (1895) I kept my " eye in " for several weeks, and scarcely ever failed to score heavily. But when the rain came and damaged the wickets I was master of the situation no longer.

Though I was in my very best batting form, my position was seriously challenged by two brilliant young amateurs who are now generally acknowledged as among the best half-dozen batsmen in the world—I refer, of course, to Mr. A. C. MacLaren and Prince Ranjitsinhji. The Lancashire amateur has established a threefold reputation in about ten years. He was one of the best of the Harrow Team during his schooldays, the finest batsman in the Lancashire Eleven, and the most brilliant bat during Stoddart's tour in Australia. Playing for Lancashire against Somerset, he beat all previous records in first-class cricket, by making the gigantic score of 424. Moreover, he headed the first-class batting averages of the year with an average of 51.5 — a fraction above my own. Ranjitsinhji's fame was not then made, but his extraordinary batting powers soon received popular recognition, and his aggregate of 1775 runs in first-class cricket established the Indian Prince's reputation.

The promotion of Derbyshire, Warwickshire, Leicestershire, Essex, and Hampshire to the rank of first-class counties, who now numbered fourteen, made it obviously impossible for each county to

play out-and-home matches with all the others.
As a result, the old system of reckoning points in
the Championship contest was to some extent
disorganised. The M.C.C., however, instituted a
rule that each of the counties should play a
minimum of out-and-home matches with eight
other counties, and that a point should be counted
for each win and a point deducted for each defeat,
the county securing the number of points in
greatest proportion to the finished matches to be
adjudged champion. No fewer than 131 inter-
county matches were played, as against 71 the
previous summer. The multiplication of engagements under the new arrangement had the natural
effect of diminishing interest in the County
Championship, but the justice of the inclusion of
the newcomers in the list of first-class counties
was amply demonstrated by the positions they
took in the Championship table — Derbyshire
coming out fifth, Warwickshire sixth, Essex eighth,
Hampshire tenth, and Leicestershire twelfth.

In recognition of the eminent services rendered
to his county by Mr. W. W. Read, a testimonial
match was arranged for his benefit. The happy
idea of reviving the match between Surrey and
England, which had not appeared in the fixtures
for twenty-nine years, was carried out, but the
county failed to rise to the occasion, and fared
almost ignominiously in the contest. The England
Eleven was scarcely representative, but it found
no difficulty in inflicting an overwhelming defeat
on Surrey.

The return to the cricket-field of George Lohmann, after an illness which had necessitated his spending two years in the sunnier clime of South Africa, was welcomed by all cricketers, but the famous all-round professional had lost his cunning with the bat, and even in bowling had to play second fiddle to Tom Richardson, to whose herculean efforts Surrey owed much of the glory of the Championship this season.   From the day that "Archie" MacLaren found himself able to put his services at their disposal, the Lancashire Eleven never looked back, for, though they had lost three matches out of seven before the old Harrovian joined the team, only one match was lost subsequent to that event.   In addition to creating a new record by his score of 424 against Somerset, Mr. MacLaren earned the distinction, hitherto monopolised by myself, of playing an innings of over a hundred in three successive matches.   Tyldesley, who is now one of Lancashire's most reliable run-getters, made his first appearance in inter-county cricket this season, and acquitted himself creditably.   Although I scored very freely in County Cricket, making 1424 runs during the season, and although Charlie Townsend did wonders with the ball—taking 124 wickets for 12.73 runs apiece—Gloucestershire had a bad season, winning only two matches out of sixteen.   Mr. G. L. Jessop, who had commenced first-class County Cricket in the previous season, helped the county materially, not only by his dashing batting, but by his bowling.   Mr. J. J.

Ferris returned to Australia this year, and although he had done very little for Gloucestershire for some time as far as bowling was concerned, his batting was greatly missed. For the first time for about thirty-five years E. M. took no part in first - class cricket. Ranjitsinhji's appearance under the residential qualification vastly strengthened the batting of the Sussex team, which also received a valuable accession in Mr. C. B. Fry, but the weakness of Sussex cricket this season, as it had been for many years, was the need of really good bowlers. I sometimes think that the remarkable run-getting qualities of the Hove Ground are a serious detriment to Sussex cricket, as their opponents generally find it easy to pile up big scores against the Sussex bowling, when aided by the singularly fast wickets always obtainable at Brighton.

During this summer two amateur teams of English cricketers crossed the Atlantic for short tours. Mr. R. S. Lucas formed a team for a tour in the West Indies, and had a very pleasant experience in the islands. They played sixteen matches, winning ten and losing four against Colonial Elevens, which, though easily beaten, played the game with considerable skill. Apart from the fact that the tour opened new territory for English cricketers, it had little significance. The team taken by Mr. Frank Mitchell to America in August consisted principally of University men, and the tour was successful in the cricketing sense, and, in spite of intense heat, was thoroughly enjoyed in its social aspects.

The tour of the English cricketers which Lord Hawke took out to South Africa in the winter of 1895–96 was to some extent overshadowed by the disturbance of public feeling which followed Jameson's Raid in the Transvaal. The team consisted of Lord Hawke (captain), Sir T. C. O'Brien, C. B. Fry, A. J. L. Hill, S. M. J. Woods, H. T. Hewett, R. H. M. Bromley-Davenport, C. W. Wright, A. M. Miller, C. Heseltine, Hayward, Lohmann, Butt, and Tyler. Sixteen matches were played, of which seven were won and two lost.

1896   The Australian team of 1896 came over without very sanguine hopes of success, but at the end of their four months' sojourn in England they had proved themselves equal to any Colonial team which had preceded them. England won the rubber in the Test matches, it is true, but the team won nineteen matches out of thirty-four, and lost only six, a superior record to that of any team since 1884. Though they were twice beaten by England, once by the M.C.C., once by the Midland Counties at Birmingham, once by Earl De la Warr's Eleven at Bexhill, and by Mr. C. I. Thorton's Eleven at Scarborough, not a single county club lowered their colours. Mr. G. H. S. Trott proved an admirable captain, and the tour was singularly free from hitches and unpleasantnesses of any kind. No less than seven of the visitors—Gregory, Darling, Clement Hill, Iredale, Trott, Giffen, and

Donnan—exceeded a thousand runs, but the
bowling honours fell to Trumble and Jones.
The strength of the bowling was the secret of the
team's success, as may be judged from the fact
that only three centuries were scored against
them in their thirty-four games. Following the
example of the 1893 team, the Australians slightly
curtailed their English programme in order to
make a brief tour in the United States.

This season will long be remembered for K. S.
Ranjitsinhji's many great performances. He did
well in 1895, but in 1896 he astonished the world
with the brilliance of his batting. Throwing in
his fortunes with Sussex, he played regularly
through the season, and scored more runs in first-
class cricket than had ever been made by any
single batsman in the whole history of cricket.
My own 1871 record of 2739 had to take second
place to Ranji's 2780, though his average was 21
less per innings than mine was in my record year.
Ten times he scored upwards of a century—five
of them in not-out innings. During the season
he made upwards of a hundred in three successive
first-class matches—a feat also achieved this year
by Abel and Storer.

The presence of the Australian team slightly
reduced the number of inter-county matches, but
did not appreciably affect public interest in the
struggle for the Championship, which ultimately
fell to Yorkshire. In their match against Warwickshire, Yorkshire eclipsed all previous records
by compiling 887 runs in one innings, a total which

has never since been exceeded. During the same season Yorkshire played another innings of 660. one of 543, and no less than five of over 400. Towards the score of 887 against Warwickshire no less than four Yorkshire batsmen contributed a century apiece, thereby establishing another record.

A sensation was made in cricket circles this season by the strike of the professionals who had been asked to play in the England *v.* Australia match at the Oval. On the eve of the match five of the professionals who had been selected demanded a larger sum than is usually paid them for their services in the contest. Wide publicity was given to the demand, which was accompanied by an ultimatum. The Surrey Committee naturally felt aggrieved at the dictatorial tone adopted by the players, four of whom were on the Oval staff. Declining to discuss the question of terms with the discontents, the Selection Committee proceeded to engage substitutes for the match, when three of the striking professionals withdrew their demand, and unreservedly submitted themselves to the Surrey Committee. The fourth Surrey professional subsequently apologised for his action. The incident was regrettable, not only because the strike was ill-timed, but because it led to an unseemly controversy, in the course of which many irritating statements of an absolutely false character were made with regard to prominent amateur cricketers. The question as to the remuneration a professional cricketer should receive for his services in a test match is not one which I need discuss here ; it is a matter for private negotiation between the cricketers and the committee responsible for the test matches. Every one is anxious that players should be fully remunerated for their services in the test matches, but the professionals who took part in this inopportune strike damaged their own cause by a course of action which alienated public sympathy and brought discredit upon themselves.

Two separate teams of English cricketers visited the West Indies in the early part of this year. Both were entirely composed of amateurs, and, though necessarily their engagements somewhat clashed, each team returned with excellent records. Lord Hawke's combination won nine matches and lost two, while Mr. Arthur Priestley's team won ten and lost five out of sixteen games. Mr. A. E. Stoddart bore off the honours of Mr. Priestley's team in both batting and bowling; he made 1079 runs in twenty completed innings, and took 104 wickets at an average cost of 7.89 runs. Mr. P. F. Warner conducted a team of amateurs to America, and had a brief but completely successful tour.

In the absence of any Australian team public **1897** interest was this season concentrated once more on County Cricket, and the severe struggle for the premiership, which was gained by Lancashire, whose record of sixteen victories, three defeats, and seven draws was adjudged superior to Surrey's seventeen victories, four losses, and five draws. During this season Lancashire found two good men — a brilliant bowler in W. R. Cuttell, who took over a hundred wickets in county matches alone, and Lees Radcliffe, whose wicket-keeping proved of immense service.

The tour of the Philadelphian cricketers in England this summer excited but little interest. Hitherto American teams had been content to test their strength against second-class clubs and amateur elevens, but, having been led to imagine by occasional victories over English teams in America, and their success against the Australians in Philadelphia, they were fit to fly for higher game, they sought engagements on the occasion of this tour with some of the leading counties, the Universities, and the Marylebone Club. When their tour opened in June their achievements were watched closely, but the curiosity of the public died away when it became only too patent the Philadelphians were not so strong as some people thought. When faced by English professional bowling, they generally went to pieces. Indeed, throughout the tour of fifteen matches they were only successful against Sussex and Warwickshire. The most notable member of the team was Mr. J. B. King, a fast bowler, who had the baseball trick of making the ball curve in the air after leaving his hand. For a time he did extremely well, especially against Sussex, where he took seven wickets for thirteen runs, and clean bowled Ranjitsinhji with his first ball.

Gloucestershire, which for some years had been in the Slough of Despond, came out of the season's engagements with a creditable record, and was the only county which succeeded in inflicting defeat on both Surrey and Yorkshire. Though Charlie Townsend did not repeat the brilliant achievements with the ball which made him famous in 1895, he materially helped towards the success. Even more valuable was the batting of Mr. G. L. Jessop, who on four occasions exceeded a hundred, and by his magnificent hitting helped to snatch several matches out of the fire. The innings of 101, which he made against Yorkshire in forty minutes, was a display of batting worthy of C. I. Thornton, T. C. O'Brien, or G. J. Bonnor. His hitting was simply terrific, and the nerve which he threw into his play stimulated every other member of the team. I did not—perhaps it was not to be expected—retain the exceptional form in which I had batted in 1895 and 1896 ; nevertheless, I scored 1532 runs in first-class cricket—a record with which I personally was thoroughly satisfied.

The main events in the tour of the English team, which Mr. A. E. Stoddart, by invitation of the Melbourne Cricket Club and the Trustees of the Sydney Cricket Club, took out to Australia at the end of this season are probably still fresh in the memory of my readers. Mr. Stoddart selected an admirably representative team, composed of A. E. Stoddart, A. C. MacLaren, K. S. Ranjitsinhji, N. F. Druce, J. R. Mason, Richardson, Briggs

J. T. Hearne, Board, Storer, Wainwright, and Hirst. Captain Wynyard, who had been asked to join the team, fell out of the combination in consequence of his military duties. Nine out of the thirteen men constituting the team had not previously been to Australia. In batting, the team was expected to distinguish itself. With six such batsmen as Stoddart, Druce, Mason, MacLaren, Ranjitsinhji, and Hayward, it could scarcely fail, while with such bowlers as Jack Hearne, Hirst, Richardson, and Briggs as mainstays, and Stoddart, Wainwright and Hayward, as changes, the bowling department was scarcely less powerful.

Nevertheless, the tour was a disappointment to the cricketers themselves and their friends at home, and the team, which left home buoyant, and almost sanguine of success, came back having lost more matches than they won. Four times they were severely beaten — twice in a single innings — in the five test matches. To some extent this poor record was due to misfortune, Ranjitsinhji suffering from bad health, while Stoddart was prostrated with influenza, and unnerved by the death of his mother during his absence from England. Ranjitsinhji, in his capital little book, " With Stoddart's Team in Australia," frankly confessed that the comparative failure of the English team was to be attributed to meeting opponents who were better than themselves, and better than people in England had any idea of.

Their strength on their own wickets, he says,

is not at all realised in England, as it is impossible
for any one to realise correctly the ability of
Australian players without seeing them on their
own ground.   Mr. Stoddart himself declared that
the Australian Eleven which opposed the English
team in the test matches was the finest in every
department of the game that he had seen in
Australia in an experience of four visits ranging
over a period of ten years.   Speaking of Australian
bowling, Ranjitsinhji declared that it was not the
superlative merit of one bowler, but the excellence
and judgment of nearly half a dozen, all different
in style, method, and pace, that made them so
deadly and unconquerable.   It was obvious, however, that the English team did not play up to
its true form.   MacLaren and Ranjitsinhji met
with wonderful success, and J. T. Hearne maintained his reputation as a bowler, but Richardson,
handicapped by rheumatism in his right arm, was
almost ineffectual, while Hayward, Briggs, Wainwright, and Hirst were almost harmless on the
good, hard, dry wickets upon which the great
matches were fought out.

The harmony of the tour did not go unbroken,
as unpleasantness arose on one occasion because
Phillips, the English umpire, twice no-balled
E. Jones, the South Australian bowler, for throwing, and on several occasions the Englishmen had
to complain of the hostile demonstrations—known
in Australia as " barracking "—of certain rowdy
sections of the spectators.   The marriage of
Archie MacLaren, which took place after the last

match at Melbourne, was an interesting event in the tour. Ranjitsinhji, who returned to India at the close of the tour, made a great impression upon the Australians. Indeed, he created something like a *furore*, and Ranjitsinhji matches, Ranjitsinhji sandwiches, and Ranjitsinhji hair-restorer were said to be as common in Australia as Jubilee etceteras had been in England in the previous year.

1898   The outstanding event of the cricket season of 1898 was the wonderful stand made by J. T. Brown and J. Tunnicliffe at Chesterfield in August. The achievement was in every respect extraordinary, as the two Yorkshire professionals, playing against Derbyshire for W. Sugg's benefit, opened the Yorkshire innings on the Thursday morning, and remained in partnership until Friday afternoon. In five hours and five minutes this record partnership produced no fewer than 554 runs, a stand which completely overshadowed all previous first-class records, not only for the first, but for any wicket. Tunnicliffe, who was out first, made 243, and then Brown, having reached his 300, hit his wicket down. While Brown and Tunnicliffe were compiling their unprecedented score at Chesterfield, Tom Hayward was achieving a magnificent feat at the Oval. He went in on the Thursday morning, and batted until half-past three on the Friday afternoon, carrying out his bat for 315—the highest individual score of the season. Telegrams were flying between the two grounds whilst Brown and Hayward, a hundred and fifty miles apart, were passing and repassing each other's totals. This see-sawing proved a source of intense excitement to the spectators at the Oval, and the delight of the Surrey crowd knew no bounds when, after the tidings had reached Kennington that Brown had hit his wicket down, with his score at 300, Hayward carried his total to 315.

In both England and Australia this season seems to have been remarkable for high scoring, and though the match itself is unimportant, it is interesting to record that the Melbourne University, playing against Essendon in March, compiled 1094 runs in one innings, which is described by "Wisden" as the highest authenticated total in the history of cricket. Whether a thousand runs will ever be scored in a first-class match is a point upon which I do not care to risk an opinion, but I have wondered, if made, how it could be registered on our cricket telegraph-boards, which have spaces for only three numerals in the division set apart for the total. Apparently a score of a thousand does not enter into the calculations of the makers of cricket telegraph-boards, and, I think, rightly too, as, unless we play matches out, like they do in Australia, it will not often happen.

County Cricket presented but few features of special interest this year, as, owing to abnormally high scoring and broken weather, an exceptionally large proportion—considerably more than a third—of the inter-county matches were left unfinished. Yorkshire, who secured the Championship, played so brilliantly that at one time it seemed as if they would go through the season unbeaten ; but once defeated, their luck, or at any rate their form, forsook them. In Wilfred Rhodes, Yorkshire found a bowler to take the place of Robert Peel, whose connection with the county club had closed under distressing circumstances in the previous year. Rhodes is a left-hand slow bowler, who on bad wickets revives memories of Peate and Peel, even when at their best, in the eighties. His delivery is easy and graceful, and he seems to bowl with a natural action which involves very little effort. His record for Yorkshire this season was 126 wickets taken in a thousand overs, at the average cost of 13.84—a sensational start to what promises to be a great bowling career.

Middlesex, who secured second place, owed their success to their bowling rather than their batting. J. T. Hearne, now one of the best bowlers in England, had a brilliant season, and Albert Trott, the Australian, who had qualified to play for Middlesex, met with wonderful success in spite of an injury to his hand. During June and July Middlesex met with nothing but misfortune ; then luck turned, and from the beginning of August to the end of the season an unbroken succession of victories crowned the efforts of the team. A severe strain kept Mr. Stoddart out of the cricket-field until the middle of the season, but in August he batted with conspicuous dash and consistency, and in nine matches scored 603 runs.

In inter-county matches he scored 1005 runs, and secured the splendid average of 52.89. During this season Sir Timothy C. O'Brien, whose spirited hitting had often saved Middlesex in an emergency, dropped out of the team, while Mr. A. J. Webbe, who had played for the county for twenty-five years, and captained the team for fifteen, retired from first-class cricket.

The reappearance of Mr. W. A. Troup and Mr. C. O. H. Sewell, together with the success of Mr. G. Jessop with the bat, and Charlie Townsend with the ball, so strengthened the Gloucestershire Eleven that the county rose to the third place in the Championship, and closed the season with the admirable record of nine victories and only three defeats. Two features of the Gloucestershire season deserve notice—they did not lose a single home match, and they closed their programme with five victories in succession. Once more I was in good form, scoring 1141 runs in twenty-four completed innings, and topping the county batting averages. I exceeded the hundred on three occasions this year. Up to this season I had never in any first-class match made 93 runs, or rather played an innings of 93, but at Bristol against Sussex I stopped my score at that figure, and so achieved what I think no other batsman has ever done—*i.e.*, made every possible score between 0 and 100 in first-class cricket. I am glad to say, however, that I have never yet distinguished myself by making a pair of spectacles in a first-class match.

In honour of my fiftietl birthday, the Committee of the M.C.C. fixed the Gentlemen *v.* Players match at Lord's for July 18. Two splendid representative elevens were selected for the match, which was apparently regarded by the public as the event of the season, as the number of spectators present on the three days established a record for the Gentlemen *v.* Players match at Lord's. I shall not readily forget the exceptionally enthusiastic reception accorded me on my appearance, nor the congratulations which were heaped upon me after my innings—in which I scored 43 and 31 not out—though I was lame at the time, and suffering from the effects of a damaging blow on the hand. The cricket proved very interesting, as the match was fought out with the utmost keenness. Eventually the Players scored a signal victory by 137 runs, and the game finished amid a scene of great enthusiasm.

Though Mr. C. B. Fry batted with remarkable brilliance—adding his name to the list of batsmen who have scored two innings of a 100 in the same match—Sussex severely felt the loss of Ranjitsinhji's batting, and for a time the probabilities seemed great that the county would drop to the bottom of the Championship. Happily, at the eleventh hour, they won three matches, and so escaped that ignominy. Mr. Fry's doubtful delivery called upon him the censure of three different umpires this season. Though he only bowled in four county matches he was no-balled for throwing on three occasions—by W. A. J. West at Trent Bridge, by James Phillips at Brighton, and by Mordecai Sherwin at Lord's. No doubt the no-balling of Mr. Fry and of Hopkins, the young Warwickshire bowler, by V. A. Titchmarsh at Tunbridge, was the outcome of Phillips' initiative in penalising Jones, the Australian fast bowler, during Mr. Stoddart's tour in the colony in 1897–98. The action of the umpires in no-balling a bowler, who had escaped being penalised for six years, created some sensation, but as the masterly inactivity of the umpires had been a source of dissatisfaction for many years, their determination to put into force the law permitting them to no-ball any bowler of the absolute fairness of whose delivery they were not satisfied was generally regarded as a step towards putting an end to a source of grievance and bad feeling. There is no doubt that the immunity which bowlers with a doubtful action had enjoyed had encouraged an abuse of the bowling laws which was fast becoming a nuisance, and, though I was sorry for Mr. Fry, I felt that he was the victim of a step which will tend to make future bowlers more scrupulous and fair in the cultivation of their action. The law prohibiting no-balling was becoming obsolete, and the time had come when the interests of cricket demanded drastic measures to suppress throwing and discountenance anything like dubious delivery.

The whole question of the management of future test matches in this country between England and Australia was thoroughly discussed

this season, and as the outcome of a meeting of
county representatives held in the pavilion at
Lord's, on July 18, under the presidency of the
Hon. Alfred Lyttelton, M.P., a board to govern
future test matches at home was established. The
suggestion had come from Lord Hawke, who had
publicly expressed the opinion that the time had
come for test matches to be placed under the
control of a specially constituted body. All the
counties welcomed the proposal, and their representatives at the meeting at Lord's unanimously
agreed to ask the M.C.C. to constitute such a
board to be composed of the President of the
M.C.C., who was to have a casting vote, five of
his club committee, and one representative from
six of the first-class counties, selected for the
purpose by the M.C.C. Accepting the responsibility, the M.C.C. constituted a board, and selected
the six first-class counties highest on the list to
send their representatives. Lord Hawke, Mr. A.
J. Webbe, Sir Richard Webster, C. Green, and
Mr. A. N. Hornby (or Mr. S. H. Swire) were
nominated by the counties, and the M.C.C. completed the board by nominating their President,
the Hon. A. Lyttelton, M.P., the Earl of Lichfield,
Lord Harris, Mr. W. E. Dennison, Mr. H. D. G.
Leveson-Gower, and Mr. W. H. Patterson, as their
representatives. The new board met on November 11, and agreed that in 1899 five test matches
should be played—viz., at Lord's, Kennington Oval,
Manchester, Nottingham, and in Yorkshire. The
suggestion that a test match should not extend

beyond three days was unanimously adopted. The board decided to delegate the selection of teams for test matches to a small sub-committee, and also agreed that the remuneration given to professionals and reserve men for taking part in a test match should in the future be £20 each. As under the new financial arrangements each first-class county participates proportionately in the profits derived from the test matches, any possibility of difficulty in securing the service of professional cricketers on the ground that they are engaged elsewhere is removed.

During 1898 three batsmen achieved the distinction of scoring over a thousand runs and capturing over a hundred wickets in a season of first-class cricket—F. S. Jackson for Yorkshire, Charles Townsend for Gloucestershire, and W. Cuttell for Lancashire. This had up to this year been done eighteen times since 1874—seven times by myself, twice each by C. T. Studd and G. W. Hirst, and once each by Flowers, Davidson, Peel, Wainwright, Mr. G. J. Jessop, and Hayward. It is a striking indication of the development of all-round play in individual cricketers that this feat, which has, as a rule, been a rare performance, was achieved by four men in 1897, and three more in 1898. George Giffen, who will soon be able to boast of having obtained 10,000 runs and 1000 wickets in his first-class cricket career, accomplished the feat of scoring 1000 runs and taking 100 wickets during his visits to England in 1886,

1893, and 1896, while Mr. G. E. Palmer performed the double feat in 1886.

The cricket season is still in its infancy, as I write in the early days of June, but, though anything like a review of the events of this year is obviously impossible, and any attempt to prophesy events might be falsified before these pages are in the hands of the reader, one or two points worth notice may be mentioned. We have with us the Australians, who have come over with great reputations, and are achieving signal triumphs in the name of the great colonies whom they represent. Australian critics tell us that no better all-round team has ever visited the mother country, and as the men composing it have been selected on the ground of their performances against Mr. A. E. Stoddart's team in 1897–98, we have welcomed them in a hearty fashion, and are prepared, now we have tried their strength, to take them at their own estimate. Several of the fourteen are old friends whom we have met in England before. J. Worrall, of Victoria, came over here with McDonnell's team in 1888, Gregory and Trumble accompanied Murdoch's team in 1890, and revisited us in 1893 and 1896; Hill, Jones, Darling, Iredale, Johns and Kelly were members of the 1896 team, but Howell, Laver, McLeod, Noble, and Trumper are new to English cricket-fields, while the manager, Major Ben Wardill, is known to all cricketers as the Secretary of the Melbourne Cricket Club.

I have had several opportunities of judging the

form of the Australian team, since their match against the South of England, with which they opened their tour, on the ground of the London County Cricket Club — of which I am now secretary — at the Crystal Palace. My matured opinion confirms my first impressions, for as the result of that match, I came to the conclusion that the team was a good one, and likely to justify all that had been claimed for it. I believe that Trumble is now the best bowler Australia has sent us. He has extraordinary command over the ball, and through his great height and high delivery his bowling leaves the ground at a very fast pace. On slow wickets Trumble and Howell are baffling the best of our English batsmen. Howell has already distinguished himself by the feat of taking all ten wickets in an innings (against Surrey on May 15), which has never been done before by an Australian bowler on English wickets. Howell seems capable of varying his pace to an extraordinary degree, without any apparent indication or change of action. In batting the team is undoubtedly strong, and I expect that the Colonials will make a brave fight for the rubber in the test matches, especially as a cold and rainy May has prevented most of our batsmen from playing into form, while most of our best bowlers seem to be distinctly off colour. Altogether, I do not regard the outlook for England in the test matches as hopeful, as the dearth of really good English bowlers is almost phenomenal—the old and well-tried hands seem to be failing, while as yet no very promising youngsters have shown signs of coming up to first-class form. The new Essex left-handed bowler, Young, created a sensation by his brilliant performance against the Australians at Leyton, when, by taking eleven wickets for 74 runs on May 13, he practically won for Essex the first victory over the Australian team. Young, who was formerly in the Navy, played for Essex in several matches last year, and when I batted against him I thought he was a very fair bowler, with a nice action and a useful break, but I was not prepared for his sensational triumph over the Australian batsmen, for, though the wicket was bad and helped him very materially, his achievement did him credit.

As I have already said, very few of our batsmen have got into form, but Mr. C. B. Fry has opened this season auspiciously, and, if I am not mistaken, will be as he was in 1898, one of the greatest run-getters of 1899. Mr. Jessop also has given proof that his hitting propensities have not forsaken him, and that he may again be relied on to score freely, and to delight spectators with his dashing cricket.

One of the most notable events of the season up to the end of May was the last wicket stand made by Board and Wrathall for Gloucestershire against Surrey on May 19. The Surrey bowling has apparently lost its sting, and these two professionals put on 106 runs in a little over an hour, giving a display of the liveliest running seen at the Oval for many a long day. The audacity with which they stole short runs reminded me of some of the performances of A. N. Hornby and my brother E. M., who were unrivalled as run-stealers. Board and Wrathall made, or, rather, stole, about 60 runs in half an hour, and if Board had not then been completely exhausted by the effort, they might have kept on scoring by the same tactics for any length of time, so completely had their audacity demoralised the Surrey fieldsmen.

Another sensation was the remarkable Whit Monday match between Somerset and Middlesex for Wilfred Flowers' benefit. The drenching rain on the first day made play impossible at Lord's, and when the match was begun on Tuesday (May 23) the wicket was found to be in a most treacherous condition. The bowlers had a harvest, and in the first two overs of the match eight wickets fell for 5 runs. The match was all over in three hours and five minutes, thirty wickets having fallen in that incredibly short time for 195 runs. Albert Trott and J. T. Hearne won the match for Middlesex, the former getting eleven wickets for 31 and the latter eight for 44.

A third sensation, and the greatest of the three, was Abel's grand performance against Somerset (May 29–30), which is still a theme of general conversation. Up to now it is the event of the season, and though a cricket prophet rides for a fall, I doubt whether it will be excelled for a long time. Bobby's not-out innings of 357 has broken

a number of records and surpassed anything he
had done hitherto. Hayward's 315 against Lancashire in 1898, the biggest individual score made
for Surrey at the Oval ; my own 318 for Gloucestershire against Yorkshire in 1876 ; W. W. Read's
famous 338 against Oxford University in 1888,
which until Bobby beat it was the greatest
individual score made for Surrey, and my own
344 for the M.C.C. against Kent in 1876—all these
were one after the other beaten by the little
professional. I did not see Bobby's great feat,
but from all accounts, personal as well as Press,
it was a magnificent innings. He went in first as
usual, had two partners (Hayward and Mr. Crawford), who stayed with him long enough to make
centuries on their own account, shared the honour
with Hayward of putting on 334 runs—a record
for the fourth wicket—saw all ten batsmen dismissed, and was at the wickets for eight hours and
a half, and while 811 runs—the highest aggregate
ever scored on the Oval—were compiled ! I
believe I am right in saying that up to that time
no other batsman had ever been at the wickets
while 810 runs were scored.

While these pages have been undergoing final
revision several very notable events have taken
place, and two new records have been established.
Mr. Stoddart's innings of 485, which since 1886
had held the record as the highest individual
score ever obtained in any match, has been far
surpassed by a Clifton College boy—A. E. J.
Collins—who has compiled the stupendous score

of 628 not out in a match between Clark's House and North Town. Further, the record for the best stand for the last wicket in a first-class match held by the 173 made by Briggs and Pillings fourteen years ago has had to take second place to the score of 230 made by Roche and Mr. R. W. Nicholls for Middlesex against Kent.

CHAPTER IX

AT one time I made a reputation of a somewhat novel character. Somehow I seemed to invariably make a century whenever I played in a professional's benefit match. One outcome of this was that I was always being asked to play in benefit matches. When John Lillywhite was having a benefit at the old Hove Ground at Brighton he asked me to come and play for him. I went down, and when our innings began took my place at the wicket to bat. It was a very bright sunny day, and the glare dazzled my eyes. Anyway I was bowled by the first ball. I went to Lillywhite and told him how sorry I was at my ignominious failure. "Never mind," he said. "Here's a couple of sovereigns. You can have them, if you agree to give me sixpence for every run you make in the second innings." I accepted his conditions, put the money in my pocket, and on the next day went in to bat again. Before stumps were drawn I had made 200 not out, so I went up to Lillywhite and said, "I owe you £5. Here it is, but if you don't let me off any further liability I shall knock down my wicket with the first ball to-morrow morning." Lillywhite laughed and said, " All right, we'll cry quits."

I had another funny experience at Canterbury in 1876. I was playing for the M.C.C. against Kent. In their first innings Kent scored 473—Lord Harris contributing 154—while we of the M.C.C. were all out for 144. It was Friday afternoon when we went in again for our follow-on innings, and as the game seemed lost, and I had to play at Gloucester on the Monday, it crossed my mind that I would hit out whether I lost my wicket or not. Even if I got out, I thought, it didn't matter much, and I should be able to travel down to Gloucester on Saturday instead of Sunday. Anyway I went in and hit out for all I was worth. In forty-five minutes I had made 100, and when stumps were drawn the M.C.C. total was 217— of which I had contributed not out 133—with several wickets to fall. Next morning the high pace of scoring continued and the M.C.C. total was advanced to 323 in ninety minutes. By five o'clock in the afternoon I had made 344, and the M.C.C. aggregate was 557 for eight wickets. As the result the match, which it was thought was going to be a soft thing for Kent, was left drawn—if anything in favour of the M.C.C.

After that match I travelled off to London and thence to Bristol, which I reached on Sunday night. Next morning I had to play for Gloucestershire against Notts at Clifton. I won the toss and went in first. This time I scored 177, and we won the match by ten wickets. As the Nottingham men were travelling back towards the North, they met some of the Yorkshire team who were journeying South to play against us (Gloucestershire) at Cheltenham. Tom Emmett, the Yorkshire bowler, shouted out, " How many did 'the old man' make ? " One of the Notts men replied, " 177." " That's all right," said Tom. " He won't make three centuries in succession. If he does I'll eat him." Well, I won the toss again, and Yorkshire went out to field. They didn't get me out at all that match, for I made 318 in the first innings. I think I did as well in 1876 as ever I did in first-class cricket. In five successive innings I scored 1008 runs, which is almost as good as my 1895 record of a thousand runs in May.

Another interesting reminiscence is the match we had down in the West Country between the Graces and the Robinsons. My brother E. M. married a Miss Robinson, a member of the well-known Bristol family. The Robinsons played cricket, and as the result of a little friendly chaff between the two families, a match was arranged between eleven Graces and eleven Robinsons. It was played at the County Ground at Bristol in the presence of a few friends who came by invitation. I had an injured knee at the time, and was unable to bowl, so I kept wicket.

That reminiscence reminds me that I once kept

wicket in a test match between England and
Australia. The Australians were in rare batting
form, and we Englishmen had a grand outing in
the field. As a last resort Alfred Lyttelton was
put on to bowl his lobs and I, who had been in
every place in the field except behind the wickets,
seized his gloves, and soon caught Midwinter on
the leg side. I am sorry to say that the umpire
gave poor Midwinter out on an appeal from the
bowler, although I am sure the ball only grazed
his leg as it passed. I had no time to prevent
the umpire giving his decision, so Midwinter had
to go.

Once when we were on a tour with the West
Gloucestershire team in Wales, E. M. and I made
a practice of keeping wicket to each other's
bowling. Although I say it myself, we proved
pretty good behind the wickets. But our hands
wouldn't stand the hard treatment, and we gave
up the experiment. As a general rule, I think it's
stupid for a safe batsman or a good bowler to put
on the wicket-keeping gloves, as sooner or later he
is certain to get his hands damaged.

When E. M. was in his prime he was made the
subject of a curious bet. He was playing at
Manchester in an All England Eleven against
Eighteen of Manchester. While he was at the
wicket—I think he had made about twenty runs—
somebody made a bet of 20 to 1 that he would
not score 100. E. M. was hitting tremendously
hard at the time, and the man who gave the odds
had a very narrow shave of losing the bet, because

when the innings closed E. M. had made 97 not
out.   If the last man had survived another over it
was more than probable the bet would have been
lost.

A few weeks ago a London pressman told me
a funny story about Alec Hearne, the Kent
bowler.   When J. T. Hearne made his first appearance for Middlesex in 1890 some of the cricket
reporters in the Press box at Lord's were curious
as to the identity of the new player.   Just before
the match began Alec Hearne happened to pass
just below the Press box, and one of the reporters
leaned down and said, "Alec, is this new man
Hearne any relation of yours ? "   " No," came
the reply.   A couple of hours later, when J. T.
Hearne made a great impression by his bowling,
and captured several wickets with very small loss,
Alec Hearne again happened to pass the Press
box.   Mr. Edgar Pardon, scenting an opportunity
for a joke, said to one of the other reporters,
" Ask Alec now if this new man's any relation."
" Alec," shouted the pressman, equally eager for
the joke, " is this young Hearne any relation of
yours ? "   " Yes," came the reply, " he's a cousin
of mine."   Apparently the cautious Alec wanted
to see how his relative got on before he claimed
the relationship.

In the sixties cricketers did not worry their
heads about records as they, or rather the public,
do nowadays ; otherwise I think my brother
E. M. and Colonel Fred Campbell would have
made a reputation for the fastest bit of sprinting

ever known on a cricket-field. They were playing for the Gentlemen of the South against the All England Eleven, and were batting together, when E. M. did what he was very fond of doing—had a "go" at a fast ball which was pitched a little short. It caught the edge of his bat, and soared mountains high in the air. Colonel Campbell and E. M. both declare that before the ball came down and dropped into the hands of the wicket-keeper (who, by the way, missed it) they were just finishing their third run. I have seen two run while a ball was in the air, and before a catch was made, but though I know that both E. M. and the Colonel were very smart in getting between the wickets, the yarn taxes one's credulity.

The following story, which was new to me when I heard it a few weeks ago, but which may be a chestnut to some of my readers, amused me greatly. A cricketer who was to go in sixth on his side, seeing that the preceding batsmen were making prolonged stands, betook himself to the refreshment tent, where he imbibed too freely of his favourite beverage. Suddenly wickets began to fall, and his captain, on hunting up the man to tell him to prepare to bat, found him in a state bordering on intoxication. " I am afraid," said the batsman, " that I can't do much good. I am sure I shall see three balls." " Never mind," said the captain, "smack at the middle one." The batsman survived one over, and was then bowled by a straight one. As he walked back to the pavilion his captain went out to meet him, and imperiously asked why his advice had not been taken. "I did exactly what you told me," replied the batsman. "I struck at the middle ball, but in a moment of indiscretion I struck out with one of my outside bats."

It was the custom in the seventies for the Jockeys to play a match against the Press. The event usually took place at Brighton in the beginning of August, and though it was not often remarkable for good cricket the encounter always provided a fund of amusement. For the Jockeys, R. I'Anson, who was one of the finest steeplechase riders of his time, and is now a very popular handicapper, was a host in himself. He was always superior in his cricketing ability to the other members of his team, and in 1874 he made 74, and would not have been dismissed then but for the timely assistance of a friendly umpire, who gave him "Run out." I have often been amused by the very comical description George Fordham used to give us of the batting of Jimmy Goater, the great jockey of those days. I remember seeing Fordham in the old saddling paddock on Bath racecourse, showing a little circle of friends how Jimmy used to stand at the wicket. Fordham struck an attitude, flourished his whip, just as Goater used to flourish his bat, and imitating Goater's voice, said, "'Now, then, you bowlers, I'm ready for you'; but the next minute," added Fordham, "Jimmy's wicket was down."

Although everybody knows Lord's Ground, it is possible that everybody does not know how it got its name.   Among the men attendants at the White Conduit Club was one man named Lord, who used to bowl to the members. It was suggested to him that if he took a private ground he would be supported.   Accordingly, in 1787 he hired a piece of ground, which he called by his own name, on a spot now forming Dorset Square. The gentlemen of the White Conduit Club kept their promise, patronised Lord's Ground, and ultimately established themselves as the Marylebone Cricket Club.   The club soon became the nucleus of surrounding counties, and finally came to be recognised as the source and fount of cricket law.   When the ground was required for building purposes the club, still calling its ground Lord's, removed to a spot through which the Regent's Canal has since been cut.   In 1864 the present ground at Marylebone was acquired, and is now the most magnificently equipped cricket-ground in the world, although the new stands have somewhat disfigured it.

Perhaps the most extraordinary cricket match on record is one which took place at Bishop Auckland in 1875.   A local auctioneer made a bet with a local innkeeper who had boasted that the auctioneer could not bowl him out in twelve hours.   They agreed to put the case to the test of experiment, and it was agreed that the auctioneer could provide his own ball and the innkeeper his own bat.   The batsman appeared first on the scene, with a bat made specially for the occasion; it was ten inches wide, and the height of the wicket, which it completely obscured from the bowler's sight. The bowler, however, was equal to the occasion; he appeared with a potshare ball, similar to those used in the game of bowls, and weighing twenty-seven ounces. Under these circumstances the men were apparently evenly matched, but in less than ten minutes the bowler, after splintering the bat to pieces, won the bet by bowling his adversary.

My cousin, W. R. Gilbert, once paid the penalty for treating slow lobs contemptuously. He was playing for the United South against Twenty of Keighley in 1876, and had got well set, when Armytage went on with slow underhands. Armytage, who bowled round the wicket, sent down a very slow ball, which kept close to the ground all the way, and had a slight break from the leg. Gilbert, when he saw the ball creeping towards him, thought it was not worth playing, and instead of hitting it, kicked at it. To his astonishment, and the amusement of all the spectators, the ball hopped up, went over his foot and bowled him out.

I suppose all old cricketers have heard the story of the ball bounding into my shirt, and of the curious difficulty which arose about it, but I may repeat it here for the benefit of youngsters and of old stagers with short memories. I was playing at Clifton for Gloucester in 1878, and while batting with Frank Townsend (father of

Charlie Townsend) made a hit for which we ran three. As I got back to the wicket the ball, which was being thrown in, bounced into my shirt and lodged there. Townsend and I ran three more, I carrying the ball with me inside my shirt. The difficulty which arose was unique, and there was no precedent to guide our procedure. Obviously we could not go on running for ever. But how were the Surrey men to get the ball? If they stopped me they were breaking the rule which forbids fieldsmen to impede the batsmen; if I took it out of my shirt, I should have been out for touching the ball before it was dead. However, Jupp and Southerton got hold of me and asked me to give them the ball. I, however, laughingly declined, but invited Jupp to take it out, which was done. I don't think the incident has ever repeated itself—certainly not in first-class cricket. Of course it would be impossible for such an incident to happen now, as a new rule decrees that the ball is dead if it lodges in a batsman's shirt or pad.

At one time Tom Emmett was engaged as professional bowler to a local club in Yorkshire. One Saturday afternoon he was bowling for his club, but the fieldsmen dropped catch after catch with such systematic persistence that Tom lost his temper, threw the ball on the ground, and said with asperity, " I'm not going to bowl any more. There's an epidemic on this ground, but, thank God, it ain't *catchin'* ! "

This *bon mot* of Emmett's reminds me of Jack

Crossland's remark to two fieldsmen who had both run for a catch and missed it. " I'll tell you what it is," roared Crossland (whose language I expurgate). " One of you's as good as two, and two of you's as good as one, for neither one nor both of you can hold a catch."

The origin of words is always interesting, and some readers may be surprised to know that William Barnes was the inventor of the term "stonewaller." It was in 1882 that R. G. Barlow, playing for Lancashire *v.* Nottingham, made his famous record of five runs in two hours and a half's play. After the innings Barnes went up to Barlow and said, "Bowling at you is like bowling at a stone wall!" The name stuck to Barlow, who, though not the first to play slow cricket, was literally the first "stonewaller" of the cricket-field. Of course the *sobriquet* "Stonewall," as applied to Jackson, the famous Confederate general, is of an older date.

Mr. J. M. Barrie, the Scotch novelist—who is an ardent cricketer, and when playing for the Authors against the Press at Lord's is said to have fielded "brilliantly with his hands in his pockets"—tells a story of a man notable for his pedantry who was batting one day when Mr. Barrie was wicket-keeping. " If I strike the ball with even the slightest degree of impulse," remarked the batsman, addressing the wicket-keeper, " I shall immediately commence running with considerable velocity." There was no occasion (adds Mr. Barrie naïvely) "for him to commence."

While these reminiscences were appearing in serial form I received the following interesting communication from Mr. William Hearder of Plymouth :—

"As an old Amateur Cricketer I have been taking a great interest in your chatty articles, and I thought you might be glad to hear of an incident that happened at Plymouth on Wednesday, May 3, 1882, when a team of Australians landed here.

"They drove up to my business house and explained that a bet had been made on board the vessel that Mr. G. J. Bonnor, who was one of the team, would not throw a cricket-ball 110 yards. The conditions were to be, *first throw on landing,* and no other attempt to be made previous. I took them to our cricket-ground, as both parties concerned asked me to act as judge.

" On arriving at the cricket-ground, Mr. Bonnor objected to the grass, and said he would prefer a hard road or parade-ground. We then drove to the Raglan Barracks, where there is plenty of space. And he said that would suit very well. The distance was marked off by newspapers, and he took his stand, toeing a line. The ball, which he had previously purchased from me, was an ordinary match-ball. This I handed to him, and I had placed in my hand the two cheques for £100 a piece.

" He threw the ball from where he stood to the line and did not run. It was a grand throw ; it seemed as if the ball would never stop rising ; and it pitched on a spot which was measured after to be 119 yards 5 inches from where he stood. As there was no objection made I handed over the two cheques to Mr. Bonnor, who then said, ' I will back myself for £200 to throw the ball 125 yards the next throw.'

"Of course 120 yards is a fair throw, but the conditions were that it was to be *first throw on landing*, and after he had been cooped up on board ship for six weeks you can imagine he would be out of training.

"Mr. Bonnor kindly presented me with the ball after the event and we adjourned to their hotel to wash off the dust."

CHAPTER X

HINTS FOR YOUNG CRICKETERS

In devoting a chapter of this volume to Hints for Young and Aspiring Cricketers I shall endeavour to avoid reiterating the copy-book maxims concerning cricket which are to be found in every sixpenny treatise on the game. To experienced hands it may be that many of my remarks in this chapter may seem to be so obvious as to be scarcely worthy of expression, but as new generations of cricketers are always coming up a few pages of advice, founded on thirty-five years of first-class cricket, may prove helpful to some aspirants for cricket honours.

Cricket, like most games of skill, is best learned in early boyhood, and my first advice to young cricketers is to begin early enough. To some boys cricket comes naturally. They take to the game like a duck does to the water ; others are exactly the reverse, and are as wooden and awkward as can be when they begin to bat, bowl, or field. The former need a little oversight, and should be encouraged to stick to correct form ; the latter should have constant supervision, while at practice, by some one, either a coach or parent, who can show them their faults and correct them before they become settled habits. In cricket, as in all games, style is ease, and ease is strength. The most stylish cricketers are, as a rule, good players. For this reason I lay stress on the necessity of cultivating correct and stylish play. It is so much easier if a boy commences in the right way. But though a boy may frame—or, as they say in the North, shape—badly at first, his clumsiness may be overcome if he is taught the correct form when young, and, having overcome his initial difficulties, he may become quite as good a cricketer as the boy who intuitively played correctly from the first. As every rowing-man knows, an oarsman who has never rowed before may become a better rower than one who has acquired bad habits, such as bucketing, or snatching at the beginning of his stroke. It is the same to some degree in cricket, where early defects may become settled habits beyond eradication. On the other hand, there are young cricketers, whose style is awkward and ugly, who nevertheless succeed with both bat and ball.

I would begin by offering some suggestions as to batting.

In the first place, a boy should not play with too heavy a bat, nor should he use a full-sized bat until he is tall enough and strong enough to wield it freely and control it completely. This is extremely important, as many a boy's style is utterly ruined by playing with a heavy and unwieldy bat.

Above all a bat should be well balanced, as a boy will play better with a well-balanced bat that is slightly too heavy for him than with an ill-balanced bat that is the correct weight. I strongly recommend boys at odd times to play, or, rather, practise, with a stick or broom-handle and a soft ball, as by this method they may acquire the quickness of eye and perfect union of eye and hand which are among the essentials of a good batsman. Whilst speaking of bats, I may say that a great point in a good bat is that it should have some springiness in the handle.

As boys grow up they should be provided with bats according to their style of play. It stands to reason, for instance, that a hard hitter will want a heavy bat, or, at all events, a heavier bat than a batsman who plays quietly. Driving, or hitting straight forward, can be best done with a heavy bat, while, of course, it is easier to cut with a light one. I never saw a good cutter use a heavy bat. Personally, I play with a bat weighing about 2 lb. 5 oz., which, I think, is heavy enough for anybody; but, as I have said before, a few ounces make very little difference if the bat is really well balanced. Of course perfectly balanced bats are hard to secure, and a batsman who possesses one regards it as a treasure.

I am often asked who are the best makers of bats, and I find it difficult to reply. Years ago it might have made a good deal of difference whose bats you used, but nowadays all well-known makers are much of a muchness. You can get a good bat, and you can get a very inferior one, from almost any maker, the reason being, I suppose, that, owing to the great demand, makers are bound to make use of every available piece of timber, and some poor blades slip in.

I am firmly convinced that a boy should never be allowed to buy a bat for himself. Of course he should be allowed some word in the choice, but a capable judge should be consulted before a final selection is made. I do not know that I need confine this advice to boys. I know many good cricketers who are shockingly poor judges of a bat. Nevertheless, an experienced cricketer, though he may be a bad hand when it comes to selecting a bat, soon realises when he has got hold of a good one. Apropos of selecting a bat, an old Lancashire slow-bowler, who keeps a cricketing depôt, once told me a good story, which illustrates my point. A gentleman entered his shop one day, and said he wanted to buy a bat. "What sort do you want?" asked the shopman. "Oh," replied the customer, "I want a slipper." The shopman was puzzled, and asked what he meant. "Well," said the gentleman, "I want a bat that I can guide the ball down the slips with." The shopman, a cute and canny Scot, recognising the sort of gentleman he was dealing with, said : "I've got the very thing you want." Walking to a case, he took down a bat which he had had in his shop for six years, which no one would look at because it was very thin in the blade and very badly balanced. It had been kept well oiled and

had a good brown face on it, and the customer
seemed vastly taken with it. It ended in the
gentleman deciding to have that particular bat,
and the shopman, thinking it was a pity that the
gentleman should not go on thinking that he had
something extra good, asked thirty shillings for
it, on the ground that he had had it in stock and
bestowed great care upon it. Nothing loath, the
gentleman paid the thirty shillings, and went
away perfectly satisfied with his prize. At the
end of the season he went to the cricketing
depôt again, and told the attendant that that bat
was the very best he had ever handled. The
story shows how little some men know about bats,
and I have no doubt this was no exceptional case.

As to the price of a good bat, I consider that for
fifteen or sixteen shillings an excellent one can be
procured, but, as a rule, a guinea is about the
price charged for a reliable, well-balanced, and
properly finished bat.

The position of a batsman at the wicket is a
matter of great importance, and a few guiding
maxims should be taken to heart. My first advice
to a young batsman is to stand firm with the
right foot planted just within the popping crease,
and almost parallel with it. The toe of the right
foot should be just clear of a line drawn between
the off stump of the distant wicket and the leg
stump of the wicket at which the batsman is
standing. Of course I mean an imaginary line,
although I think it is a very good plan for any one
who is coaching a boy to draw such a line from a

point about half a yard outside the popping crease to the leg stump, so that the boy can see for himself when his toe gets in front of the wicket. The right leg and foot should bear the weight of the body and be, as it were, a pivot ; the left foot should be planted about a foot's length away from the right, and in such a position that the batsman can move it readily and change the position of his body with sufficient rapidity to play the ball, no matter which side of him it may come.

Though many good players stand with their left foot and knee covering part of the wicket, I think it is advisable to teach youngsters to keep their left as well as their right foot absolutely clear of the wicket. Nevertheless, this should not be made an arbitrary rule in the case of boys who have got into the habit of standing with their left foot slightly in front of the wicket. Undoubtedly it is safer to keep the left foot clear of the wicket, but if a boy has contracted the habit I have mentioned, and does not take readily to the change, I should not insist on it, lest interference should prejudicially affect his play, because, as a rule, right-handed batsmen seldom get out leg before wicket through the ball hitting the left leg or foot, though that sometimes happens in the case of a slow yorker dropping on the batsman's toe.

In batting the left shoulder should be thrown well forward, that is, in the direction of the bowler. This is a most important principle, and cannot be too emphatically emphasised, because

a batsman with his left shoulder thrown well forward is almost bound to play with a straight bat,
which again is one of the essentials of correct style.

At almost any cost a boy must be made to play
with a straight—*i.e.*, a perpendicular—bat. There
are, no doubt, exceptions to every rule, and even
this may be a counsel of perfection. I have
known first-class cricketers who played with a
cross—*i.e.*, a horizontal—bat, but they have been
men possessed of wonderful eyesight, and their
success has been achieved in spite of their defect.
There are, and always have been, players who have
defied what I may call the "straight-bat" principle. They were incorrigible, but their prowess
does not shake my conviction that a boy should
be trained to play with an upright bat. For the
benefit of small boys, who are often unable to
comprehend why it is necessary, or at least advisable, to play with a straight, when they find that
they can make runs with a cross bat, it should be
pointed out that an upright bat strengthens their
defence, because, whereas a cross bat covers only
two or three inches of the wicket, an upright bat
shields them almost completely.

I do not believe so implicitly, as some cricketers
and writers upon cricket do, in watching the
bowler's hand. I prefer to watch the ball, and
not to anticipate events. If when batting you
watch the bowler's hand, and you see that he
gives a twist to the right or the left, as the case
may be, you know—or at least you think you
know—which way he intends the ball to break.
Then, before the ball reaches you, you get

ready for a twist in the direction which in the ordinary course of things the ball ought to take ; but the unexpected very often happens in cricket—it's a glorious thing for cricket that it does—and instead of coming in the way the bowler meant, and you anticipate, the ball breaks a little in another direction, and you are beaten by it. So my advice is, " Keep your eye on the ball." I don't want to be misunderstood. I think it is as well to notice the action of the bowler, as most bowlers, when they are going to send down a very fast ball, generally change their delivery or their run, and it is certainly well to know when a fast ball is coming.

For boys who are learning to bat, an important piece of advice is to play forward as much as possible. On good hard and true wickets nearly every ball can be played forward, and if a boy has once learned to play forward confidently he will soon adapt himself to playing backwards at balls that demand it. The old-fashioned habit of back play has almost entirely gone out. I can remember when batsmen regularly played the ball when it was only a few inches from their wickets. Nowadays most batsmen either play forward or adopt what is called the "half-cock stroke," which means playing the ball when it is level with the batsman's body. Owing to this new style of play the old "draw," which used to be a very favourite stroke, has entirely gone out. Tom Hearne used to play this stroke very skilfully, and to score from it very freely. Of course the half-cock is a purely defensive stroke, though runs are occasionally made from it.

I am afraid I may be condemned for heterodoxy, but I believe that young batsmen, who are quick on their legs, should be encouraged to step out of their crease to play slow bowling. I do not think we step out often enough nowadays, and I am surprised that we do not, because it is so much easier to score off slow bowling by running out to meet the ball than by staying in the crease. Moreover, a batsman who leaves his ground now and again to drive a slow ball demoralises the bowler. When I first began playing first-class cricket, many of the old players made it a habit to run out to meet slow bowling, and they somehow managed to smother the good balls while driving the loose ones to the long field. I do not by any means suggest that batsmen should run out to every slow ball bowled, but when a ball is at all over-pitched I consider it distinctly good policy to rush out and take it as a full pitch. It is no use advising a boy who is slow on his legs to leave his ground, as a slight mistake would be fatal to him, as he would not be quick enough to get back to play the ball defensively, and would run no small risk of being stumped. To decide which ball a batsman should run out to meet, and which should be played while retaining his ground, is a great problem, but instinct will gradually teach a young batsman which course to pursue, and pages of advice on the point would be useless.

From my long experience I have formed the opinion that beginners should be encouraged to continue playing in the style which comes most naturally to thém, provided, of course, that the style is not radically wrong. The idea I mean to convey is that if a young batsman is naturally a slow scorer, he should not be urged to hit out, and that if, on the other hand, the beginner is naturally a hard hitter, he should not be discouraged in that practice. I have no affection for stonewallers, and a boy who shows any tendency towards that odious style should be weaned away from it, but no attempt should be made to make a hitter of a boy whose disposition is towards steady, patient play. A natural aptitude for hard and free play should certainly not meet with any discouragement. It would not do for everybody to be a hard hitter, nor for every one to be a stonewaller, but it should be remembered that batsmen who get runs quickly and play freely all round the wicket are not only more appreciated by the onlookers, but are often, by their rapid scoring, able to snatch a victory for their side when time is short and runs are needed. There is no doubt that big hitters draw crowds and delight spectators, who would sooner see an hour of spirited play than spend an afternoon watching the most perfect slow batsman compiling runs in monotonous singles. Even men with short memories must recall the intense excitement which used to be aroused when C. I. Thornton, Bonnor Percy Macdonald, Massie, and other hard hitters of the past were making big scores. Jessop and Ford are popular at the present time for the same reason. Say what you will, the cricket-loving public likes lively batting, and for this reason, that is, for the good of cricket, I think hitters should be encouraged. Moreover, if there were more hard hitters, there would be fewer drawn games. As a proof that the public do really prefer rapid scoring to the most finished and perfect batsmanship of the slow order, it is only necessary to remind readers of the way that the steady, not to say tedious, play of Scotton, Shrewsbury, and sometimes even Gunn killed for a time all interest in Notts county cricket. I am glad to say that the Nottingham men have abandoned that style of play, though I still think that they play too slow a game for the public taste. I confess that this ultra-patient batting is not to my own liking, and that I sympathise with the public craving for a little excitement. I know nothing more exhilarating than the feeling that the spectators are on the *qui vive* and eagerly watching every ball, and it is because I realise that spectators are always in this mood when a notorious hard hitter is at the wicket that I say : "Encourage a young batsman who has a disposition to hit out." It is very delightful, no doubt, to watch good and perfect cricket, but slow play does get terribly monotonous, and for the good of the game it should not be given too much encouragement.

Many young cricketers make the mistake of grasping the handle of the bat either too high or too low.   Experience has taught me that it is most advantageous to hold the bat with the right hand about half-way up the handle, and with, of course, the left hand just above it.   By this means the bat can be controlled more effectively than if held nearer the blade, and more firmly than if held right at the top of the handle.   The bat should not be held too stiffly, as facility of motion and freedom of wrist action are essential.

Do not get into the irritating habit of flourishing your bat in the air.   Nothing is gained by it, and sometimes a good deal is lost by it. Personally, I find that the greatest scope for freedom of play is secured by holding the bat in what is called the pendulum fashion, which tends to facility of movement, without diminishing in the slightest degree the batsman's power of defence.   I await the attack of the bowler with the top of the handle of my bat just above my waist, and the bottom of the blade almost on a level with the centre of the middle stump.

One of the primary essentials of a batsman is judgment in timing the ball.   This depends on the accuracy of the eye and the nerve of the batsman.   Above all, take care that the bat hits the ball, and not the ball the bat, by which I mean, let the ball receive the full force of the bat.

Confidence comes with experience, and until confidence is acquired a batsman's defence cannot be good.   An uncertain and vacillating style spells failure, for in batting he who hesitates is assuredly lost. So make up your mind how you intend playing a ball, and then play it confidently and resolutely, hitting hard if you are going to hit, and blocking vigorously if you intend to block. Do not allow the bat to passively await the impact of the ball.

Take every possible precaution to protect the body when batting. Do not face fast bowling without leg-guards, and do not dispense with batting gloves. I know that some cricketers dislike the gloves, but I think it is a mistake to discard them, as sooner or later a batsman who dispenses with these protections will get his fingers smashed, or a hand injured, and nothing is more annoying than to be disabled when in good form by some trivial accident, which might have been avoided by taking ordinary precautions.

Quickness of determination and promptitude of action must be cultivated by practice, and for their cultivation I can recommend nothing but practice.

Every young cricketer is ambitious to cut well, and it is a most desirable accomplishment. From no stroke does a batsman get more satisfaction, or the onlookers more delight. In the hands of a good batsman the cut is admittedly one of the most brilliant and effective hits. In cutting the left leg takes the place of the right as the pivot on which the weight of the body is thrown, while the right leg is brought briskly across to the off-side. The blade of the bat should be brought sharply upon the ball with an action which some one has aptly described as a cross between a pat and a push. The stroke requires considerable wrist flexibility, and must be practised assiduously if it is to be successfully performed.

A batsman must always be prepared to back up immediately the ball leaves the hand of the bowler, but I would caution the beginner against leaving his ground until he has made sure that the ball has actually left the bowler's hand, otherwise the bowler may retain the ball and promptly "run out" the batsman. This has sometimes been called sharp practice on the bowler's part, but if there is any sharp practice I think it is really on the part of the batsman, who tries to take an unfair advantage by getting out of his ground before the ball is bowled.

Watch where the ball goes, and at once call for a run if you intend to attempt one. There should be no hesitation in this matter. If you feel inclined to run, do not hesitate, but call, and, having called, on no account alter your mind and send your partner back, as you can get to the opposite wicket easier than he can return and recover his ground.

Do not hesitate to steal runs if you think it is possible to get between the wickets in time. By saying this I do not recommend any reckless attempts at impracticabilities. The real value of a stolen run, or rather of a succession of stolen runs, is the effect upon the bowler, who gets irritated, and upon the fieldsmen, who get demoralised.

Cultivate patience in the early stages of your innings, and get accustomed to the bowling before you begin to take any liberties with it. An impatient desire for fast scoring engenders recklessness, than which there is nothing more fatal. However much at home you may be when set consistent care should be exercised from beginning to end of your innings. There is an old maxim, which I recommend you to take to heart, viz., take care of the stumps and the runs will take care of themselves.

The imperative necessity for making their practice consonant with their play during a match cannot be too forcibly impressed upon the minds of young players. The fate of many a promising young cricketer can be traced to the baneful habit of reckless batting into which he has relapsed during practice hours, and young cricketers should sedulously avoid these suicidal tactics.

I do not believe in over-coaching, though I do think that boys should be put in the right way of playing. After they have been shown the right way to play, and the advantages of correct form have been explained to them, they should to a certain extent be left alone to benefit by their own experience. Most boys are naturally sensitive, particularly in their games, and those who coach young cricketers should take great care lest by over-coaching and excessive fault-finding they frustrate their own purpose by making the boys dislike the game. A boy soon tires of being constantly told of his defects and hardly ever praised for his good points. This is perhaps more of a suggestion to coaches than a hint to young cricketers, but I have seen so much of the peril of over-coaching that I want to impress this point upon all who have anything to do with teaching the young idea to shoot.

Perhaps it is superfluous to say that continual practice is the secret of success in batting. Sir Isaac Pitman used to say after studying the rules and principles there were three great maxims to be taken to heart in learning shorthand. The first was practice, the second was practice, and the third was practice. It is the same in cricket. Get as good, level, and true a wicket as possible, and practice regularly and patiently, and skill at the game will come to a young cricketer.

It is a good rule when boys are practising that they should have boys to bowl to them, or some old cricketer who does not mind having his bowling knocked about a little. It is an excellent thing for a boy when big and strong enough to learn to play to good bowling—it cultivates his defensive faculties ; but he needs, also, to learn how to hit loose bowling, and if he gets all his practice against a bowler who gives him no opportunities for hitting, and takes his wicket every few balls, discouragement is inevitable. I have seen the professional bowlers at schools bowling their hardest and their best at a youngster who more than anything else ought to have been given the chance to hit out. It is a great and

almost incorrigible fault of Public School coaches
that they cannot resist the temptation to see how
often they can bowl the wickets down irrespective
of any consideration for the boys who are there
to learn to bat.

Some youngsters have what we call a good and
natural action—they bowl correctly by intuition ;
others have no action at all—they bowl clumsily,
and with the expenditure of infinitely more effort
than is necessary. Again, command of the ball
comes naturally to some boys ; others send it
anywhere but in the direction they want it to go.
It is perhaps more important in bowling than in
batting that beginners should be shown their
defects and have their faults corrected.

Boys should be taught to bowl with a high
action. Some of the old cricketers believe that
fast round-arm bowling below the shoulder would
still pay, but I cannot think that this style of bowling would be very effective on the billiard table
wickets of the present day.

Young cricketers should not be allowed to
bowl the full distance (twenty-two yards) until
their frames are knit and their muscles firm,
otherwise they would overtax their strength and
acquire a clumsy style. Boys should begin bowling, say, at fifteen yards and gradually as they get
older and stronger increase the length to eighteen
yards, then twenty yards, and finally the regulation
length.

Strict attention to the rules governing bowling
should be paid by young cricketers, who should

be scrupulously careful not to bowl "no balls," that is, not to pass the wicket before delivery, and to avoid any suspicious action suggestive of a throw.

When a boy is learning to bowl it is a good thing I think to have the bowling crease marked out just as if it were for a match. A boy can then see for himself that his foot is behind the bowling crease when the ball leaves his hand.

Young cricketers sometimes ask me whether they should bowl round or over the wicket. My advice is to get accustomed to bowl from either side, and then to adopt whichever suits you best. The advantage of being able to bowl either round or over the wicket is to be found in the fact that the ground, especially towards the end of a long match, often gets cut up by the constant wear of the bowler's feet, and a bowler often finds it useful to be able to bowl from that side of the wicket which happens to be least worn and torn. Further, it is sometimes a great advantage when bowling against a left-hand batsman to be able to change to the other side of the wicket. If a batsman makes a stand and plays the bowling easily, it is often as good as a change of bowling if the bowler reverses from round the wicket to over it or *vice versâ*.

One great reason why most bowlers bowl over the wicket is because this course heightens the chance of getting the batsman out for leg before wicket, but in spite of this it is a drawback to any bowler if he can only bowl one side of the wicket.

A young cricketer should not bowl for too long at a time, as exhaustion is certain to make him bowl loosely.

To keep a good length should be the constant aim of a young bowler. It is an excellent plan to put a white feather or bit of paper about four yards from the middle and off stumps, and then try to pitch the ball upon that spot. By means of this device a young bowler will soon acquire the habit of bowling good length balls, and will moreover very quickly see that when he pitches the ball near the mark the batsman finds it difficult to play. A little practical exhibition like this teaches a boy better than any amount of precept the value and necessity of keeping up a good length.

The secret of good bowling is length and straightness. To secure these desiderata the bowler must have control over the ball, which can only be acquired by unremitting practice and patient vigilance. I do not suggest that every ball should have the same length, or should pitch in the same place. The ideal bowler can, if necessary, vary every ball in an over, and pitch it almost exactly where he wants each time. One of the great examples of this triumph of skill in bowling was Alfred Shaw in my own day, and, from what I hear, old William Clarke, who they used to say could pitch a ball on a half a crown with almost unerring certainty.

When once a boy has learned sufficient command of the ball to bowl straight with a good length and a varied pace, he should try to acquire a break, that is, to be able to make the ball deviate from a straight course. The ability to bowl with a good break is a valuable acquisition, and like most things of much value is not easily attained. Some of the best bowlers have a natural break, and scarcely know when they are going to do it ; others acquire the faculty of breaking after infinite practice and assiduity. There is no infallible recipe for making a ball break—it is done by twisting the fingers and hand just as the ball leaves the hand, and in cultivating this bowlers with long arms and long fingers have an advantage over short-armed and short-fingered bowlers.

As to pace, I suggest no hard-and-fast rules. As I said about youthful batsmen, natural tendencies should be respected, and a boy should be encouraged to bowl fast or slow as suits his inclination, style, and strength. It is useless to attempt to make a slow bowler into a fast one, or a fast bowler into a slow one. It is in helping a boy to decide what his pace and style should be that the advice of a good coach is most valuable. If such advice is not obtainable the best I can say to a young cricketer is that he should not bowl beyond his strength, and should not at too early an age attempt a really fast delivery. No boy should be discouraged or depressed because he cannot bowl fast. He should remember that though fast bowling is invaluable, slow bowling has its uses, and often captures wickets which fast

bowling has failed to secure. Moreover, a fast
bowler does not last so long as a slow bowler.

Nothing should be done to discourage left-
handed play. On the other hand I think it
should be encouraged. The idea of making
every one right-handed is dying out, and it is a
good thing that it is. Both as a bowler and as a
batsman a good left-handed player is a source of
strength to his side. Very few batsmen feel as
comfortable with a left-hand bowler as with one
who bowls right-handed, while a left-handed
batsman invariably puzzles the bowlers, and by
necessitating constant changes in the field
harasses the fieldsmen. In my opinion the reason
why the last English team which Mr. Stoddart
took out to Australia lost the test matches was
because the English bowlers were unable to bowl
as well to the left-handed players as they did to
the right-handed batsmen. Hill and Darling, the
two Australian left-handers, practically won the
test matches for the Colonials. Of course, it is a
great advantage to a boy to be ambidextrous,
but very few cricketers can use one hand as well
as the other.

Though I have committed myself to the opinion
that cricketers are not born but bred, I firmly
believe that some bowlers come very nearly
within the category of being to the manner born.
To bowl well is natural to them, and a nice easy
action seems to be their birthright. But what is
more to the point, they have the subtle power
which is a bowler's greatest gift, of making the

ball increase its velocity after striking the ground. From some unknown cause the ball rebounds from the ground like a billiard-ball comes off the cush. It is this strange unaccountable faculty, which is an endowment and not an acquisition, which marks the natural bowler. The trick cannot be taught or learned ; it comes as a natural aptitude to a few, and is denied to the majority. No doubt it has something to do with the way the bowler quite unconsciously allows the ball to leave his fingers, but the bowlers themselves cannot explain the secret.

In the whole course of my long experience I have come across very few of these natural bowlers, but it is a curious fact that this gift is not confined to fast bowlers alone—medium and slow bowlers sometimes possess it, and, when they do, they are if anything more deadly than the fast bowler. My Uncle Pocock has often told me that this natural aptitude was the source of William Clarke's phenomenal success with his slow lobs. My Uncle thought the increased velocity with which Clarke's lobs left the ground was produced by his peculiar delivery, as Clarke —unlike most slow under-hand bowlers of the present day who crouch to bowl lobs and deliver the ball from about the height of their knee— used to make the most of his height, and discharge the ball from the level of his hip.

A young bowler ought not to rest satisfied until he has learned to bowl a yorker. It is difficult to give an exact definition of a yorker, but roughly speaking, it is a ball which pitches a few inches in front of the block hole, and of which the batsman cannot quite make a full pitch. A yorker may be either fast or slow, but fast or slow, it is an extremely difficult ball to play. The temptation of a batsman faced by a slow yorker is to fancy that he can hit it easily, and not only defend his wicket, but score from it. A slow yorker, however, is nothing if not deceptive, and the batsman who plays it with too much *sang-froid* is likely to misjudge it and fall a victim. A fast yorker is even more troublesome, and many good bats confess that it is the most awkward ball they can receive. A really fast yorker, such as Albert Trott sends down with pitiless frequency, often scatters the wickets before the batsman has time to prepare to play it. There is another kind of yorker which, though not a true yorker so far as the bowler is concerned, is made so by the batsman stepping out to it. If he misjudges it in the least the batsman plays over it, and loses his wicket.

There is one hint I would like to offer to young bowlers who have either a natural or an acquired break, and it is that they should overcome the temptation to exercise their power too freely. One of the greatest mistakes a bowler can make is to break too much. In the first place, he often sacrifices length and straightness, and in the second he loses sight of the fact that a small break is more deadly than a large one. If a bowler can only manage to make a ball break about three inches, and to do that quickly and imperceptibly, and at the same time hit the wicket if it gets past the batsman, he has learned the great secret of successful breaking. Everything in break depends upon the pace at which the ball comes off the ground. A slow ball which breaks a foot is easy to play compared with a fast ball which breaks three inches quickly.

Obviously there are only two ways in which a ball can break—from the off or from the leg. The break from the off—or, as it is called, the break-back—is the one which usually gets most wickets by bowling batsmen out, whilst the leg break leads to most catches, as the ball, breaking from the leg, is liable to touch the outside edge of the bat and fall into the hands of a fieldsman at cover-point or in the slips. Some bowlers have the ability to break both ways, and a valuable acquisition it is. Slow balls with an off break are nowadays frequently pulled round to leg, even by first-class batsmen. The best men at this stroke seldom try to pull a straight ball, but when they get one a foot or so to the off they pull it round with impunity.

Young batsmen ought not to be allowed to practise this stroke ; indeed, they should be severely reprimanded if they show any tendency towards pulling. Some of my readers may say : " But I have seen ' W. G.' himself pulling balls to leg." My answer to that is : " But I never pulled a ball until I was forty years of age," and I advise all young cricketers to emulate my example, and not to try it until they reach that age, because, though plenty of runs are scored off the stroke, lots of wickets are lost in the attempt to achieve it.

The worst ball a bowler can possibly bowl is the long hop, and a boy should studiously avoid it. A long hop from a slow bowler is a ball which pitches six or seven yards in front of the wicket, and so gives the batsman plenty of time to see it. An experienced cricketer never fails to take advantage of a long hop, and if it comes slowly he is pretty certain to despatch it to the boundary. A long hop from a fast bowler will, of course, fall two or three yards still shorter—will, in fact, pitch only about half-way down the wicket. A very fast long hop is not nearly so likely to get punished as a slow one, as, if the ground is at all rough, it bumps terribly, and occasionally is very unpleasant for the batsman. On a true wicket a fast long hop can be punished by some batsmen with almost as much certainty and ease as a slow one. In every respect a long hop is a very bad ball, and my final word is that boy bowlers should at all costs avoid bowling them.

A young bowler should learn to vary his pitch and pace with almost every ball in the over. If he can succeed in doing this without altering his action so much the better, as he will then be more likely to baffle the batsmen. True skill in bowling involves head work—a good bowler bowls with his brain more than his arm. I have known many good bowlers who have had perfect command of the ball, but for some reason or another have had no head. They seemed incapable when bowling of grasping the situation and ascertaining by experiment what balls puzzle the batsmen most; consequently they kept pegging away and did not get nearly as many wickets as they ought to have secured. There are many such bowlers to-day, but, on the other hand, there are others who cannot bowl nearly so well, but who use their brains more, rapidly detect the weak spots in a batsman's defence, and attack his most vulnerable point until at last he falls into their snare. A bowler, and especially a slow bowler, who uses his head is incomparably more valuable than the plodder, who, without much thought, keeps up a perfect length and accurate pitch, but bowls like a machine. It is by the machinations of the slow bowler who uses his head that batsmen are most frequently tempted into the indiscretions which cost them their wickets. Such a bowler may perhaps toss up a ball to a batsman, who jumps out and promptly sends it to the boundary. This is no source of discouragement for the bowler, who is biding his time, and in the next over, perhaps, sends down another ball apparently similar in elevation and pace, but it may be a few inches shorter. The batsman, thinking it is the same ball, again attempts to repeat his boundary hit, only to find to his disgust that he has either played over it and been bowled, or skied it and been caught in the long field. Thus a bowler who uses his head generally has the satisfaction of capturing the wickets by his head work, whereas the purely mechanical bowler plods away, hoping that the batsman will make some fatal mistake.

The supreme importance of good fielding cannot be too strongly emphasised. One of the most essential things for a young cricketer to learn is the art of fielding. The fortunes of a team very largely depend upon good or bad fielding. Success in cricket depends not only upon a team making good aggregate scores, but upon getting its opponents out at the minimum cost of runs. The best bowling in the world is thrown away unless the bowlers are backed up by sure and quick fieldsmen. I go so far as to say that a really good fielder often saves as many runs as the best batsmen on his side score, and I firmly believe that a thoroughly efficient fieldsman is worth his place in any team, even if he get no runs at all. As a rule, it is generally found that good batsmen are pretty sound all-round cricketers, whereas we frequently come across first-class bowlers who can neither bat nor field. Such a one, if he should happen to be off colour and out of form with the ball, is a dead loss to his side, or, as they put it in rowing parlance, " a regular passenger in the crew." I have an almost morbid dread of a bad fieldsman, for in my experience I have on the one hand seen many matches lost by poor fielding, and on the other hand have known many a match won almost entirely by smart fielding. A captain who has one untrustworthy fieldsman in his eleven is on tenter-hooks as long as his side is in

the field ; he scarcely knows where to put the
" passenger," and he feels sure that catches are
certain to go in his direction wherever he puts
him.

What to do with a " duffer " is a knotty problem
which I cannot pretend to have solved.   In the
old days, when I was a young cricketer, we always
used to put him at short leg, but why I never
could conceive, because, if there is one place
where you may get a harder catch than another,
it is at short leg.   On the whole, I think the easiest
position in the field, and the one to which I
should give the duffer his place, is mid-on, for
though the ball may come quickly to that fieldsman, it generally comes straight from the bat.
But, of course, everything depends upon who is
bowling and who is batting.   While one batsman
is at the wicket a particular fielder may find his
place a perfect sinecure, whereas with the very next
man in he may be kept perpetually leather hunting.

These references to bad fieldsmen and the loss
they entail call to mind the fact that in a Gentlemen *v.* Players match many years ago over a
hundred runs were scored by one of the Gentlemen, who, however, fielded so badly, and missed
so many catches, that on talking the match over
afterwards a member of the eleven aptly remarked
that although the Gentleman had scored a hundred
and twenty he still owed his side ninety-five runs,
because, if he had made no runs, and had brought
off the catches he missed, his side would have
been ninety-five runs better off.

After showing the practical value of good fielding I need scarcely recommend young cricketers to practise fielding with as much persistence as they practise batting and bowling. In these days, when practice-nets are all the vogue, the opportunity for learning fielding is less than it was when we practised without them. I think it is a good plan, when boys are practising, to occasionally dispense with the back net, and let one of the boys act as long-stop. There is more to be learned by long-stopping than at first sight would seem to be the case, because—especially if the ground is at all rough—the ball jumps about in all directions, and has to be watched carefully to ensure its being picked up cleanly.

Skill in catching should be cultivated, either by the boys throwing the ball from one to another at varying distances, or by the coach or parent, as the case may be, hitting balls for catching off the bat. In hitting for catches the batsman should be careful not to hit too hard to small boys lest their fingers should get damaged or their hands bruised, which engenders a kind of funk detrimental to their chances of becoming expert in fielding. Perhaps I may here parenthetically remark that in my judgment it is a grave mistake for small boys to play with men if they can possibly get any practice with cricketers of their own age.

In effecting a catch, and in fielding a fast ball, there is one little knack which is worth noticing The fieldsman should let his hand give to the ball ;

in other words, as the ball reaches his hand he should let his hand move in the direction the ball is going. This checks the impetus of the ball, and enables the fieldsman to secure it, whereas if the ball came to his hand when rigid it would probably bounce out again and fall to the ground. The principle is exactly the same as that which leads a man who is getting off a train or carriage in motion to step or jump in the direction the vehicle is going. With a little practice this knack of letting the hand give to the ball is soon acquired, and when once learnt is applied naturally and easily in fielding.

When the ball is coming slowly in the direction of a fieldsman, he should not wait for it to reach him, but should run to meet it. By this means time and perhaps even a run is saved. On the other hand, this must not be carried to extremes, as it is not always advisable to run to meet a fast ball. If the ground happens to be rough, it is almost impossible to judge the direction the ball will bound with any certainty, and the fieldsman who runs to meet a fast ball stands a good chance of missing it. Men who dash in often do brilliant things, but they frequently make very bad and costly mistakes.

"Throwing in" accurately is almost an art. Until a boy has learned to return the ball promptly and with certainty to the bowler or wicket-keeper, he must not regard himself as a good fieldsman. The ball should be picked up and returned with one action of the arm. This

cannot be easily learned, but a young fieldsman
should practise until he can do it. If a fieldsman
is standing near the wicket the difficulty is comparatively slight, but if he has to throw in a ball
from the long field, say seventy or eighty yards,
it is admittedly hard to achieve. A batsman soon
realises this, and if he perceives the inability of a
fielder to return the ball with absolute precision
and promptitude, he knows that he can often steal
a run with safety.

Besides trying to pick up and throw in with
one action, a fieldsman should learn also to
return the ball so that the wicket-keeper or
bowler can take it easily. This is a matter of
vital importance. The best advice for a boy is
that which the late H. H. Stephenson, the well-
known old Surrey player, used to give the boys of
Uppingham when he was coaching at the school :
" Throw it right in my face, if you please, gentlemen ; not at my feet." Fieldsmen stationed near
the wicket should make it a practice to return the
ball to the top of the bails or a little higher.
Careless throwing-in, even when close to the
wicket, is expensive. I have often seen a ball
which should have been returned to the bails
drop into the block-hole or on ground roughened
by the bowlers' feet and bound away. A sharp
return often gets a batsman " run out" unex-
pectedly, and when a fieldsman has earned a
reputation for returning the ball in a smart
fashion batsmen think twice before attempting to
steal a run from a ball which has gone in his

direction. Of course, when a man is out in the long field, he should return the ball with a long hop, that is, let it bounce a little distance in front of the wicket-keeper or bowler, so that on its first bound it will be well within easy reach. Fieldsmen, both near the wicket and in the long field, should always bear in mind that, when there is no chance of running a batsman out, the ball should not be thrown in too wildly. As a general rule, boys should get into the habit of returning the ball to the nearest wicket, but if there is any doubt it should go to the wicket-keeper, as this saves extra exertion to the bowler, and spares him the risk of damaging his hand or stinging his fingers unnecessarily. Consideration should always be shown to the bowler, who should, as far as possible, be saved unnecessary effort. Anything calculated to flurry a bowler should be scrupulously avoided, as much of his success may depend on his nerve and equanimity.

A fieldsman should be constantly on the alert—nothing looks more slovenly than a fielder with his hands in his pockets—and should watch every ball bowled with the utmost vigilance. Whatever may be the odds against effecting a catch, a fieldsman should always make a desperate try at anything approaching a chance. When a ball is in the air—whether it be a skier or a long low drive—the fieldsman in whose direction it is coming should never make up his mind that he cannot get to it. Directly he is determined where it is coming, he should run backwards or forwards to get to it. I have seen many a catch which was apparently hopeless brought off by a man who has made it his practice never to admit failure a foregone conclusion. Sometimes, for some mysterious reason, a ball seems to hang in the air and drop slowly, and the man who strains every nerve to get under it frequently dismisses the batsman by a brilliant and totally unexpected catch.

Every cricketer, whatever his standing, should unhesitatingly go to whatever position the bowler tells him, and when the "over" is called, he should return to the same spot. This may seem a detail, but attention to these small things makes all the difference between good and bad fielding. It is especially important for a fieldsman to remember the exact spot where he has been placed, as a bowler who uses his head often bowls a ball for the express purpose of tempting the batsman to hit it in a certain direction, and nothing annoys such a bowler more than to see a ball hit towards a point at which he had previously placed a fieldsman, and then to find that the fieldsman is some ten or twelve yards away from the spot to which he had been directed. Valuable opportunities are frequently thrown away through these little acts of negligence on the part of fieldsmen.

When an "over" is called, fieldsmen should assume their alternative positions with all possible despatch. If two slow bowlers should be bowling at the same time, a fieldsman at, say, long on or off, may have a considerable distance to traverse between the overs, and in this case he should take

the precaution of asking the bowler to wait
until he has assumed his proper position in the
field.

Every cheap treatise on cricket gives a diagram
showing the various positions of fieldsmen, and
this serves a beginner for a while, but as soon as
a cricketer has gained a little experience he will
learn to arrange the field according to the pecu-
liarities of the batsman and the character of the
bowling. Some batsmen are strong on the off-
side, others on the leg-side; and for them the field
must be arranged accordingly. In the same way,
the positions of the fieldsmen must be altered for
slow bowling. A little experience is the best guide
in this matter, and no arbitrary rules can possibly
be laid down.

Of course, in the arrangement of the field, the
bowler, if he has a mind of his own, and any
judgment at all, will be allowed to place his fieldsmen as he chooses. If the captain does not
acquiesce, trouble often ensues, as the bowler is
made unhappy and imagines that if a ball is hit
anywhere near a spot on which he wanted a fieldsman placed it would have been caught if he had
been allowed his own way. I have played with
not a few cricketers who had absolutely no idea of
how to place a field, and very little judgment as to
what sort of ball should be bowled for a particular
batsman. When Gloucestershire first started its
County Cricket club, and was carrying everything
before it—I think I am fully justified in claiming
that it did carry everything before it, when it is

remembered that for two years the county team
did not lose a single match—we had one of this
type of cricketer in the eleven. In those days
E. M. stood at point, and was by a long way the
best man I ever saw in that position—(though he
is my own brother I can say this conscientiously,
for most experts are undivided on the point)—
while I went to mid-on or mid-off, and when
this gentleman was bowling I occasionally whis-
pered, " Pitch him one up a little wide on the off."
The bowler—a smooth-tempered cricketer, who
did not resent a word of advice—had a remarkable
command over the ball, and he would accept my
suggestion, and pitch a ball just where I told him.
The result was often immediate.

This was really the starting-point of the " off
theory "—*i.e.*, the pitching of balls rather wide to
the off, and the placing of an extra cover-point in
the hope of catches. For many years this theory
was applied, and even in the present day some of
the slow left-hand bowlers adopt it, but batsmen
nowadays are more wary, and many of them, instead of hitting this ball to the off, pull it to leg.
E. M., Mr. W. W. Read and Mr. O. G. Radcliffe
played this stroke to perfection, and of late years
I have found it useful and much easier than I had
expected. It is not a stroke I recommend to
young cricketers, though old stagers at the game
may find it profitable. Of course, it must not be
forgotten that, in those early days of Gloucestershire County Cricket, we had some of the best
fieldsmen in England in our eleven, and that a

catch anywhere within their radius very seldom went a-begging.

When a young cricketer is placed at third man or at long leg, he should remember that a ball coming off the edge of the bat in either of these directions will twist in a most unaccountable way. Sometimes the ball will deviate a yard or even more, according to the spin it has received. Only experience at third man and long leg will teach youngsters how to allow for this mysterous twist and to field the ball properly. In my own experience I have noticed cricketers who ought to be at home anywhere in the field blundering outrageously in attempting to field at third man and long leg. I have seen them run straight to meet a ball, which immediately hit the ground, twisted sharply away from them so that they have not even touched it, let alone stopped it. The extent to which a fieldsman may be deceived by one of these curling balls can be forcibly illustrated by the simple statement that I have seen a man prepare to field a ball with his right hand which, in the end, he only just stopped with his left. For this reason long leg and third man are two of the most arduous positions in the field, and should only be occupied by reliable fieldsmen whose judgment is sufficiently sound to enable them to stop the ball, whether it deviates merely a few inches, or, as it does on some occasions, twists a yard or more.

CHAPTER XI

SOME OF MY CONTEMPORARIES

SINCE I commenced on my career a few thousand, more or less, notable men have figured in the cricket-field. Some of them have left names which stand out in the annals of a game like beacons on a hilltop; others have made a brief splash in the cricket world, and then sunk into oblivion. In this chapter, in which I purpose to gossip about my contemporaries, I shall make no attempt to be biographer to every cricketer of my time. My selection of a few of the men whom I regard as notable is not made in a haphazard manner, nor is it planned on an elaborate scale. There will be omissions by the score, due not to my personal choice, but to the inexorable limits to which I am tied by a volume of this character.

ROBERT ABEL (born at Rotherhithe, November 30, 1859) is a wonderful little cricketer. I remember Bobby when he first came out in 1881, and when he played for Surrey against Gloucestershire at the Oval that year I never imagined that he would ever be among our best professional batsmen. His style was poor, and he played badly, and he certainly gave no promise of his subsequent brilliance. In 1883 he began to improve rapidly, and in 1885 he did extremely well. Since that year, with scarcely an exception, he has stood high in the first-class averages, and in more than one season has been Surrey's principal run-getter. His innings of 357 not out against Somerset this May is the crowning feat of a great career. For a man of his height (5 ft. 5 in.) it is marvellous how he gets over the ball, especially as he plays with a crooked bat. I think his best stroke is a cut, but he drives well, and plays freely all round the wicket. Although at times he is rather slow, his batting is seldom dull to watch. At one time Bobby was one of the best short-slips in the cricket-field, but as he gets older he, like everybody else upon whom age is creeping, is not so safe in the field as he was, and at slip more than anywhere else a fieldsman needs to be particularly agile, and to have the best of eyesight. When Lohmann and Abel were in the slips together it was terribly difficult for a batsman to get a ball away in that direction. Abel was never a first-class bowler, but he often got a wicket when better bowlers had tried in vain. Bobby was one of Lord Sheffield's Team in Australia, and on the homeward voyage he was the hero of a comical incident. While waiting for mails at Aden, we amused ourselves by fishing and caught a number of fish with prickly fins and a sort of spike near their gills. My son, C. B., now at Clifton College, caught several of the fish, which I

took off the hooks.   In doing so the fish stabbed
my hand with their spikes. While we were fishing,
Abel came on deck, and one of the members of
our team picked up a fish and dropped it over
Bobby's shoulder. Somehow the fish got its spike
into his leg, and stuck there. Bobby, who had
been told that the fish belonged to a poisonous
variety, was in an awful funk. Bean sucked the
wound, and, as Bobby thought, saved his life.
Then he was put to bed, and poultices were
ordered, but poor Bobby was inconsolable, until
I showed him the wound which the fish had made
in my hand, and assured him that the fish were
harmless, as of course they were. On another
occasion, while in Australia, somebody killed a
harmless snake, and put it in Abel's bag. Bobby
had another fright when he found the creature
coiled up in his bag next morning. While we
were at Gippsland, a kangaroo and emu hunt was
arranged for us. Bobby joined in the sport, and
cut an amusing figure mounted on a fleet little
pony, to which he had to cling with one hand in
front and the other behind the saddle. Bobby
was to the front in the first run, because the pony
ran away with him, but he took care not to let it
break into a trot afterwards.

Mr. ARTHUR APPLEBY (born at Enfield, near
Accrington, July 22, 1843) was Lancashire's best
amateur bowler until A. G. Steel came upon the
scene. He made his reputation in local cricket,
then played for his county, and on several occasions represented the Gentlemen against the

Players. He bowled a fast ball with a good off
break, and had a beautiful left-hand action. He
was not a reliable bat, and he took more pride in
his bowling than in batting. Unfortunately his
business responsibilities took him out of the
cricket-field at an early age, and made it impossible for him to accept repeated invitations to
accompany English teams to Australia. He was
one of Mr. R. A. Fitzgerald's Twelve in Canada
and America in 1872, and distinguished himself
on several occasions, particularly at Ottawa, where
he got eleven wickets for 3 runs. As the result
of a chaffing remark, he was generally known as
the " Tormentor "—a *sobriquet* which stuck to him
for many years. His bowling feat at Ottawa inspired a Canadian rhymester to enshrine Appleby's ·
name in song :—

" Here's the left-handed bowler—that Lancashire swell—
  Whom Ottawa batsmen remember so well.
  He bowled a whole innings (and bowled like great guns),
  In Apple-pie order for—only three runs."

Poor Appleby : his bowling always inspired the
poets (?). I'm not sure that it wasn't the poets
who drove him out of cricket.

Mr. C. W. ALCOCK (born at Sunderland, December 2, 1842) is well known as Secretary of the Surrey
County Cricket Club, but before he entered on
secretarial duties in 1872 he had distinguished
himself in the football field. His knowledge of
cricket and cricketers is profound and comprehensive. He is a cricket encyclopædia, full of

reliable information and is always ready to serve cricket by any means in his power.   The service he has rendered to visiting teams for Australia and America have won him friends in far-distant lands, while his geniality, courtesy and ability as Secretary of the Surrey Club have made him deservedly popular among frequenters of the Oval.   Surrey has had its up and downs during his Secretaryship, but the Club was never more prosperous than it is to-day, with its membership of about 4000.   Mr. Alcock is an old Public School boy, having received his education at Harrow (1855–59).   At school he played no games until his last year, when he took to football.   He and his brother were the founders of the Forest Football Club, which was practically the first football club on any organised basis.   It existed for four years, and was then merged into a club called the Wanderers, whose members were all Public School men.   Mr. Alcock was elected captain of the first three International Association Football matches, but was kept out of the field by illness, and only played in the third match.   He captained the Wanderers for many years, during which period the club won the Cup five times out of the first seven years after its institution.   As centre-forward he had no superior.   He played the Rugby game well enough to represent Blackheath on one occasion.

Mr. Alcock is very fond of telling two stories against me.   In our younger days he often came down to Downend and stayed with my father and mother. On one occasion he and my brother Fred and my brother-in-law, John Dann, were following the Duke of Beaufort's hounds, and to save climbing a hill cut along a valley. Alcock says he looked up and saw me and the grey horse I was riding go head over heels. They all three saw me tumble, and I got chaffed for a good many years about my horsemanship.

The other story—also against myself—I must give in Mr. Alcock's own words—my version of it spoils the joke. " Once," he says, " W. G. played football on Clapham Common, when the Wanderers were playing a match against the Rovers. I was centre-forward, and had got the ball right in front of the Rovers' goal, and was just going to kick it between the posts when, in his great big rough sort of way, W. G. bowled me over and kicked the goal himself. It was "—Mr. Alcock always adds—" the most blackguard thing that ever happened to me in the whole course of a long sporting career." All I can say is that my behaviour on that occasion was not half as bad as Alcock's when playing at the Oval v. Scotland. In those days you were allowed to use your shoulders, and the way Alcock used to knock over a fellow when he was trying to pass him I shall never forget. A friend of mine said Alcock made catherine-wheels of those fellows.

Mr. ALEXANDER CHAMBERS BANNERMAN (born March 21, 1854) was one of the famous Australian Team of 1878, the first of the series to visit England, and no one who ever saw Alec

Bannerman bat will forget him. He was a stonewaller of the most stubborn type, and vexed
the soul of every bowler who opposed him. His
defence was invulnerable, and though he was
a treasure to his side he was tedious to watch.
But though he would sometimes stay at the
wickets for two hours for as many runs, he could
punish loose bowling with great severity. His
patience was inexhaustible and his zeal for the
game unbounded. George Giffen tells a story of
an erratic lightsome player who brought upon
himself the censure of Alec Bannerman by
beguiling the time between the overs by singing
music-hall ditties. " Do you know," asked Alec
with severity, "you are playing cricket ? If you
want to play cricket play it, and if you want to
sing go and sing, but for Heaven's sake don't
sing comic songs in the slips." The story was
characteristic of Alec Bannerman, who played
cricket as if dear life hung upon it. He was a
rattling good field, especially at mid-off, and threw
in with great precision and smartness.

WILLIAM ATTEWELL (born at Keyworth, June 12,
1861) has represented his county since 1881, and
has done good service at Lord's, where he is
on the staff. He is one of the most, if not the
most, successful bowlers England has ever sent to
Australia. He bowls right-handed at a medium
pace with a high delivery, and exercises a great
command over the ball. His action is so easy
and graceful that bowling seems no effort to him,
and he is capable of keeping up a good length

throughout a long innings. Aitewell is a bowler who never gives his captain any trouble. When in Australia with Lord Sheffield's Eleven he was always willing to change ends, however well he was bowling, if another bowler had a preference for the end at which he was bowling. He always does his best, working hard and loyally, and is one of the best type of professional cricketers. Occasionally he has proved a useful bat, and if he had paid more attention to batting might have been a fine batsman.

RICHARD GORTON BARLOW (born at Bolton, May 28, 1850) was the Lancashire stonewaller for twenty years. The story goes that Barlow was originally a porter at a country railway station in the North, and was "discovered" by a gentleman, greatly interested in Lancashire cricket, who found himself stranded at the station with three hours to wait for the next train. He asked the station-master what he could do in the interval, and received the reply, "You can join us in a game of cricket if you like. Come and have a bowl at our porter ; he's been batting for six weeks, and we can't get him out." The story may not be true— I don't vouch for it—but I'm not sure that Barlow was not quite capable of keeping up his wicket for six weeks. He had the most stubborn defence I ever saw, and of patience he had no end. Once, when Mr. Justice Hawkins had been listening to a barrister making a long prosy speech, he sent down a note to a friend sitting among the counsel engaged in the case. The note contained the following words : "Award of Merit in the Patience Competition—Mr. Justice Hawkins, 1st; Job, nowhere." Barlow's batting gave one the impression that he would excel even Sir Henry Hawkins in patience. His play was monotony incarnate, and could be relied on to send spectators to sleep on a sultry day. I have seen Mr. A. N. Hornby, who always opened the Lancashire innings with Barlow, score a century while his partner made a tedious dozen—principally in singles. Stonewallers have their uses, but it is a blessing that Nature is sparing with the supply of the requisite patience necessary for making a stonewaller. One in a team is sometimes very useful, but a second is more than spectators can stand. Barlow once, to my knowledge, took two hours and a half to score five—an average of one run for every thirty minutes—and on another occasion batted one hour and twenty minutes for a duck. A record surely ! He bowled left round-arm medium pace, kept very straight and a good length, and was a very useful bowler, and when the wicket was at all cut up he often bowled with deadly effect. His fielding was excellent, as he was always on the alert. He was left out of the Lancashire team long before he had lost all form.

Barlow went through his cricket career without making a pair of spectacles. He and I share, I think, the monopoly of that honour. Barlow kept an athletic requisite establishment in Manchester, and tells a good tale of a man coming into his shop and asking, " Do you keep a full supply of cricket requisites?" "Certainly," replied Barlow. "Then let me have a bottle of arnica, three penn'oth of court plaister, two yards of bandaging lint, and an arm sling. I'm playing in a cricket match against Jack Crossland this afternoon." Barlow generally opened the innings for Lancashire with his captain, Mr. A. N. Hornby, as partner. Both were incorrigible run-stealers, and had such a reputation for running each other out that spectators at Old Trafford used to bet on which would run the other out.

WILLIAM BARNES (born at Sutton-in-Ashfield, Notts, May 27, 1852: died April 1899) played for his native county for over twenty years, and was at one time by far the best all-round professional Notts could put in the field. He was a reliable bat, an effective bowler, and a sound fieldsman, and in all three departments served not only his county but the M.C.C., the Players, and England. His batting was marked by clean hitting, especially on the off-side—a "late cut" was his *forte*—and his scoring, when once he got comfortable, was often very rapid. His 266 for M.C.C. against Leicestershire in 1882, when Midwinter and he put on 473 runs in five and a half hours, was his most brilliant effort, but he scored a century and upwards almost every season. His fast medium bowling with a slight off-break was deadly on a damaged wicket, and when in form with the ball he performed some extraordinary feats. He went to America in 1879, to Australia in 1882, and again in 1884, when he headed

both the batting and bowling averages of the tour,
and once more in 1886, when he was second in
the batting and first in the bowling averages.

Mr. JOHN MCCARTHY BLACKHAM (born May 11,
1855) was the finest wicket-keeper Australia has
produced, and when at his best was never surpassed. He was discovered by Conway, who
brought the first Australian Team to England
in 1878, and in twenty years represented Australia thirty-four times in test matches. His
reliability as a wicket-keeper was marvellous.
Clean, quick as lightning, and quiet, he stood as
close to the wickets as the laws of cricket permit
and took the fastest bowling with consummate
ease. To stand up to Spofforth's fastest bowling
was in itself an achievement, but to keep wicket
against the Demon without permitting a bye to
pass was a phenomenal performance. The batsman who stirred out of his ground when Blackham
was at the wicket knew he had to hit the ball or
his innings was over. There was no element of
chance in Blackham's stumping ; it was a case of
inevitability. His hands might get damaged, or
the ball might bump on a rough wicket, but
Blackham was upon it. Pilling was his only rival
behind the wicket, and Pilling was only in the
cricket-field for a few years, while Blackham
stuck to his guns for twenty. Moreover, as a batsman he was an eleventh-man-in of whom it was
never safe to assume that he would soon be dismissed. He was not a pretty bat, but I confess
that he saved his side in many an emergency, and

would hit out with a fine recklessness which dismayed his opponents. As a captain he was a failure, as, owing to his nervous, high-strung temperament he worried himself and his men over trivialities and fretted his heart out with needless anxiety as to the result of matches.

Mr. GEORGE J. BONNOR (born February 25, 1855) was one of the grandest specimens of manhood that ever stepped upon a cricket-ground. As a lady spectator once said of him in an audible voice, he was "a beauty." Six feet six he stood, erect, broad-shouldered, straight-limbed, splendidly proportioned—a giant of strength and an Apollo of grace. His own strength he scarcely knew, but when he got a ball well in the centre of his bat people made guesses as to the horse-power he had put behind it. When he threw in from the long fields the ball whistled as it clove the air. On the day he landed at Plymouth, in 1882, Bonnor established a record by throwing a cricket-ball 119 yards, and thereby won a bet of £100 from some one who had doubted his ability to throw it 115 yards. It is said that on another occasion he threw the ball 130 yards. But Bonnor will be remembered for his hitting. He was the C. I. Thornton of Australia, and while in England he gave us many a taste of his powers. Once, at Cambridge, he made 66 (including four 6's) in half an hour; again, at Scarborough, against I Zingari, he made 20 runs off one over. He was a born "siogger," but somehow he got the notion into his head that he could bat with scientific patience. It was rubbish; he was made to smite for all he was worth, and could no more play slow cricket than R. G. Barlow could "slog." His temperament was against patient batting, while his enormous reach and tremendous strength designed him for "hitting." Two of the most memorable catches ever seen in the cricket-field were made off strokes by Bonnor. One was the famous catch (to which I have referred elsewhere) by which my brother G. F. dismissed Bonnor in 1880. The other was a catch made by George Ulyett at Lord's. Ulyett was bowling to Bonnor, who got a ball well on the blade of his bat, and drove it with terrific force. Ulyett put up his hand, but the spectators waited to see the ball dropping somewhere out of the ground, when to their amazement they saw Ulyett quietly drop the ball and examine his hand. The wonder was that the impact of the ball coming at express speed had not shattered Ulyett's hand, but the old Yorkshire bowler merely remarked that it was a good job he caught it, as if it had hit his fingers there would have been no more cricket for him that year. As to Bonnor, he looked thunderstruck at being caught off such a hit.

Mr. HENRY FREDERICK BOYLE (born December 10, 1847) was a member of the first Australian Team which came to England in 1878, and with Spofforth shared the bowling in the memorable match against the M.C.C., when the Australians first showed us the stuff of which they were made. On that occasion (when the M.C.C. Eleven was dismissed for 19) Boyle had a better average than Spofforth, getting six wickets for 3 runs, and headed the bowling averages of the 1882 tour with 144 wickets, obtained at a cost of 11.98 runs apiece. Boyle was a medium-pace right-hand bowler, breaking both ways. No matter how severely he was punished—and occasionally he did get punished—he kept up a superb length, and bowled doggedly on without slackening his energy. Boyle could bat with freedom, and in the field was exceptionally brilliant, especially at short mid-on, then a new position colloquially known as "Boyley's silly mid-on." Though he ran great risks in standing so close to the wicket and in the direction of on-drives, he always said he could use his hands to protect his body, and often miraculously escaped injury. He visited England four times—in 1878, 1880, 1882, and 1884, and on each occasion met with marked success with the ball.

JOHN BRIGGS (born at Sutton-in-Ashfield, Notts, October 3, 1862) has for many years been one of the best all-round players. At one time an English representative Eleven would be incomplete without the little Lancashire professional, who excels in batting, bowling and fielding. He began his first-class cricket career as a batsman, but gradually rose from the position of change bowler to the mainstay of his county team. He bowls left handed at a medium or slow pace, breaking both ways at will and capable of perplexing the most confident batsman on a sticky wicket ; he bats

right-handed, and in spite of his diminutive stature
(5 ft. 5 in.) plays with wonderful freedom all
round the wicket. The way he can take a high
long hop at a level with his head and bang it to
the boundary greatly surprises spectators who
see him for the first time. In the field he is as
agile as a cat, and in fielding his own bowling
does the work of mid-off and mid-on as well.
When not bowling he generally stands at cover-
point, and in that position has few equals and, as
far as I know, no superior. Moreover, he is the
soul of energy, and his endurance seems inexhaustible. He is game and alert from beginning
to end of a match, and seems all the happier when
he is kept incessantly at work. Good-humoured
and full of vitality, he is one of the "characters"
of the cricket-field. His merry antics—sometimes carried a little too far—make him extremely
popular. "Let's give Johnny a clap" generally
goes round the ground when Briggs comes out to
bat. Briggs visited Australia in 1884 and 1886,
1887, 1891, 1894, and 1897—indeed since 1884 he
has been one of the first men to be selected for
every team going out to the colony. He was one
of Lord Sheffield's Team, which I captained in
Australia in 1891, and was one of the mainstays of
our bowling. Peel and he (both left-handers)
between them did most of the bowling, and when
the wicket was good it was often a question
with me as to which was to go on first, and
for a curious reason. On apparently similar
wickets Peel would fail when Johnny was doing

brilliantly, while on another day Peel would carry everything before him when Johnny could do nothing. The why and the wherefore of it all were a puzzle to me, as it happened not once but many times, and I could never determine which was the right man to put on bowling, as both seemed to bowl equally well, but with fluctuating results. Briggs is one of the best head-bowlers we have ever had. He varies nearly every ball in an over, and if he has any fault it is the fault of trying to do too much with the ball. Johnny is sometimes a very dangerous bat, but as a rule he slashes and cuts at the ball immediately he gets to the wicket. If he does make a hit the ball generally goes to the boundary, but too often he gets caught in the slips. When out in Australia he played beautiful cricket in the first match— making 90 before he was dismissed—but throughout the rest of the tour he went in for slashing hitting. He would go in and return to the pavilion in a few minutes, and if you had not seen how he got out it was generally safe to assume that he had been caught at slip.

One good story about Johnny occurs to my mind. He was playing against the Australians at Leighton, Wiltshire, for Mr. Laverton's Eleven, and on the third morning of the match joined a small party of us who went out rook shooting. Johnny enjoyed the fun immensely, and when he got back to the cricket-ground bounced a good deal about his shooting. But at lunch time his happiness vanished as a policeman served him with a summons for shooting without a licence. Moreover, the summons was made returnable at Leighton on the first day of the Gloucestershire *v.* Lancashire match, in which Briggs was, of course, engaged. Mold, who had been one of the shooting-party, was included in the joke, but somehow he got wind of the ruse. Of course the summons was a dummy, but, as it was written on a proper summons form, Johnny was completely taken in. We kept the joke up for some time, and while Briggs believed that the summons was genuine he got plenty of offers of bail.

WILLIAM BROCKWELL (born January 21, 1866) lost his chance of distinguishing himself until he was twenty-seven years of age, owing to the fact that Surrey had almost a plethora of first-rate cricketers, and could not give him a fair opportunity until 1893—although he had played for his county as far back as 1886. His path to fame was thus beset with obstacles, but when in 1893 he was regularly included in the Surrey Eleven, he leaped to the front by capital all-round work and was selected to play for England in the test match at Manchester that season. But better things were still in store for Brockwell, and in 1894 he met with great success, making scores exceeding the century on no fewer than five occasions—all at the Oval—and by topping the batting averages with an aggregate of 1491 runs. An invitation to join Mr. Stoddard's first Australian team was the immediate result of the grand form he had shown, but he scarcely maintained his reputation. Since 1894 he has been one of the mainstays of Surrey's batting, and seldom fails to make a useful contribution to the score. Along with Bobby Abel, Brockwell in August 1897 scored 379 for the first wicket for Surrey against Hampshire—Brockwell's individual innings eventually realising 225 ; while in the same year the same batsmen made 204 for the first wicket in Surrey *v.* Warwickshire at Birmingham. Brockwell is deservedly popular among spectators, who appreciate his attractive style, his splendid defence, and his spirited hitting. One of his prettiest strokes is a late cut between short and deep slip. The way he manages to guide it through the slips is delightful to watch. Brockwell is a good change bowler, and on occasion has given Surrey timely assistance in this department, and he is an exceedingly smart fieldsman in the slips or long field. He commands the respect and esteem of every one who knows him by his gentlemanly bearing, geniality and modesty.

J. T. BROWN (born at Driffield, August 20, 1869) began playing for Yorkshire in 1889, when he was twenty years of age, but his powers matured slowly, and it was not until 1893 and 1894 that his batting attracted any considerable notice. In 1893 he headed the county averages, and by scoring 712 runs materially contributed to Yorkshire's triumph. In 1894 he did even better still, and indeed took rank among our best professional batsmen by scoring 1397 runs in first-class cricket, and by making upwards of a century on three occasions. Since 1894 he has improved steadily, and is now equal to Shrewsbury and Gunn at their best. Some of Brown's great achievements are historic. His score of 203 against Middlesex in May 1895, when he and Tunnicliffe put on 139 for the first wicket, and then in the second innings made the 147 runs necessary to secure the victory for Yorkshire without being separated, was a remarkable feat. In 1897 the same two batsmen, playing against Sussex at Sheffield, scored 378 before the first wicket fell, while Brown carried his individual total up to 311. But both these feats pale into insignificance before the memorable first-wicket stand by the same batsmen against Derbyshire in August 1898, when they stayed together while 554 runs were scored —a record partnership for any wicket in first-class cricket. On that occasion Brown made 300, and then hit his wicket with the deliberate purpose of closing his innings. Brown, like all batsmen, is at his best on hard wickets, but even when rain has damaged the turf he often succeeds in defying the bowlers and compiling a big score. His defence is excellent and the number of his strokes is almost legion. He hits high balls with remarkable skill, considering his height, and scores all round the wicket with confidence and freedom. The way he manages to make runs off short bumping balls or balls that rise rapidly off the ground is very notable. He accompanied Mr. Stoddart's first team to Australia, and batted creditably throughout the tour. At point he is a great fieldsman, often bringing off brilliant catches. He bowls slow round-arm leg-breaks, and when put on generally takes a wicket or two.

Mr. JAMES ARTHUR BUSH (born in India, at Cawnpore, July 28, 1850, and educated at Clifton College) was one of the best amateur wicket-keepers of his day, and played for Gloucestershire for many years both in the cricket and football field. He accompanied the team I took to Australia in 1873–74 and kept wicket so well out there that on his return to England he was selected to keep wicket for the Gentlemen against the Players, and right well did he do it. "Frizzy" not only played cricket well, but at football he took a lot of beating. He learnt his football, like his cricket, at Clifton College. After leaving the College he played for the Clifton and Bedminster Football Club, where he sometimes played three-quarters, but his proper place was forward. He worked like a lion, being a good runner, and his tackling was very safe. He played for England *v.* Scotland in 1872–74–75–76, and no doubt would have done so in 1873 if he had not been in Australia. Bush was a splendid place-kicker, and I have seen him kick many a goal when you would have thought it impossible. After giving up Rugby football for some years, he started playing the Association game, and "Frizzy" as a goal-keeper and kicker-off was as good as any one could be.

WILLIAM CAFFYN (born at Reigate, February 2, 1828) was a member of the first English team to visit Australia.   Of the twelve men who went out under H. H. Stephenson in 1862, Caffyn and T. Hearne are, I think, the only survivors.   Caffyn was the pillar of Surrey's strength for many years before County Cricket had any organised existence, and was one of the finest players of his time.   He was a reliable bat, a capital bowler, and a sure field.   When Stephenson's team returned, Caffyn remained in Australia, and by coaching and example he helped to raise the standard of colonial cricket.   He returned to England, but although he played for Surrey he never again took his place amongst the leading first-class cricketers. Since writing the above, the old man—now over seventy—has published his reminiscences of cricket under the attractive title, "71, not out."   It is an interesting volume, especially in its relation to cricket in the middle of the century, concerning which no living man is more competent to speak.

RICHARD DAFT (born at Nottingham, November 2, 1835) is one of the few cricketers—Diver of Warwickshire is the only other man I can think of—who entered first-class cricket as an amateur and then became a professional.   At a later stage in his career he became an amateur once more. When most professionals excelled in bowling and neglected batting, Daft was distinguished in the batting department.   He was one of the most elegant bats I have ever played with, and though he had done most of his best work before I entered the cricket-field, I have vivid recollections of his graceful and stylish batting.   His confident hitting and his incomparable defence always excited my admiration. In 1867, and again in 1870, he had an average of over 50, but I believe I am right in saying that he never scored a thousand runs in a season ; but in those days very few matches were played. During the period that he captained Nottingham the county invariably took a high place among the counties, and on two occasions won the Championship. He is now a first-class umpire, and takes as keen an interest in cricket as ever.

Mr. NORMAN F. DRUCE (born January 1, 1875) leaped into fame while a comparative boy, and soon matured into a brilliant batsman. He began to excel with the bat when at Marlborough, and got his "Blue" without delay at Cambridge. The season of 1895 saw him in grand form, and though he did not rise to the occasion in the University match, he did brilliantly for the Gentlemen against the Players at both Lord's and the Oval. 1896 was an off-year with him, but in 1897, when he captained Cambridge, he had an average of 66 runs per innings and scored 227 not out against C. I. Thornton's Eleven—the largest score ever made on Fenner's Ground. He went out to Australia with Stoddart's Team in 1897, and scored consistently. He has not yet distinguished himself in County Cricket, though he played for Surrey during two seasons ; but he is still a young man, and may yet be expected to take a good place in County Cricket. He is a grand field, and when at Cambridge brought off some very fine catches at short-slip.

THOMAS EMMETT (born at Halifax, September 3, 1841) was at once one of the most popular and proficient professional cricketers of his time. "Tom" deserves a biographer who can do justice to himself and his performances, for he was an odd "character" as well as a first-rate cricketer. He is the hero of a hundred good stories, as he was the life and soul of every team of which he was a member. His great bowling feats are legion in number—so numerous that to enumerate even a few would give a very inadequate idea of the man and his work. Fast round-arm left-hand with a high delivery, curious and puzzling in itself, a leg-break varying from an inch to a foot— that describes his bowling, but the description is incomplete if no mention is made of Tom's extraordinary antics, of his quaint appearance, and erratic recklessness. As a rule, when Tom went on to bowl he sent down two or three wides— not doubtful wides, but thoroughly out-and-out, unquestionable, glaring wides. This was generally called "Tom's preliminary canter," and Tom's comrades smiled at the eccentricity, because they knew that at any moment he might send down a ball which it would pass the power of any batsman to play. He had one impossible ball— it pitched between the batsman's leg and the wicket, and breaking towards the off would just displace the bails. Tom almost invariably got my wicket when he bowled that ball (happily it was not a ball he could put in very often), but I always took consolation from the thought that that particular ball would beat any batsman on earth. Emmett bowled on the "off" theory before it became fashionable, and many a capital bat fell a victim to a ball he used to send to the off with a deceptive break to the off, which, when the batsman touched it with the edge of his bat, gave an easy chance in the slips. Tom Emmett bowling was a terror, but Tom Emmett batting was a sight for the gods. He was reckless and excited as a rule when he began his innings, and would start for a run immediately he touched the ball, never thinking to look where it had gone, or caring whether it had been fielded. I remember throwing down his wicket on one occasion when, having just played a ball to short-slip, he set out for a run. If he survived the first two or three overs he generally batted with conspicuous skill, his driving being especially fine. For one story of Tom I must find space, though readers with memories extending over ten or fifteen years will remember that it was then current among cricketers. Tom was batting for England against Gloucestershire in 1878 and Frank Townsend was bowling his curly lobs. Emmett made a show of contempt for underhands, and held his bat up over his shoulder, and left alone one or two balls on the off. At last Townsend got a ball to break in more than usual and it hit his off stump. Emmett, apparently mortified at his own stupidity, walked back to the pavilion in high dudgeon. Some one went up to him and asked, "What is the matter, Tom?" "Don't you 'Tom' me," was the answer. "Well, Emmett, then." "Don't you 'Emmett' me." "Well, then, *Mr.* Emmett." " Don't you *'Mister'* me." "What must I call you then?" "Why," replied Tom, bursting with inward wrath, "you must call me a stupid fool." Emmett played for Yorkshire and captained the team until he was forty-six, and even then was in very fair form. He went to Australia with the 1876, 1878, and 1881 teams, and played for the Players on many occasions. He had any number of friends and no enemies, and he was sadly missed when his first-class cricketing-days ended.

Mr. CHARLES B. FRY (born April 25, 1872) is, I should say, the best all-round athlete in England. As a long jumper he astounded the world by his extraordinary leap in the University Sports in 1892; as a sprint runner he carried off cups and trophies in great numbers; as an Association footballer he has won his International Cap as well as a University "Blue"; while as a cricketer he made his reputation as a schoolboy at Repton, improved it at Oxford, and has established himself as one of the best amateur batsmen playing in first-class cricket. He was captain of the Oxford Eleven which in 1893 won a brilliant victory by eight wickets over Cambridge, and contributed to that result by scoring 100 not out. His services to Sussex have been invaluable. His batting is free and stylish and his hitting hard and clean. He fields brilliantly, and up to last year bowled with considerable success, but his delivery was condemned by the umpires last season. Fry is one of the most genial and popular amateurs in the cricket-field.

Mr. GEORGE GIFFEN (born at Adelaide, March 27, 1859) was one of the finest all-round cricketers Australia ever sent to England. With both bat and ball his success was unequivocal. When I first went to Australia in 1873–74, George Giffen, then a boy of fifteen, was living in Adelaide, and when the Englishmen were practising at the nets young Giffen amused himself by bowling to us. In his own capital book, "With Bat and Ball," he speaks of the pride which animated him when he was permitted to send an occasional ball to me. "Never in my life," he says, "did I try more earnestly to secure a wicket than I did when bowling at Grace's team in practice, but I had to be content then with getting an odd ball past the striker without once hitting the sticks, and pleased enough was I with the measure of success." As Giffen adds, he never dreamed then that in a few years he would be bowling against me in serious though friendly conflict. But, after some five years of second-class cricket, Giffen made his *début* in an inter-colonial match, and when James Lillywhite's team went to Australia the redoubtable George was chosen to play for South Australia. His repeated successes for South Australia led to his selection for the Australian team, which visited England and went back with a splendid record, to which Giffen had contributed handsomely. In 1884 and 1886 he was with us again, and seemed to have improved during each period of absence. Indeed, in 1886 he topped the Australian averages in both batting and bowling. In 1891 he scored 271 against Victoria for South Australia, and in 1893 and 1896 he revisited England, still the same superb bat and brilliant bowler. He was not a good captain, as he never knew when to take himself off, and always seemed to think that the best possible change of attack was for him to give up bowling at one end and go on at the other. Once at Sydney, in 1884, Giffen achieved the great feat, then unique in Australian first-class cricket, of taking all ten wickets in one innings, and on three occasions he has performed the "hat trick" in first-class cricket.

WILLIAM GUNN (born at Nottingham, December 4, 1858) is beyond all doubt one of the greatest professional batsmen England has seen. It is a little curious to recall now that Gunn's first engagement as a professional cricketer was as a ground bowler at Lord's. He was late in coming to the front as a batsman, for though he gave early promise his powers matured slowly. Once ripened, however, they have never faded. He has made a thousand runs in a season for the last twelve years, and, though he is now forty-one years of age, he looks as if he were going on for ever. Nottingham has had the benefit of his invaluable services for nearly twenty years, but some of his grandest achievements have been in representative matches. His scores of 228 for the Players against the Australians—the highest individual score made against an Australian team in England—of 169 against the Gentlemen at Hastings in 1891, of 139 at Lord's in the Gentlemen v. Players match of 1898, his partnership with Shrewsbury when 398 runs were scored against Sussex in 1891, his partnership with Shrewsbury in the Smokers v. Non-Smokers match at Melbourne in 1887, when this redoubtable pair of batsmen made 310 before they were separated, and his partnership with Barnes for the M.C.C. against Yorkshire in 1885, when 330 runs were put together, are a few of his best feats. But even more remarkable than these performances was the regularity with which he made thirties, forties, and fifties for Nottingham. Gunn's batting is a revelation in patience. He scores at an almost uniform pace throughout an innings, and makes his last twenty in a prolonged innings with all the care he bestowed on the first twenty. Six feet three inches high, he has an enormous reach, and he plays forward with great precision. In the long field he covers an extraordinary amount of ground, and is as safe a catch as we have in England. Of course he misses catches now and again, but I should not advise any one to give him a chance if they wish to continue their innings.

Lord HARRIS (born at Trinidad, February 3, 1851) permitted political ambition to interrupt a brilliant cricketing career. It is the only bad thing I know about Lord Harris, whom I knew when he was the Hon. George Harris, and whom I am proud to have had for a friend for many long

years. We were comrades together in Mr. R. A.
Fitzgerald's Canadian tour in 1872, and colleagues
or opponents on hundreds of subsequent occasions. He was always the same—a rare sportsman, a true-hearted gentleman, and a keen
cricketer. His cricket career began at Eton and
he played for Oxford in his undergraduate days,
but his best work and thought was thrown into
Kent County Cricket, of which he was at one time
President, Captain and Secretary combined.
How much he did for cricket generally I cannot
here say, but he was one of its best supporters.
Up to 1885, when he became Under Secretary for
India, he played cricket regularly, but from that
year, until his term of office as Governor of
Bombay expired in 1895, first-class cricket was
crowded out of his life by Governmental duties.
He was a free and stylish bat—in 1884 he scored
1417 runs in forty-two innings—a brilliant field, and
a fair change bowler.   He played cricket for the
love of the game, and got more delight out of a
close finish than an overwhelming victory. Once,
I remember, when I wanted a few runs to complete a century in both innings of a match which
could not be finished, he put on an underhand
bowler, so that I might, as he said, get out or complete the hundred before " Time" was called.   It
was just one of those chivalrous little acts which
mark the true sportsman.   Lord Harris took an
English team to Australia in 1878.

THOMAS HAYWARD (born at Cambridge,
March 19, 1871) comes of a cricketing stock, and

has added lustre to the name which was borne by his father, Daniel Hayward, the old Cambridgeshire cricketer, and his uncle, Thomas Hayward, who in the sixties was unrivalled among professional batsmen. Tom Hayward, the son and nephew of this famous pair, learned his cricket in connection with the Y.M.C.A. at Cambridge, which has produced some first-rate oarsmen as well as good cricketers. He qualified by residence to play for Surrey, and in 1893 made his first appearance in the County Eleven. In his second match—against Leicestershire—he made 100, and at the end of the season the Surrey authorities realised that in the young professional they had found a batsman of incalculable value, for in his first season of first-class cricket he scored 637 runs. He slightly improved his average in 1894, and since then has gone on from better to the best form. He has done many brilliant things, but his greatest triumph has been his not-out innings of 315 against Lancashire at the Oval in 1898. His consistent run-getting and good fielding fairly won him his place in test matches this season. Hayward is a stylish bat as well as a good scorer. He cuts and hits with freedom, and yet at the same time has an almost invulnerable defence.

JOHN THOMAS HEARNE (born at Chalfont St. Giles, May 3, 1867) came of the Buckinghamshire branch of a family whose deeds in the cricket-field have made their surname famous. The nephew of Old Tom and George Hearne, and the cousin of Alec Hearne, might have been expected to do something creditable in the cricket-field, but "Jack" has exceeded all expectations. He was tried by Middlesex in a tentative way as early as 1888, but it was not until 1890 that he got into the county team. Since 1891, when he took 118 wickets for 10.39 runs apiece, and came out top of the first-class bowling averages, he has been indispensable to the metropolitan county. Ten years' hard work has not revealed any deterioration from his original form, and in almost any England team he is sure of a place as long as his bowling maintains its standard. On a sticky wicket he has no superior, while even on hard wickets his excellent length and varied pace and deceptive break make him formidable. His height and high delivery make his bowling leave the ground very rapidly. He is one of the few bowlers who have got into form early this season, which he has opened auspiciously by a marvellous bowling feat against Somerset. Jack Hearne has the virtue of patience—he will bowl for hours without fatigue and without sending down many loose balls, and he seems, like George Lohmann, to feel always confident that he will get the wickets. He has visited Africa, India and Australia, is a capital shot, a fairly good horseman, and a rare sportsman in all respects. Genial, good-natured, and courteous, he is respected throughout the cricket world.

Mr. HERBERT TREMENHEERE HEWETT (born at Horton Court, Taunton, May 25, 1864) is admittedly one of the finest left-handed batsmen in England. An Harrovian and Oxford man, he first won some little renown in Public School and 'Varsity Cricket, but it was not until he joined Somersetshire that he forced himself to a prominent place in County Cricket. As captain of the Somersetshire team he materially assisted his county in the bold bid it made for supremacy, and at the same time he leaped to the front among amateur batsmen. Left-handers are not, as a rule, attractive batsmen, but Mr. Hewett is an exception, his dashing and fearless hitting atoning for any awkwardness of style. In 1892 he was third in the amateur batting averages, but distinguished himself most by a wonderful innings against Yorkshire, when he made 201 himself, and in association with Mr. L. C. H. Palairet established a new record in first-class cricket by putting on 346 runs for the first wicket.

Mr. ALBERT NEILSON HORNBY (born at Blackburn, February 10, 1847) is another of the rare good sportsmen I have been lucky enough to include among my friends. At cricket and football, with the gun and in the saddle, he was equally in his element—always keen, invariably good-humoured, and seldom beaten. His cricket reputation dated from his school-days at Harrow, but his best work was devoted to Lancashire. How he captained the county team during some of its palmiest days and led his men from victory unto victory every one knows. He was a model cricketer, game from first to last, daunted by no difficulties, and cheerful under adversity. His batting was of the dashing variety, and he often lost his wicket through trying to hit out in the first minute of his innings. I should not hesitate to say that A. N. Hornby stole more runs than any cricketer of his time. Sometimes he would literally play tip and run, and I've often heard batsmen say that he ran them off their legs. It is years ago now, but I never forget being at the wickets with him at Prince's Ground. For half an hour we ran immediately the other touched a ball. Some of the attempts we made were suicidal, but we kept it up with impunity till I had such a narrow escape of being run out that I protested against running further risks. In 1881 and 1882, when he was at his best, Hornby made over a thousand runs in the season—in the former year heading the first-class averages. In the field he was superb, especially at cover-point and long-leg. I am glad to see that his son, who made a promising *début* in first-class cricket by playing for Lancashire against the M.C.C. early in May of this year, is likely to carry on his father's traditions. They also tell me he is, like his father, fond of a short run.

Lord HAWKE (born at Gainsborough, Lincolnshire, August 16, 1860) has been a good friend to cricket for the last twenty years, and still influences what I again call the "politics" of the game. He began his cricket at Eton, getting in the Eleven in his fourth year; he then went to Cambridge, and in 1882, 1883, and 1885 played for the 'Varsity *v.* Oxford, being captain of the team in 1885, and made his *début* in County Cricket in 1881. He took up the captaincy of the Yorkshire team in 1883, and succeeded in introducing an *esprit de corps*, and standard of discipline, from the absence of which the county club had been suffering. In his first year as captain Yorkshire went to the top of the tree, to which place it had not attained for many years, but which it has since occupied on many occasions. He is a splendid captain, inspiring his men by the example he gives them of pluck and resource. He bats with great confidence, hitting hard, and driving, especially on the on side, in fine style. He went out to Australia— he was then the Hon. M. B. Hawke—as captain of Mr. G. F. Vernon's team in 1887, but on the death of his father returned home before the completion of the tour. He has captained two English amateur teams in India (1889 and 1892), two in America and Canada (1890 and 1894), two in South Africa (1895 and 1898), and one to the West Indies (1896), so that in various ways he has materially assisted in extending the area of the cricket-playing world.

Mr. F. STANLEY JACKSON (born November 21, 1870) has in turn captained Harrow and Cambridge, and is now vice-captain of Yorkshire. He is generally admitted to be one of the most brilliant all-round amateur cricketers in England, and has been one of the first to be selected for the test matches this year. At Harrow he showed exceptional promise, at Cambridge he made a reputation as both batsman and bowler, and for Yorkshire he has done great feats. While still at Cambridge he was selected by the M.C.C. to play for England in the test match at Lord's, and played a splendid innings of 91 on a wicket which made run-getting difficult. He plays a forcing game with wonderful confidence and scores with remarkable rapidity. He is a capital field and good bowler : he took 104 wickets in first-class cricket last season, besides making 1566 runs in thirty-eight complete innings.

Mr. GILBERT L. JESSOP (born May 19, 1874) is the C. I. Thornton of to-day—*i.e.*, he is the most fearless hitter in first-class cricket. It goes without saying that in these days, when spectators have a positive hatred of slow cricket, he is a popular figure wherever he goes. His daring is delightful, and the way he punishes the best bowling is simply astonishing. The number of times that Jessop has changed the aspect of a match by hitting out at bowling which some batsmen have found unplayable is legion. He first established his reputation for Gloucestershire before he went to Cambridge. No one needs to be reminded of his famous innings in the 1897 'Varsity match, when, going in when the game was anybody's, he knocked up 42 runs in about eighteen minutes, and so put heart into his side that they won a brilliant victory. Nor need I say anything about his memorable innings in the Gentlemen *v.* Players match at Lord's in the same year, when

in thirty-five minutes he scored 67 runs by terrific hitting, which kept the spectators in a frenzy
of excitement and helped to win a sensational
victory for the Gentlemen. I go so far as to say
that up to that time no batsman had ever treated
Tom Richardson's bowling with such contempt
as Jessop did that day. In his first fifteen
minutes at the wicket he made 39 runs out of 44.
F. G. J. Ford, who was his partner, is not a
slow bat by any means, but Jessop's vigorous
hitting made his partner's play seem tedious.
While Jessop made 67, Ford made about 20,
which for half an hour's play would have been
regarded as rapid scoring if Jessop had not
scored at such a pace. Since 1897 he has often repeated such performances—he has already done
one wonderful feat of the kind this season—and
though he sometimes fails, no one more highly
appreciates his value than I who have had him for
six years as a member of the Gloucestershire
team. All great hitters are uncertain, but one in
a team is invaluable. Like his great prototype,
C. I. Thornton, Jessop has a partiality for certain
grounds and bowlers. With Thornton it was
Scarborough ; with Jessop it is against Yorkshire
and at Harrogate, where the boundaries are short,
and he can hit out with assurance. His score
of 101 against Yorkshire in July 1897—made in
forty minutes—revived memories of C. I. Thornton's memorable feats on the Scarborough ground.
He is a good change fast bowler and a capital
field in any position. His selection to play for

England in one of the test matches this year, in spite of the fact that Selection Committees are often shy about including men of his type in test matches, was justified by results.

Mr. K. J. KEY (born October 11, 1864) was educated at Clifton College and Oxford. He made his first appearance in first-class cricket as one of the Oxford University Eleven. He then began to play for Surrey, and since the retirement of Mr. John Shuter has captained the Surrey team. Mr. Key was at one time a consistent run-getter; he scored at a good pace and often came off when other men failed. Though not a graceful or polished batsman, he hits well and scores freely. Fielding has always been his weak point, and in throwing in he is seldom accurate. Indeed he gets chaffed a good deal over his fielding. But even if he were a worse fieldsman and a far less effective bat he deserves his place in the Surrey team as a captain.

W. H. LOCKWOOD (born March 25, 1868) is one of the great all-round cricketers which Nottinghamshire has bred and passed on to another county. He was playing for Notts in 1886, but his prospective value was not realised by his native county, and he found an opening for his services in the Surrey Eleven. By the time he had qualified for Surrey, it dawned upon the Nottinghamshire Club that he would be a serviceable man, but Lockwood stuck to the county of his adoption, and with the exception of 1896 and 1897 has ever since rendered Surrey conspicuous service. He is a very fine bowler, and his batting is exceptionally good. It was by the bat that he got his place in the Surrey team in 1889—his bowling ability revealed itself later—but his batting and bowling now entitle him to rank as one of the best of living cricketers. The secret of the deadliness of his bowling is his combination of pace and break, with a faculty for deceiving the batsmen by sending down slower balls without perceptible change of action. His best years with the ball were 1892, 1893, and 1894, but from 1894, when he went to Australia, to 1898 he fell off his form, and was even dropped from the Surrey Eleven. He was himself again in 1898—scoring freely and bowling with his old sting—and is in form this season, though a strained muscle kept him out of several matches. Lockwood went out to Australia with Mr. Stoddart's first team in 1894, and has also visited the Cape, where he was for a time engaged as a ground bowler.

GEORGE LOHMANN (born at Kensington, June 2, 1865) was not only one of the best all-round cricketers of his time, but one of the best I have ever come across during my thirty-five years' experience of first-class cricket. Moreover, he was one of the best of good fellows, though on one or two occasions he permitted himself to be ill-advised in actions he took. He began to play for Surrey in 1884, and for ten years was the idol of the Surrey crowd, who almost lionised "George." If I believed in cricketers being "born," I should say that George Lohmann was prenatally designed for cricket. In bowling, batting and fielding he was first-class. As a bowler he had no superior. I do not remember meeting a bowler who used his head more than Lohmann. The work he got on the ball, the variety of his pace, which ranged from slow to fast, the excellent though varied length which he kept up, combined to make him pre-eminent. His action was easy, graceful and natural, and he contrived to vary his pitch and pace without giving the slightest evidence of his intentions. The better the batsman the better Lohmann bowled. He soon discovered, and never forgot, a batsman's weak point, and he seemed to throw all his soul into his work. Capable of making the ball break both ways, he always accommodated his bowling to right- and left-handed batsman. One of his most deadly balls was a straight fast one, with a good length, which usually beat the batsman simply because he expected it to break in one direction or the other. A tireless worker, he always had the idea, even when he was being hit about, that he was going to get a batsman out, and even when his captain thought it was time to make a change George always thought he could get the wicket if he went on at the other end. I was often amused by that characteristic of Lohmann when I was his captain out in Australia. "George," I used to say, "it's time for a change, isn't it?" Yes," he would reply readily; "don't you think I'd better go on at the other end?" It was not selfishness that prompted the reply, but simple

keenness for the game, and a sanguine feeling that
he was going to get the wicket in a minute or
two. He always worked desperately hard, and
was game until the last minute of a match.
Though he was played at first for his bowling, he
improved rapidly as a batsman, and established a
reputation as a reliable run-getter. George had the
faculty of " coming off " with both bat and ball
when the need was greatest. I never knew any
one rise to an occasion better than Lohmann.
He was generally most dangerous as a batsman
when runs were most needed, and his bowling
was, as a rule, most deadly when the odds were
against his side.

From 1888 to 1892, when he was at his best as
a bowler, Lohmann was one of Surrey's most
productive batsmen. He might have been an
even better batsman than he was but for his great
idea of hitting certain bowlers out of the ground.
When he was in Lord Sheffield's Australian team,
George Giffen's bowling was to Lohmann like a
red rag to a bull—he always had a "go" at
Giffen, and after one or two good hits generally
lost his wicket. He could play steady cricket
when he wanted, as he showed at Sydney when
playing against New South Wales (where Giffen,
of course, was not one of our opponents),
when he and Peel got together after we had
lost six wickets, and by careful, consistent batting
(against Turner's bowling) pulled off the victory
for the English team. As to his fielding it is
impossible to speak too highly. At slip he covered

more ground than any one I ever remember seeing in that position, and brought off most unexpected catches. Towards the end of his cricket
career in England he got into the habit of
"showing off" by falling full length on the
ground when he could have reached the ball
without much effort. Lohmann went out to
Australia three times, and played for England in
nearly every test match between 1886 and 1892,
when, owing to failing health, he had to leave
England and live in South Africa. He continued
his cricket in the colony, and returned to England for the summers of 1895 and 1896, resuming
his place in the Surrey team, and meeting with
his old success in bowling, though his batting had
gone off.

Lohmann was as popular among cricketers as
with the public, for though he was made so much
of he was unspoilt by his success, and was a
gentleman to his finger-tips. I remember how
delighted everybody was with Lohmann when we
were in Australia together in 1891–92. At one
place a picnic was arranged, and George, who
was always at everybody's service on a social occasion, undertook responsibility for the luncheon.
Provision was made for thirty people, but about
fifty turned up, and the possibility of the eatables
running short loomed before us. But George
got over the difficulty. How he did it I don't
know, but the provisions for thirty did duty for
fifty, and no one went on short commons. The
ladies were all in love with George for the attentive

care with which he saw that everybody had what they wanted.

Lohmann often told a story against himself. Once, when a match with Lancashire ended on the second day, George was asked—as professionals often are—to play for a local club on the Saturday. He consented, and had a comical experience. His presence had been advertised, and a big crowd had assembled to see him make havoc of the local team. The wicket was in a terrible condition, rough and worn bare. George distinguished himself by making a duck, much to the delight of the bowler, who from that hour boasted that "he once bow'ed Lohmann, the Surrey crack." George hoped to redeem his failure with the bat by a good performance with the ball, but on such a wicket he was helpless. His bowling jumped in all directions, and the local slogger knocked the great Surrey bowler all over the ground. George used to confess that he never felt so happy in his life as when that match ended and he had packed his bag ready for home.

Mr. PERCY STANISLAUS MCDONNELL (born November 13, 1860: died September 24, 1896) was another of the famous Australian hitters, but he combined the faculty of slogging with the qualities of a sterling batsman. When runs were wanted badly he hit out with almost reckless freedom, but when other occasions demanded other methods, he played stylish cricket and charmed spectators with his graceful batting. Once he scored 124 and 83 in a test match at Adelaide, and while in England he let us judge the quality and variety of his hitting. A batsman of McDonnell's type, capable alike of getting runs against time in an emergency and of playing steadily when need arose, is of inestimable value to his side. He rose to the occasion, whatever the difficulties, and was often instrumental in staving off a defeat or snatching a victory when the odds were against his side. In the field he was a safe catch and a smart fieldsman. Genial, good-natured, light-hearted, and generous, he was popular among cricketers in both hemispheres, and his early death was deeply deplored.

Mr. GREGOR MACGREGOR (born at Edinburgh, August 31, 1869) has distinguished himself in both the cricket and football field. As full back he was very hard to beat, and played for Scotland in all the International Rugby matches as far back as 1890, while in the same year the signal honour of selection to play for England in the test match was conferred upon him, though at the time he was still at Cambridge. Since Alfred Lyttelton's days no amateur has approached MacGregor as a wicket-keeper. I saw him wicket-keeping for Middlesex against Gloucestershire in May this year, and he is still the same quiet and unostentatious but safe and smart stumper as when he played for Cambridge ten years ago. His batting is not, perhaps, as good as it was, but he is generally safe to make runs. Mr. MacGregor was a member of Lord Sheffield's Australian team, but for some reason or other never kept wicket up to his proper form in Australia.

Mr. ARCHIBALD C. MACLAREN (born December 1, 1871), though scarcely twenty-eight years old, has been before the cricket world for twelve years, has had a distinguished career, and has still a brilliant future before him. The son of an old friend of the game—his father is Treasurer of the Lancashire County Cricket Club—"Archie" MacLaren began to show promise as a youngster, and when a boy of sixteen earned distinction by his batting in the Eton *v.* Harrow match in 1887. He played in the annual encounter at Lord's on four occasions — captaining his school team in the last match in 1890, and contributing to the victory for Harrow by a fine innings of 96. In the same season he was selected—on his brilliant form—to play for Lancashire. I doubt if any young cricketer ever made such a sensational *début* in first-class cricket as did Archie MacLaren for Lancashire at Brighton on August 14, 1890. He was expected to do well, but I question whether any one imagined, when he went in fourth on that Thursday afternoon, that this boy, fresh from school, would make a century. Nevertheless, the unexpected happened, and MacLaren with Briggs as partner punished the Sussex bowling for two hours, at the end of which time MacLaren had scored 108 by the most dashing and confident cricket. The achievement was without parallel. Since 1890 Mr. MacLaren has been identified with Lancashire cricket, and has captained the team

PLATE IN COMMEMORATION OF W. G. GRACE'S "CENTURY OF CENTURIES,"
1895.

(1)   (2)   (3)   (4)   (5) (6)   (7)   (8)   (9)   (10)

A FEW BATS AND BALLS IN THE POSSESSION OF W. G. GRACE.

(1) and (2), *Bats presented to W. G., by Surrey Cricket Club, for his innings of* 173 *not out for Gentlemen of the South v. Players of the South,* 1866 ; *and for his innings of* 268 *for South v. North, at Oval,* 1871. (3) *Ball used in this match and presented to W. G. as a memento.* (4) *A bat as used in eighteenth century cricket.* (5) *Ball used at Kadina (South Australia), in* 1874, *when the* 22 *scored only* 13 *runs against W. G.'s team, and the ball was worn rough by the stony wicket and fielding ground.* (6) *A cork-faced bat.* (7) *The bat with which W. G. scored* 1,000 *runs, in May,* 1895. (8) *Ball presented by the Surrey Club to W. G. for his bowling in the match South v. North, June* 22*nd and* 23*rd,* 1865, *when he took five wickets in the first innings and eight in the second.* (9) *Unspliced bat presented to W. G. by the South Wales Cricket Club, for scoring* 170 *and* 56 *not out against Gentlemen of Sussex, July,* 1864. (10) *Bat used by W. G. when with Lord Sheffield's Team in Australia.*

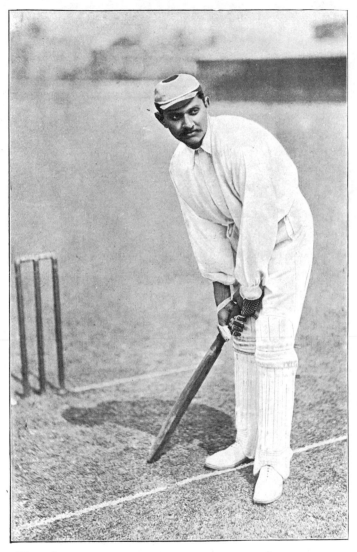

PHOTO BY]   [REINHOLD THIELE.

PRINCE RANJITSINHJI AT THE WICKET.

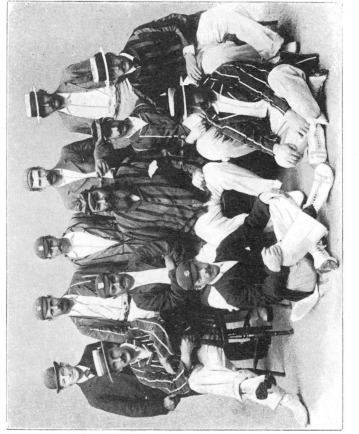

WM. HEARNE (UMPIRE) T. HAYWARD.   A. A. LILLEY.   T. RICHARDSON.   J T. HEARNE.
A. C. MAC LAREN.   K. S. RANJITSINHJI.   W. G. GRACE (CAPTAIN).   F. S. JACKSON.   CAPT. WYNYARD.

PHOTO BY]   R ABEL.   R PEEL,   [HAWKINS, BRIGHTON.

THE ENGLAND ELEVEN.
The Final Test Match, Oval, 1896.

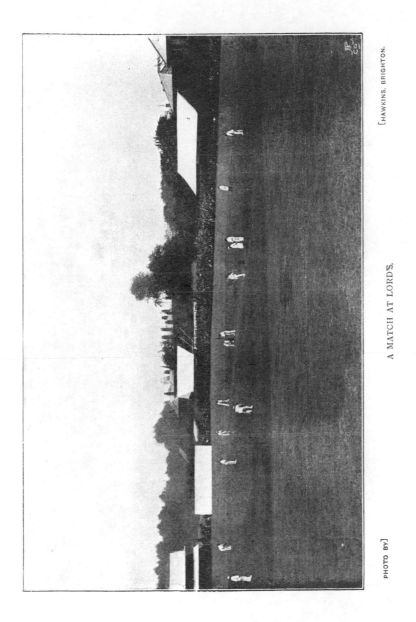

PHOTO BY]

A MATCH AT LORDS.

[HAWKINS. BRIGHTON.

SMITH (SCORER).   W. H. MURCH.   W. H. HALE.   H. WRATHALL.   W. S. A. BROWN.

F. G. ROBERTS.   C. L. TOWNSEND.   W. G. GRACE (CAPTAIN).   W. TROUP.   G. L. JESSOP,

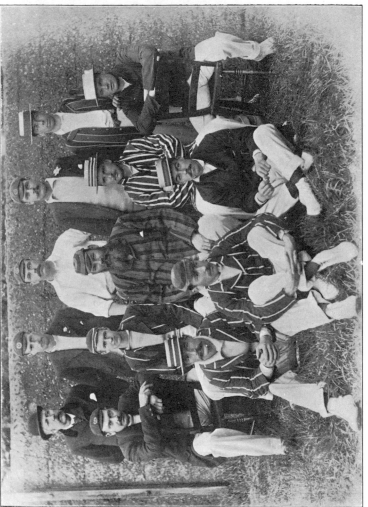

J. H. BOARD.   H. S. GOODWIN.   C. O. H. SEWELL.

THE GLOUCESTERSHIRE ELEVEN (1898).

PHOTO BY]

[HAWKINS, BRIGHTON.

LORD HAWKE.

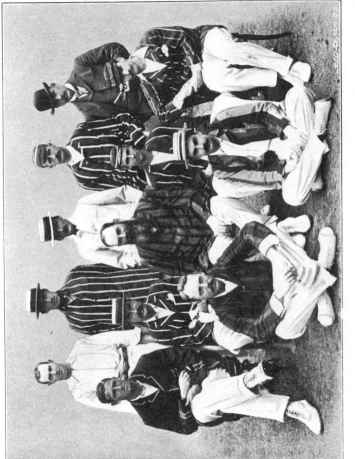

THE GENTLEMEN'S TEAM,

W. G.'s Jubilee Match, Lord's, 1898.

PHOTO BY] [HAWKINS, BRIGHTON.

W. G. GRACE AT THE WICKET.

W. G. GRACE PLAYING A BALL TO SHORT LEG.

W G. GRACE, CUTTING.

J. KELLY.   M. A. NOBLE.   H. TRUMBLE.   G. McLEOD.   MAJOR WARDILL (MANAGER).

E. JONES.   F. LAVER.   J. DARLING (CAPTAIN).   S. E. GREGORY.   A. JOHNS.   W. P. HOWELL.

C. HILL.   V. TRUMPER.   F. A. IREDALE.

PHOTO BY]   [HAWKINS, BRIGHTON.

THE AUSTRALIAN TEAM, 1899.

SNAP-SHOTS AT THE FIRST TEST MATCH, 1899.—NOTTINGHAM, JUNE 1st.

Photos by Jasper Redfern, Sheffield.

THE FIRST BALL OF THE MATCH.

CLEMENT HILL COMPLETES HIS 50, AND CELEBRATES IT THUS

SNAP-SHOTS AT THE FIRST TEST MATCH, 1899.—NOTTINGHAM, JUNE 1st.

Photos by Jasper Redfern, Sheffield.

COMING IN FOR LUNCH.

THE END OF THE FIRST DAY'S PLAY.

SNAP-SHOTS AT THE FIRST TEST MATCH, 1899.—NOTTINGHAM, JUNE 2nd.

Photos by Jasper Redfern, Sheffield.

THE CLOSE OF THE AUSTRALIAN INNINGS.

W. G. GRACE—"c. KELLY, b. NOBLE, 28."

THE OLD ALBERT CRICKET GROUND AT SYDNEY.

from time to time. Unfortunately he is seldom able to join the Eleven until the season is well advanced—a circumstance which is a distinct misfortune to Lancashire. It is curious to notice how vast a change comes over the spirit of the Lancashire team immediately MacLaren assumes the reins. He is popular among his men, who follow his lead with confidence, and emulate his dash and spirit, which he throws into his play. No one needs to be told that Mr. MacLaren is now one of the finest amateur batsmen in the world. He won his spurs by magnificent achievements at an early age ; he has maintained his reputation by consistent success. Nor is any one likely to forget MacLaren's wonderful and epoch-making innings of 424—surpassing all previous individual scores in first-class matches—against Somerset, July 15 and 16, 1895. The Lancashire innings on that occasion is not likely to fade from the memory of cricketers. In the astonishingly short space of eight hours the Northern team scored 801 runs— an average of 100 per hour. MacLaren was at the wickets seven hours and fifty minutes, and while 792 runs were made. With Paul as his second partner, 363 runs were added for the second wicket. Of course the victory of Lancashire by an innings and 452 runs, the most overwhelming defeat ever, I think, inflicted by one county upon another, was a personal triumph for MacLaren, whose individual score wiped out my own record first-class cricket innings of 344 in 1876, and excelled in merit Mr. Stoddart's mam-

moth innings of 485 in 1886, which was compiled
in second-class cricket. Mr. MacLaren has done
many brilliant things since this historic innings,
but he will be remembered by that wonderful feat
at Taunton when his subsequent triumphs are
forgotten. A detailed record of "Archie's" career
would exhaust more space than the limits of
this volume will permit, but I must mention his
success in Australia. He went out with Mr.
Stoddart's team in 1895 and again in 1897. On
both occasions he distinguished himself, on the
latter achieving what no other batsman had ever
done in first-class cricket in Australia—scoring
two innings of over a hundred in one match. I
am disposed to regard Archie MacLaren as one
of the most stylish amateur batsmen in England.
He has fewer "showy" strokes than Ranjitsinhji,
but he plays every variety of stroke with wonderful precision, times every ball with marvellous
exactness, and hits all round the wicket with
perfect confidence. His hard cutting and clean
driving are, perhaps, his finest strokes, but his
wrist-play is very pretty to watch. Though by no
means a tall man he is muscularly powerful, and
puts plenty of power into his strokes. In the
field he can hold his own with any one, being
especially good as third man, and in the long field
the number of runs he saves in a long innings is
simply wonderful.

Mr. JAMES MACLAREN (Treasurer of the Lancashire County Cricket Club) is one of the best
sportsmen it has been my privilege to know. I

made his acquaintance in 1878 when Gloucestershire played Lancashire for the first time, and have
ever since counted him among my best friends.
He was a great footballer in the early days of our
friendship, having begun playing when, as he
says, most men leave off—*i.e.*, on joining the noble
army of Benedicts in 1864. The Manchester
Football Club was started through the instrumentality of MacLaren and a few other ardent
footballers. He was the first President of
the Lancashire Football Club, and in 1882 was
elected President of the Rugby Football Union,
he being the first Northerner to fill the office.
To cricketers James MacLaren is known for his
splendid services to Lancashire County Cricket.
Besides rendering official service, he has helped
to raise the County Club to the position it now
holds, and has given Lancashire cricket a son
(A. C. MacLaren) whose brilliance as a batsman
and wisdom as a captain are likely to carry it to
pre-eminence in many a future season.

Mr. J. R. MASON (born March 26, 1874) plays for
Kent, and is sure to leave his name among the great
cricketers of the day. He laid the foundations of
his cricketing ability at Winchester College, which
he left with the reputation of being one of the best
batsmen the College ever produced. On leaving
Winchester he joined the Kent Eleven, but it was
not until 1896, when he scored 1117 runs and
headed the Kent averages, that he took rank
among first-class batsmen. In the following year
he went out to Australia with Mr. Stoddart's team

and acquitted himself brilliantly. Last season he captained Kent on the retirement of Mr. Frank Marchant, and is not unlikely to achieve still greater things. A more stylish and elegant bat no one could wish to see. His height permits him to play forward with grace and strength. His clean hard driving and cutting are magnificent. He is a good fast bowler, at times is very difficult to play, and is a very good field, especially at short-slip.

Mr. HUGH HAMON MASSIE (born April 11, 1854) made a great reputation by his dashing cricket for the Australian team of 1882. He was another of the Australian hard hitters, rash at times and daring always, but a troublesome bat to get rid of. His score of 206 for the Australians against Oxford is remembered yet, and often talked about in the old University. He had one favourite hit which always delighted spectators—an off drive between cover point and point, into which he threw all his might. When it came off—which it generally did—this stroke was brilliant, but his affection for it often cost him his wicket. Until 1882, George Giffen tells us, he was generally regarded in Australia as " an uncertain quantity," but after his success in England his value as a demoraliser of bowling was fully recognised. Besides being a good cricketer, Massie was one of the best fellows that ever visited England.

ARTHUR MOLD (born May 30, 1865) is a native of Northampton who plays for Lancashire under the residential qualification and has long been recognised as one of the most deadly fast bowlers in England. Though his delivery is graceful and apparently without effort, some people think his action is not always above suspicion. He takes a very short run, but he sends down some terrifically fast balls, as may be imagined from the fact that in August 1896 he bowled George Lohmann with a ball that sent the bail 63 yards 6 inches from the stumps ! Beginning to play for Lancashire in 1889—soon after Crossland had closed his connection with the county—he met with immediate success, and for many years has taken a high place in the averages. He is generally safe to take over a hundred wickets in each season. Without him I do not know what Lancashire would have done : he has certainly been their mainstay for years. Like Spofforth of old, Mold frightens batsmen into losing their wickets; and no wonder, for on a rough wicket his balls bump in a most dangerous way, and make him a terror to nervous batsmen. Mold is a poor bat, but his bowling more than compensates for that deficiency. He is a genial, companionable man, and a rare good shot.

Mr. WILLIAM LLOYD MURDOCH (born October 18, 1855) is generally admitted to have been the best batsman Australia ever produced. In his own country he was dubbed the Champion, and even in England he commanded great admiration. His defence is perfect, and his hitting hard and clean. Two of his big scores—his 321 against Victoria in 1882, his 211 against England at the

Oval when a member of the 1884 team—are well remembered; but his great merit was the consistency with which he scored. He seldom failed, and his high average was attained not by a few big scores and a list of failures, but by repeated success. The perfect ease and confidence of his batting is very conspicuous. Cutting is his *forte*, though his clean hard driving is delightful to watch. His placing and timing are wonderfully skilful. At one time he made a reputation as a wicket-keeper, but he was too good a batsman to expose himself to the risk of knocking up his hands for very long. On returning to Australia in 1884 he retired from cricket, of which he thought he had had enough, but in 1890 he was back again in England captaining, with his extraordinary tact and wisdom, another Australian team. Then he settled in England, qualified to play for Sussex, but met with less success in County Cricket than might have been expected. I am not sure, notwithstanding his brilliant batting, that it was not as captain of the Australian Elevens that he earned greatest distinction. He was an ideal captain, a born tactician, a genial chief, a firm though gentle ruler, and a man of singular pluck and resource. On one occasion he was captaining an Australian Eleven in a match against one of our leading counties, and when play had been in progress a little while, Murdoch, as captain, thought a change of bowling desirable. Addressing one of the bowlers—a well-known cricketer, whose name I need not disclose—he

said, "Mr. So-and-so will go on now." The
bowler objected ; said he hadn't been given a fair
chance. Murdoch said nothing, and let him
keep on bowling unchanged until the end of the
day's play. It is needless to say the bowler never
again complained that he was not given a fair
chance.

Mr. LIONEL CHARLES HAMILTON PALAIRET
(born at Grange-over-Sands, May 27, 1870), though
a Lancashire man by birth has become a Somersetshire man by residential qualification, and has
served the county of his adoption with remarkable success. Coming to the front in Public
School cricket, he got his " Blue " for Oxford in
his first term, and captained the Eleven in 1892–
1893. On leaving the 'Varsity he threw in his lot
with Somerset. The Western county, which had
just earned its place among the nine first-class
counties, welcomed the recruit with open arms,
and found his assistance invaluable. He is now
in the front rank of amateur batsmen, and usually
makes a thousand runs each season. Combining
defence with spirited hitting, and always playing
with stylish finish, he is an attractive batsman to
watch and a formidable rival to oppose. He
took ninth place in the batting averages last year,
with a total of 1126 and an average of 41.70. In
1876, 1878, 1880, and 1882 Mr. Palairet's father,
Mr. H. N. Palairet, was champion archer of
England.

RICHARD PILLING (born July 5, 1855, at Bed-
ford : died March 28, 1891) was one of the most

brilliant wicket-keepers the world has ever seen. From 1877 to 1883 he was without a rival as stumper, and his exclusion from a representative Players' team could not be entertained. Quiet and unostentatious though he was, he took the fastest bowling with consummate ease and aston-ishing quickness. It mattered not whether the bowling was fast or slow, he crouched over the wicket with his nose close to the bails, snap-ping the ball with unerring certainty, whether it came on the leg or the off side. Twice he went to Australia, and even there, in the land of Blackham, his wonderful wicket-keeping de-lighted the onlookers. Unfortunately consump-tion claimed him for her own, and made his appearances in the cricket-field intermittent after 1883. Until that date he played regularly for Lancashire, whom he frequently helped in critical moments by his batting. Though not a reliable bat he often " came off " in an emergency, and in company with Briggs at Liverpool in July 1885, made what was until this year the longest tenth-wicket partnership on record—173. His personal popularity was very great, as his modesty and good nature made him generally esteemed.

SHRI RANJITSINHJI (born in India, September 10, 1872). Without a doubt " Ranji " is one of the most interesting figures in the cricket-field. His popularity has two sources—his extraordinary skill as a batsman and his nationality. How a man of his slender physique and apparently delicate constitution has so completely mastered

the art of batting as to score with astounding
rapidity and ease off all manner of bowling upon
every variety of wicket is simply wonderful.
" Ranji" laid the foundation of his cricket career
in India, but he perfected himself in England. It
was at Rajkumar College at Kathiawar that he
learned the rudiments of the game, but it was on
Parker's Piece at Cambridge that he acquired the
different strokes, unerring judgment and faultless
style which have made him famous. It is a little
curious to recall that it was as a substitute that he
made his first appearance in Trinity College Team
at Cambridge, and it is even more remarkable
that the authorities at Cambridge did not think
the Indian Prince worthy of his "Blue" until
1893. Then he qualified to play for Sussex, and
in his first year in County Cricket played thirty-
three innings with an average of 41. It has been
said that Sussex made " Ranji," and that in return
" Ranji" made Sussex. Some one has waggishly
suggested that " Ranji" qualified for Sussex so as
to make sure of playing ten innings a year on the
Hove Ground, for which, like most batsmen, he
has a partiality on account of the facility it gives
to run-getting. In his second year in County
Cricket "Ranji" met with remarkable success,
heading the first-class averages with an aggregate of 2780 runs (which surpassed my record
aggregate by thirty-four runs). Ten times he
exceeded the century, and ` when playing for
Sussex v. Yorkshire made over a hundred in each
innings of one match. In Australia with Stod-

dart's team in 1897–98 "Ranji" maintained his brilliant form, scoring 1372 runs in all matches, with an average of 54.88. Returning *via* India he made a long stay in his native land, and so missed the cricket season of 1898, much to the regret of English spectators, with whom he is deservedly popular.

"Ranji" is unique as a batsman. Most batsmen have one or two favourite strokes of which they are masters. "Ranji" has half a dozen strokes, which he plays with perfect ease and almost mechanical precision. Some of them are what one may call "unorthodox." I am afraid that when he gets older his habit of stepping in front of his wicket to play straight balls to leg will often cost him his wicket. Even with his wonderful, almost hawklike, eyesight he frequently gets out leg before wicket in trying to play a ball to leg which keeps lower than he expects. He hits all round the wicket with extraordinary skill, but is seen at his best in a leg-glance, which with him is an exceedingly pretty stroke. This is his favourite hit, and always delights onlookers. At hitting a high long hop to leg he is almost infallible. "Ranji" can drive well, as he has been showing lately, but he prefers to score behind, or square with the wicket, and by his genius for timing often scores to leg, or behind the wicket, off balls other batsmen would have to drive. He is comfortable with any bowling, and seems to treat all bowlers with the same unconcern.

The stories about "Ranji" are numerous. His puzzling name has made him the victim of every wit in the cricket-field. It is said that the newspaper compositors struck against setting his name in type, and appealed for his patronymic to be changed to Smith. But one of the best stories of the Indian Prince is vouched for by the Cambridge journalist who collaborated with "Ranji" in writing his "Jubilee Book of Cricket." When "Ranji" was at Cambridge he went on a tour with the Cassandra Cricket Club. A member of an opposing side inquired of some of the visitors if "that dark chap could speak English?" They, speedily foreseeing possibilities, replied seriously that he knew a few words, such as "Yes" and "No" and "How's that?" When the unconscious "Ranji" went to the wickets, to his great astonishment he heard some lively criticisms of his batting. He made a characteristically huge score, and every now and again some one of the fielding side would ejaculate, "Here, isn't it time this fellow went out?" Once, when the ball struck "Ranji" in the chest and doubled him up, the fielding captain audibly hoped that it would "knock some of the steam out of the beggar!" At the subsequent luncheon, when Ranjitsinhji rose to toast genially the home side, several faces were seen to change colour.

Among cricketers "Ranji" is exceedingly popular, his open-hearted generosity and geniality having captured all their hearts.

Mr. WALTER WILLIAM READ (born at Reigate,

November 23, 1855) entered first-class cricket at
the age of eighteen, when he played for Surrey
against Yorkshire in July 1873, and for over
twenty years was one of the most brilliant batsmen in England. The services he rendered to
Surrey could scarcely be over-estimated. On
scores of occasions his dashing and fearless
batting snatched a victory or saved his county
from defeat. As far back as 1877 he was one of
the mainstays of Surrey's batting, and in that year
he with Jupp made over 200 runs for the first
wicket. From 1881 he played in almost every
match in which Surrey engaged, and materially
helped to raise his county to the prominent position it took among the counties. Between 1883
and 1892 he was at his best, and was the hero of
many a sensational score. Once—against Oxford
in 1888—he compiled the magnificent total of
338, and on three occasions within the period
mentioned exceeded 200 in first-class cricket. A
list of his centuries would fill half a page of this
volume. For many years he was the "idol" at
the Oval, and no wonder, for his hitting was free
and his scoring always rapid. Nevertheless his
defence was remarkable, and though he seldom
failed to punish a loose ball, he generally respected a good one. His favourite ball was a
long hop to the off, which he stepped back to and
hit with tremendous power in front of cover-point;
he also was an expert with the "pull stroke."
He was a capital field either at point or in the
long-field, and in an emergency could keep

wicket well. With his under-hand bowling he often separated batsmen who had defied over-arm bowling for hours, and many a batsman has rued the moment when he treated one of W. W.'s tricky lobs with contempt, only to find himself bowled or caught in the country. Until late years Mr. Read held an official post at the Oval, but when he began to lose form his services as under-secretary were dispensed with.

WILFRED RHODES (born October 9, 1877) is Yorkshire's latest, and, it may be, greatest discovery, for as a slow bowler on wet wickets he promises to equal even Robert Peel. Of course Rhodes has only been tested for one season, but the success he met with on his first appearance in first-class cricket was almost wonderful. In twenty-six county matches last year he took 126 wickets at an average cost of 14 runs apiece, while in first-class cricket he took 154 wickets for 14.60 each. This season (1899) he early showed such brilliant form that he was selected for the first test match at Nottingham—a recognition which is almost unique. Rhodes has come to the front in the nick of time. New bowlers, fast and slow, are sorely needed, and he seems likely to take the place in England Elevens so long filled by Briggs and Peel. He bowls left-handed medium, with a good break and an action which is both easy and graceful. On slow wickets he is deadly, and even on fast hard wickets batsmen have difficulty in getting him away. He is a valuable acquisition—all the more valuable because he has come just when a left-handed bowler of his type was needed.

THOMAS RICHARDSON (born at Mitcham, Aug. 11, 1870) has for some years been acknowledged as the best fast professional bowler in England. He bowls right arm with a high graceful delivery. The exceptional length of his run always surprises spectators. His bowling, as a rule, breaks slightly from the off, although now and then it goes with his arm, and even on hard good wickets he is difficult to play. He keeps up a splendid length and can stand any amount of work. However severely he is punished he works like a Trojan, and pegs away until he gets the wicket or is relieved. Richardson visited Australia with both of Mr. Stoddart's teams, and on the first occasion —in 1895—met with great success. Rheumatism kept him from bowling in his best form in several of the matches in Mr. Stoddart's second tour, and to this was attributed a great measure of the misfortune which the team met with in 1897–98. Since his return to England early in 1898 he has never been the same bowler, and this year (1899) his bowling seems to have lost most of its sting. Moreover, Richardson, who was a tall slim man when he came to the front, has added flesh at a rapid rate, and hardly seems capable of the endurance for which he was famous three years ago. There are not a few good judges who declare that, if Richardson would go into strict training, he would bowl as well as ever; he is stouter than he ever was, and could well lose a stone or more. I believe that Richardson has been over-worked, and that the comparative ease with which batsmen now score off him is directly attributable to the fact that fast bowlers cannot last for ever.

WILLIAM SCOTTON (born at Nottingham, Jan. 27, 1856 : died July 9, 1893) began to play regularly in first-class cricket in 1879, and for thirteen years was the left-handed stonewaller of the Nottingham team. At one time he was beyond doubt the best professional left-handed batsman in England, and though his batting was so slow that he made cricket monotonous to watch, he frequently saved matches for his county; and in 1884, by an innings of 90, made in five hours and three-quarters for England against Australia at Kennington Oval, helped to convert a probable defeat into a credit-able draw. On two occasions Scotton and I made big first-wicket scores against the Australian team of 1886—once for England at the Oval, when we scored 170 together, and again for Lord Londes-borough's Eleven at Scarborough, when we made 156 before we were parted. Scotton visited Australia with Shaw and Shrewsbury's teams of 1881, 1884, 1886. He had, perhaps, the most im-pregnable defence I ever saw, and I have vivid recollections of his score standing unaltered for over an hour when he was batting with me against Australia in 1886. On two occasions he made scores of 200 for the M.C.C., and on another occasion he made 123 runs, which took him **exactly eight and a half hours.** The tediousness of his play did not contribute to his popularity, and although he was a good field and a fair bowler, he was no great favourite with the spectators.

ALFRED SHAW (born at Burton Joyce, Notts, August 29, 1842) was dubbed "The Emperor of Bowlers" by Richard Daft, and for many years the exalted title was well deserved. He came into first-class cricket in 1864, but it was in the early seventies that he made his name famous by brilliant bowling exploits which made the subject for conversation wherever cricketers congregated. Between 1870 and 1880 he was perhaps the best bowler in England. He had an easy round-arm action, kept an astonishingly good length, varied his pace from slow to medium, and made the ball break slightly in both directions. He seldom bowled two similar balls in one over, and he worked with his head as much as with his body. When Morley and Alfred Shaw led the Nottingham bowling, the Midland county could boast of one of the most deadly pairs of bowlers in the cricket-field. Shaw's greatest year was 1878, when his average stood:

Overs.	Maidens.	Runs.	Wickets.	Average.
2522	1512	2084	196	10.124

Though Shaw himself has denied the cock-and-bull story that he once broke five out of six saucers placed on the wicket for him to pitch the ball upon, he was quite capable of performing the feat, as he seemed able to pitch the ball exactly where he pleased. The fact that he went through his long career without bowling a single ball very wide of the wicket, and was only once "no-balled," is eloquent testimony to his accuracy of pitch. He took all ten wickets in one innings while playing in 1874 for the M.C.C. against the North of England. In 1865 Shaw and I made simultaneous first appearances in the Gentlemen v. Players match. In later years Shaw was employed by Lord Sheffield at Sheffield Park, when he spent his energies in training young cricketers to play for Sussex. Occasionally Shaw played for Sussex, Nottingham having dispensed with his services before he had lost his form. I think Shaw has had more experience of cricket in Australia than any other English cricketer. He first went to the colony in 1876 with James Lillywhite's team ; in 1881, 1884, 1886 and 1887 he was in Australia again with teams for which he and Shrewsbury were responsible; and in 1891 he acted as manager to Lord Sheffield's team, of which I was captain, and right well did he arrange things.

MORDECAI SHERWIN (born at Kimberley, Notts, February 26, 1851) was, in his best days—between 1880 and 1892—one of the finest wicketkeepers in England. It was for Nottinghamshire that Sherwin did his best work, though he played for the Players, the North, and England on different occasions, and accompanied Shaw and Shrewsbury's team to Australia in 1886. His pluck at the wickets was only equalled by his cheerfulness. Though he was a big, burly fellow, he was as nimble and sharp as a cat, and took any bowling with absolute ease and certainty. Not even Pilling excelled Sherwin in taking leg-balls, which are, of course, the most difficult for a wicket-keeper to secure. I sometimes thought that he played a little too much to the gallery when keeping wickets, but it was his boisterous, demonstrative nature that led him to play the buffoon for the amusement of spectators, with whom he was very popular. He was a poor bat, but he often got runs when they were wanted. He was the life and soul of a travelling party, and added to the gaiety of his companions and fellow passengers when on the voyage to Australia. One day (so I am told) Sherwin slipped on deck, and fell heavily, though without getting hurt. Mordecai, however, saw the chance for a joke. He pretended to have severely cut his face, rushed off to the doctor, who fell in with the joke, and bandaged Sherwin's face in sticking-plaster. The passengers were full of sympathy, and the ladies especially compassionate, waiting upon Sherwin with tender solicitude as he sat on deck with his face enveloped in sticking-plaster. Next morning, to the amazement of the ship's company, Sherwin appeared on deck minus the sticking-plaster, and without the semblance of a scar on his face.

Sherwin was a good football-player, and for years kept goal for Notts County Association Football Club. In those days it was permissible to charge the goal-keeper, but in Sherwin's case he generally had the best of it, as weight will tell.

ARTHUR SHREWSBURY (born at New Linton, Notts, April 11, 1856) must be acknowledged as the greatest professional batsman of his age. His reputation has been built up not by a few magnificent feats which set the world talking, but by years of consistent run-getting. It was not until ten years after his appearance in first-class cricket that he reached the height of his power, but, having once reached it, he maintained his proud position as our leading professional batsman. Any detailed record of his achievements would need a volume to itself. He has been a pillar of strength to his native county, has played for the Players since 1876, and in fifty-three innings made 1749 runs in those matches, and has played for England in almost every home test match ever since 1886. Four times he has accompanied an English team to Australia, and in the four tours has twice headed, and twice taken second place in, the batting averages. His hand has lost none of its cunning, and his defence is as fine to-day as ever. Batting is as a science to Shrewsbury, who possesses all the nerve, patience, eyesight, and strength which are the essentials of the ideal batsman. His coolness is remarkable, so remarkable that it is impossible to tell from his play whether he has been batting five minutes or five hours. His caution never relaxes, and his judgment is seldom at fault. Every hit is timed to a nicety, and a lofty stroke is a thing he very seldom indulges in. He cuts with singular dexterity, and the wrist action which he brings into play when blocking a ball is a point young cricketers should observe and study. At one period of his career he showed a tendency towards stonewalling, and scored so slowly that spectators found that with all his stylish form his batting was tedious, and when Scotton and he were partners their displays were, I must confess, more scientific than exciting. In later years he has returned to his earlier and rather freer form. For eight years the score of 398, which Shrewsbury and Gunn made against Sussex on May 17, 1890, held the record as the longest partnership in a first-class match. Personally Shrewsbury commands the esteem of all who know him ; he is a representative of the best type of professional cricketer.

JAMES SOUTHERTON (born at Pelworth, November 16, 1827 : died June 16, 1880), generally known by the familiar " Jimmy," had the distinction of playing for Surrey, Sussex, and Hants in the fifties and sixties, as in those days there was no rule to prevent a man playing for more than one county at the same time. His success came late in life, as he was thirty-nine before he gained the full recognition to which his slow round-arm bowling entitled him. " Jimmy " used his head in bowling, which puzzled batsmen by its variety of length, break and pace. His action, however, was doubtful at times, and Pooley went as far as to say that " Jimmy " never *bowled* a ball in his life. With a sticky wicket to help him he enjoyed himself immensely in matches against odds which were often played in his day. Sooner or later he discovered a batsman's weak spot, and then it was only a matter of time, for "Jimmy" was nothing if not a "sticker." He played for the United South Eleven for many years, and was a familiar figure on cricket-grounds all over the world. He was an effective though uncertain bat, his hitting being free, even if his defence was shaky. We used to tease him by saying that he sometimes closed his eyes to hit ; and once, when I was fielding at point, I proved it by claiming a catch from a ball which had palpably struck the ground before I caught it. "Jimmy" opened his eyes just in time to see me toss up the ball, and I, to carry on the joke, said he had given me a "hot 'un" ; then he believed he was caught, and walked out. The fieldsmen told him he was not out, and Pooley whistled him to return, but Southerton would not believe it. We often chaffed him about it, but he always insisted that he had been caught out fairly enough, and nothing would convince him to the contrary. He accompanied my first team to Australia in 1873, and as umpire distinguished himself by giving the ridiculous decision at Castlemaine to which I have referred in another chapter.

Mr. FREDERICK ROBERT SPOFFORTH (born September 9, 1853) has left his name emblazoned on the annals of cricket. It is difficult to express all one feels about Spofforth. He was unique as a fast bowler, and practically established a school of bowlers. I made my first acquaintance with

Spofforth when I visited Australia in 1873–74. He was then a promising youngster, but none of us imagined that he would soon have a world-wide reputation. I renewed the acquaintance under changed conditions in 1878, when Spofforth came over with the 1878 Australian team. He met with immediate and signal success, his first triumph being in the second match of the tour, when he and H. F. Boyle, bowling unchanged, dismissed the M.C.C. Team for 31 and 19, and practically won for Australia the magnificent victory. It was on that day that some one christened him the "Demon," a nickname by which he was known to the end of his bowling days. His pace was terrifically fast, at times his length excellent, and his breakbacks were exceedingly deceptive. He controlled the ball with masterly skill, and if the wicket helped him ever so little was almost unplayable. A good many batsmen funked Spofforth's bowling — a circumstance which helped to his success—and a great many more found it impossible to score off him. Some of his bowling feats are historic. Who, for instance, has never heard of Spofforth's magnificent feat at Kennington Oval in 1882, when he took seven wickets in each innings at a trivial cost and got rid of Barlow, Ulyett, Read, and A. G. Steel for "ducks," and practically won the match for Australia by his own deadly bowling? He has done the "hat trick" three times in first-class cricket.

Mr. ANDREW ERNEST STODDART (born at South

Shields, March 11, 1863) is one of the few amateurs who have won world-wide renown in both cricket and football. In both he has had his International Cap and won a measure of popularity such as few athletes enjoy. As a Rugby three-quarter back he has never been excelled ; as a cricketer he is brilliant in all three departments—batting, bowling, and fielding. Coming to the front as a member of Hampstead Club in 1885, he has maintained his reputation up to the present time, and though he has intimated his intention to withdraw from first-class cricket, all cricketers indulge the hope that he will revise his decision. He held for fourteen years, the record for the highest individual innings ever made—485 for Hampstead *v.* Stoics on August 4, 1886, but he has achieved success far surpassing that feat in actual merit—notably his scores of 195 and 124 in the same match (Middlesex *v.* Notts), at Lord's, in 1893, his 215 against Lancashire in 1891 and his 151 for England against the M.C.C. in the Centenary Match in 1887 ; and many more centuries in England and Australia, far too numerous to mention here. He is a graceful, spirited and finished batsman, a rapid scorer under almost any conditions. He always acknowledges—especially when his bowling is being punished—that it is my "fault" that he became a bowler, and I am not disposed to resent the soft impeachment; indeed, I congratulate myself on introducing so good a change bowler to the cricket-field. His fielding is so sure, and his picking up and return so clean and rapid, that a bowler has no anxiety when he sees a ball go in Mr. Stoddart's direction. He has visited Australia four times—with Mr. G. F. Vernon's team in 1887, with Lord Sheffield's team in 1891, and with the teams which went out under his command in 1894 and 1897. Indeed, he is almost as popular in Australia as in England.

FRANK H. SUGG (born January 11, 1862) has in turn played for Yorkshire, Derbyshire, and Lancashire, with very varying success. He is a batsman of the dashing order, a tremendous hitter, and when he has got his " eye in " punishes any kind of bowling he may have to face. Batsmen like Sugg are the terror of bowlers, who never know to what extent they may be punished. Sugg might have made a better batsman if he had been gifted with a little more patience. His hard clean driving and his splendid hitting to leg are delightful to watch. As long as he is at the wicket he hits with splendid impartiality at good or bad balls, and generally gets out, caught at the wicket or in the long-field. No doubt these hitters are towers of strength to their side, and I am much too fond of lively cricket not to appreciate their value. I have seen Sugg keep a crowd in roars of laughter and applause by his tremendous hitting. He is a very strong hitter, and when he gets hold of a ball the probabilities of its failing to reach the boundary are remote. The drawback with batsmen like Sugg is that they are never reliable. Nevertheless, more matches are won by hitters than by stonewallers, and when my time comes for watching instead of playing cricket, I shall hope that batsmen like Frank Sugg will be plentiful. Apart from his batting, Sugg is a magnificent fieldsman, and as safe a catch as there is in the cricket-field. His picking up and throwing in are done by one action, and make him a model for young cricketers to imitate.

WILLIAM STORER (born January 25, 1868) is a first-class wicket-keeper, an excellent bat, and a dangerous change bowler. Indeed, he is one of the best all-round professional cricketers of the day. "Derbyshire born and Derbyshire bred," he is "strong in the arm" but certainly not "weak in the head," for a more alert and resourceful cricketer is not to be found. He came to the front in 1893, when he kept wicket for the M.C.C. against the Australians so brilliantly—he caught four men, stumped another, and did not give a bye — that his position among professional wicket-keepers was promptly acknowledged as pre-eminent. Moreover, he was a promising, batsman, and could always be relied on to put on some runs as his contributions to the total. Since 1893 he has maintained his high standard as a wicket-keeper, and at the same time improved as a batsman with singular rapidity. He has played for England against Australia, for the Players against the Gentlemen, and during the tour of Mr. Stoddart's team, 1897–98, in Australia did splendid service, both with the bat and behind the stumps. His wicket-keeping is almost as good as Pilling's when the great Lancastrian was in his prime. The ease with which he takes the bowling of Mr. Kortright and Tom Richardson is astonishing, and his smartness in getting the bails off always delights spectators. When he doffs the gloves and takes the ball he bowls a slow ball with a puzzling leg-break. I can't say that his batting style is elegant, but it is vigorous, and he gets runs with almost unfailing regularity. Sometimes, when his hands are damaged, he fields at point, and is quick and safe in that arduous post. In fact, he is a master of the game in all its departments.

Mr. CHARLES INGLIS THORNTON (born at Llanwarne, Herefordshire, March 20, 1850) was, when in his prime, the most prodigious hitter of the century. His name has become the synonym for hitting, and when cricketers want to convey a striking impression of a batsman's powers as a smiter, they say, "He's a regular C. I. Thornton." He began his cricket as a schoolboy at Eton, playing in the Elevens of 1866–67–68. Even as a youngster he was a hitter. In 1867 he made over fourteen hundred runs. It is curious that, though he "came off" in all three matches against Harrow, he was never on the victorious side. He began to play for Cambridge in 1869, and signalised the opening of his first innings against Oxford by driving a ball over the Pavilion at Lord's into the secretary's garden. Four times he played in the 'Varsity match, and on three occasions victory rested with the Light Blues. In 1871 he scored 20 runs off one over of four

balls bowled by David Buchanan, the famous old
Rugby bowler, who is said to have taken more
wickets than any living bowler. Once, in practice
at Brighton, he hit a ball out of the Hove Ground
and down the Western Road. When measured
it was found that the ball had travelled 168 yards,
and it is still the longest authenticated hit in the
annals of cricket. Playing for the Orleans Club
against the Australians, he drove another ball from
Boyle a distance of 152 yards. But perhaps his
most wonderful hitting performance was for the
Gentlemen of England v. I Zingari at Scarborough.
His innings of 107 was made in twenty-nine
strokes. It was made up thus : 6, 1, 6, 4, 6, 2, 1,
1, 4, 6, 4, 6, 1, 4, 4, 4, 1, 6, 4, 4, 4, 6, 4, 4, 1, 4, 2 ;
and the bowler who was most punished was
Mr. A. G. Steel. One of his mightiest hits in
that innings soared sky-high and went straight
out of the ground over a high block of houses
and dropped in Trafalgar Square ! Another hit
at Scarborough went through an open window
on the second floor of one of the houses over-
looking the cricket-ground ! Off Tom Emmett he
hit a ball—also at Scarborough—which dropped
130 yards away from the batsman's wicket ! Tom
Emmett said it had gone into the sea, which was
a quarter of a mile away ! In 1870, playing for
Cambridge against the M.C.C., he scored 34 in
ten hits ; and in 1871, playing for the Gentlemen
against the Players at Brighton, he surpassed the
feat by making 34 runs off nine balls—viz., seven
4's, one single, and one ball which he did not

hit ! At one time, when "Jimmy" Southerton (who used to lie awake at nights dreaming of what would happen if Mr. Thornton drove a ball back to him when he was bowling) and Martin M'Intyre were keen rivals, Mr. Thornton sent the first four balls he received from Southerton to the boundary. M'Intyre watched his rival's punishment with glee, but Southerton entreated Mr. Thornton to treat M'Intyre in the same way, which he did, to M'Intyre's disgust and "Jimmy's" profound satisfaction. But a chapter might be devoted to Mr. C. I. Thornton's leg-hits and scores against time. It is superfluous to say that he was the hardest hitter—he has sent balls out of the Oval on three sides of that gigantic ground—and the most speedy run-getter I ever saw in the cricket-field. A hundred runs an hour was about his normal pace. He stands quite alone as the hitter of my time, and will never be excelled, even if he is equalled. Without pads—which he said interfered with his running—and without gloves, he forced the fastest bowling, apparently without any fear of injury. Once he paid the penalty for disregarding the precautionary batting gloves by having a finger-nail ripped off by a ball from S. M. J. Woods, but even then Mr. Thornton seemed to care less about his injury than about the fact that the same ball disturbed his bails. The secret of Mr. Thornton's hitting power was his eyesight and timing the ball correctly.

Mr. Thornton has a rare collection of cricket

stories, and is very fond of telling them. One I must quote though I figure in it, and the laugh is against me in the end :

" In 1888, I think it was " (says Mr. Thornton), " I managed to bag a brace against the Australians on a sticky wicket at Scarborough. That night, when dining at Londesborough Lodge, a big parcel was brought into me. I at once smelt a rat, as I was not expecting any parcel, particularly as I saw old W. G.'s eagle eye fixed on me. However, I didn't want to spoil the fun, and I opened it. The parcel contained the biggest pair of specs. you ever saw, about a yard wide. I had three more by post next day. Well, this wasn't all. We went to the circus after dinner, where Lord Londesborough used to take seats for all the pros. and their families, as well as for us. When the clown appeared ('Whimsical Walker' by name) he was dressed up in an Eton blue cap, no pads and gloves, like me, and when he began fumbling about in his pockets the ringmaster said, 'What are you looking for, Walker ?' 'Oh,' he said, ' I got a brace of duck's eggs on the ground to-day, and I can't get them out.'

" Ultimately he did get them out, and the roars of laughter that followed, as well as the cheers that greeted his entry, I shall never forget. It was all really very gratifying to me. I always think W. G. and Harris arranged this little episode, but whoever did it carried it out wonderfully well, as I had not the slightest inkling of it in advance. I paid old W. G. out afterwards by having a letter delivered to him at dinner, purporting to come from Farrands, the umpire, who had given him l.b.w., saying he should decline to stand as umpire the next day unless W. G. apologised for what he had said about his umpiring. The Old Man took it all in at the time, but we let him know the truth during the evening."

ROBERT THOMS (born May 19, 1825)—"Bob Thoms," as every one calls him—is one of the very best umpires the world has seen. What Bob doesn't know about cricket is not worth knowing. As he is fond of saying with a wise wink in his eye, "I watch this game, my boy," and as he has been watching cricket for fifty years he has stores of knowledge, and only needs an index to make him a walking encyclopædia of cricket. I wish I could remember some of Bob's sententious remarks as he stands at the wickets and comments on everybody's form : no one resents being criticised or advised by him. Bob prides himself on being something of a prophet, and often reminds cricketers that when they were beginning their career he prophesied a great future for them. When he stands, as he often does, in a school match, he gives the youngsters scraps of valuable and timely advice, and has always a word of congratulation for a boy who has done well.

Mr. CHARLES L. TOWNSEND (born November 7, 1876) is, I believe, to be the great cricketer of the end of the century. He is a *protégé* of my own, and concerning his future I entertain hopes to

which I had better not give expression. He has
done enough already to justify my belief that he is
one of the best all-round amateurs in the cricket-
field. His father, Frank Townsend, was in his
day a famous Gloucestershire cricketer, and as
dashing a batsman as I ever saw, but Charlie
promises to surpass his father's best achievements. He has all the natural advantages of
height, nerve, strength, and eyesight, as well as
the benefit which comes from early training
and sound coaching. As a schoolboy at Clifton
College, Charlie established a reputation as a
bowler—he began as a slow bowler—and when
scarcely seventeen began to play for Gloucestershire, his first appearance in first-class cricket
being against Middlesex at Clifton in August
1893. He played till the end of the season
for Gloucestershire, and distinguished himself
against the Australians by taking five wickets for
an average cost of fourteen runs apiece. At that
time his batting was a thing of promise rather
than reality, but in 1895 he shot to the front with
both bat and ball. He was unable to play until
late in the summer, as he was then at college, but
in twelve matches he got 124 wickets for 12.73
runs each, and scored 365 in eighteen innings.
In this season he played for the South against the
North and for the English Eleven which met
Mr. Stoddart's team during the Hastings Festival.
On his form that year he would certainly have
secured a place in an England Eleven. During
1896 he fell off a little, and in 1897 his bowling

was not quite so deadly, though his batting had improved amazingly. But 1898 saw him in grand all-round form, and he added his name to the short list of cricketers who have achieved the double feat of scoring 1000 runs and taking 100 wickets in first-class cricket — his record being 1270 runs in thirty-seven innings and 145 wickets at an average cost of 20.63. For the first time he played for the Gentlemen against the Players at Lord's—viz., in my birthday match. Charlie bowls over the wicket, with a high right-hand delivery, and sends down a fast medium ball with a deceptive leg-break. Though at times his length is apt to fall a little short he commands the ball with marked ability, and puts in an occasional straight fast ball which most batsmen find dangerous. He bats left hand, and can hit hard, though he generally plays a steady consistent game. His long reach permits him to play forward easily, and he drives with exceptional cleanness. His fielding is smart and reliable, and he plays keenly from beginning to end of a match. He is a great cricketer, and I shall be disappointed in him if he does not surpass all that he has already done and prove himself a pillar of strength to Gloucestershire cricket for many years to come.

J. T. TYLDESLEY (born November 22, 1873) began to play for Lancashire late in the season of 1895, and immediately attracted attention by his capital batting. It was not until 1897, however, that he took his place among the best professional batsmen. In that year he scored nearly a thousand runs and ended with an average of 33. Last year his form was even better, and for Lancashire he scored 1801 runs in forty-six innings—heading the county averages with 39.15 and taking a good place in the first-class averages with 1918 runs in fifty-two innings. He has already gained the distinction of scoring two separate centuries in one match (106 and 100 for Lancashire v. Warwickshire in 1897). His selection to play for England in the first two test matches this season was a well-earned recognition of his batting powers. He scores freely, even on a slow wicket, and hits hard with splendid confidence. His fielding is irreproachable, and he is one of the few cricketers who can return the ball well from the long-field.

GEORGE ULYETT (born at Pitsmoor, Sheffield, October 21, 1851). For twenty years George Ulyett was one of Yorkshire's most reliable professionals, and was unquestionably the greatest all-round cricketer the county ever produced. His sustained record for many years entitled him to a place in any representative team. Though his most conspicuous successes were with the bat, his bowling was remarkably fine, while his fielding, especially in the long-field, was first rate. His hard clean hitting made him a favourite with spectators, who never failed to show their appreciation of the confidence and ease with which, when set, he would punish the bowling, irrespective of its quality. His driving was especially interesting to watch, as he threw all his gigantic strength into his strokes. The secret of his bowling success was a combination of pace and off break, coupled with the fact that he made the ball rise very rapidly. On bumping wickets it was no pleasure to play Ulyett's bowling. In the field he was almost infallible, and any one who saw the superb catch with which he dismissed Mr. Shuter at Lord's in the Gentlemen *v.* Players match in 1891 will never forget the roar of applause which went up when Ulyett, fielding at extra long-on, leaped up and caught the ball just as it was dropping on the awning over the spectators' seats. From 1876 until two or three years ago, Ulyett had his place in nearly every representative eleven. He accompanied Lillywhite's team to Australia in 1876, and revisited the colony in 1881, 1884, and 1887, went out with Daft's team to America and Canada in 1879, and with Major Wharton's team to South Africa in 1888.

Ulyett had a passion for practical joking, and once or twice carried this habit to extremes. On the occasion of the picnic down Sydney Harbour, given to the team then in Australia, Ulyett, who went out in a small boat towed by a steamer, conceived the idea of frightening one of the gentlemen in the boat. He pretended to scuffle with the gentleman, and while doing so purposely fell overboard—a foolhardy trick, as sharks are not uncommon in those waters. George, who was a splendid swimmer, struck out for the shore, but

was fished up.   Then he proceeded to frighten
the gentleman by accusing him of pushing him
overboard and demanding compensation.   On
another occasion Ulyett, who was also a good
boxer, was invited, when playing at Moreton-in-
the-Marsh, to the house of a gentleman, who, after
being introduced to some of the Yorkshire
cricketers, asked if any one would like a little
"mill" with the gloves. Some one suggested
that Ulyett should have a round or two, but he
pretended that he knew nothing about boxing.
However, after some persuasion he did put the
gloves on, and in a few minutes convinced his
host that he had him at his mercy.   It was George
Ulyett who distributed the wickets as weapons
of offence and defence—when Lord Harris's team
was mobbed at Sydney.   Luckily there was no
need for the wickets to be brought into active service.   George Ulyett armed with a wicket would
have been a desperate antagonist even for an
Australian larrikin.

ALBERT WARD (born November 21, 1865) has
been the most consistent run-getter in the Lancashire Eleven for the last ten years.   He is a
stylish though rather slow batsman, for though he
can hit out when he likes, he is often very tedious
to watch.   His defence is remarkably good, and
his judgment is seldom at fault.   Usually he
goes in first for Lancashire, and begins his innings with an apparent determination to tire the
bowlers even at the expense of boring the spectators, who nowadays prefer hitting to science.

He visited Australia with Mr. Stoddart's first team, and much of the success of the team was due to his steady play.

Mr. I. D. WALKER (born January 8, 1844 : died July 6, 1898) rendered services to cricket which could not be extolled too highly. Coming first into prominence as a member of Harrow Eleven, for whom he played four times, twice as captain of the team, he associated himself with Middlesex, for which county he played for twenty years, captaining the eleven until 1884. He was a member of the famous Walker family, whose name is indissolubly associated with Harrow and Middlesex cricket, and was perhaps the best batsman of the four celebrated brothers, who made Middlesex cricket by their instrumentality in establishing the county club. " I. D." was a batsman famed the world over for his hard hitting, especially on the off side. He was unquestionably one of the fastest scorers I ever saw, and I shall never forget his hitting when playing for Middlesex against Gloucestershire in 1883, when with Alfred Lyttelton he put on 324 runs for the second wicket—226 of them being scored in 105 minutes, a terrific pace even by two such notorious hitters. Against the Players in 1868 he scored 165 runs for the Gentlemen with almost equal alacrity. He hit out with the vigour of Bonnor or C. I. Thornton, and on one occasion sent a ball into the billiard - room at Lord's ! Driving was his *forte*, and his most characteristic stroke a high hit over cover-point's head straight to the boundary. He was a superb field too, and often amazed people by bringing off a catch which no one imagined he would reach.

Mr. S. M. J. Woods (born April 14, 1868) came to England to study, and was educated at Brighton College and Jesus College, Cambridge. He captained the University in 1890. He has become such a familiar figure to English spectators that we forget that he is an Australian, and take credit to England for producing such a fine specimen of manhood as "Sammy" Woods. A fine specimen he is!—a giant in size, in strength, and in pluck! He made himself famous by his fast bowling, but his pace has fallen off, and he now distinguishes himself more with the bat, hitting very hard. He bowled with a high action at a great pace, and on any wicket was a dangerous opponent. By residence he played for Somersetshire (of which he is now captain), joining the Western county just as it was elevated to the first-class. "Sammy" as a footballer has rendered great service to his University and College, being far away the best forward. He is not a good scrimmager, but if given a roving commission he is continually bringing off some grand bits of play. He is a wonderful tackler, and has played in International matches for many years.

Mr. John Perkins, younger brother of Henry Perkins, late secretary of the M.C.C., was born at Sawston, Cambridgeshire, on May 17, 1837, and educated at Bury St. Edmunds Grammar School, where he was captain of the School and Eleven in 1855, when he went up to Christ's College, Cambridge. In 1857 he played in the United Eleven at Lord's, but gave up cricket for reading in 1858, and thus lost all chance of his "Blue." In 1861 he was secretary of the College Boat Club and captain of the eleven, scoring in College matches 346 runs for five completed innings. In 1861, in the memorable match Cambridge *v.* Surrey, which was won by the former by two wickets at ten minutes past seven on Saturday evening, with H. Perkins and A. Diver the not-outs and Buttress *non compos*, he got 24 runs while T. Hayward was getting 26. This and 67 for M.C.C. *v.* The University, and 67 and 16 for Cambridge *v.* Kent in 1863, were his best performances, though he five times exceeded the century in minor matches. He was invited to join the M.C.C. and to play for the Gentlemen *v.* Players at Lord's in 1863, but was unable to accept the latter invitation, owing to having a reading-party in Wales. Having, in 1861, been elected to a Fellowship at Downing, he assumed the management of about 6000 acres of shooting, including two grand partridge farms, at the Fourmile Stables and Six-mile Bottom. This introduced him to General Hall, the father of partridge driving, with whom he had many grand days' sport, and also to H. R. H. the Duke of Cambridge. Downing College possesses four good coverts—notably "Gilrags," perhaps the most noted in the Cambridgeshire Hunt, and this fact led to his being made secretary of the Hunt in 1873. He was presented by the Hunt with £150 worth of plate in 1880, and has just resigned the office after twenty-five years' service, in consequence of no longer being able to look up subscriptions in the field. He considers that his career at Downing is replete with reminiscences of an amount of sport, conviviality and joviality that has never fallen to the lot of any other College Don. Many a good day's sport have I had with him at Four-mile Stables, Six-mile Bottom, Gamlingay, amongst the potatoes, and at Hatley when staying with him at Cambridge, or at the Palace. No one knows how to beat a field, when out shooting, better than John Perkins, who is one of the best sports-men I ever met. The first time I saw him was at Bishop's Stortford, in July 1868, when the All England Eleven played eighteen of Bishop's Stortford. I played for the eighteen. Mr. John Perkins was captain. I remember we stayed with Mr. A. Spencer and that we won the match by nine wickets.

Mr. HENRY PERKINS, the late secretary of the Marylebone Cricket Club, was born at Sawston, Cambridgeshire, on December 10, 1832. He was educated at Bury St. Edmunds Grammar School and Trinity College, Cambridge. He got his "Blue" for cricket and played for his 'Varsity against Oxford in the year 1854. In the second innings he made more runs than all the others of the side together—the highest score, 27, out of a total of 53 runs, coming from his bat. This was his first match at Lord's.

He was a great supporter of the Cambridgeshire County Club, and captained and managed the eleven for six years from 1858 to 1864. He was a good all-round player, a good hard hitter, bowled under-hand rather fast, and could field anywhere, being especially good at mid-wicket and at long-stop, which in those days, when the ground was rough, was a very hard post to fill with credit to oneself.

A curious incident is that R. A. Fitzgerald and H. Perkins both played for Cambridge University *v.* Oxford in 1854, and that afterwards they should both fill the post of secretary to the Marylebone Cricket Club, the former from 1863 to 1876 and the latter from 1877 to 1897.

Mr. WALTER BODEN is the success-assuring and popular President of the Derbyshire County Cricket Club.

His connection with it dates from its beginning in 1870 to the present time. In sunshine and shower, on the field and in the committee-room, his presence has always been a stimulant to success, the committee and the players always reposing in him a confidence born of his unerring judgment, which itself results from innate ability and long experience.

Mr. Boden is by no means conversant with the cricket side of sport alone, for he has played the game all round.

The success with which he has met as a shot is shown by the number of heads which adorn the walls of his house.

He has been a prominent member of the

Meynell Hunt for many years past, and seldom does a " meet" take place without his presence in the field. We believe his connection with the Meynell Hunt extends over fifty years. He is the chairman of the Derby Recreation Company, a corporation which made the County Cricket Ground and the success of the Derby Races, so well known to the sporting world, that further comment is unnecessary. As to generosity, we do not know who esteems him the more—the sportsman or the philanthropist, for with Mr. Boden generosity and love of sport walk arm-in-arm.

STATISTICS OF W. G. GRACE'S CRICKET

W. G. GRACE IN FIRST-CLASS CRICKET

| BATTING | | | | BOWLING | | |
Completed Innings	Runs	Average	Year	Runs	Wickets	Average
7	197	28·14	1865	268	20	13·40
11	581	52·81	1866	434	31	14·00
5	154	30·80	1867	292	39	7·48
11	625	56·81	1868 {	— / 686	1 / 48	— / 14·29
23	1,320	57·39	1869	1,193	73	16·34
33	1,808	54·78	1870	782	50	15·64
35	2,739	78·25	1871	1,346	79	17·03
29	1,561	53·82	1872 {	— / 736	6 / 62	— / 11·87
30	2,139	71·30	1873 {	— / 1,307	5 / 101	— / 12·94
32	1,664	52·00	1874	1,780	140	12·71
46	1,498	32·56	1875	2,468	191	12·92
42	2,622	62·42	1876	2,458	129	19·05
37	1,474	39·83	1877	2,291	179	12·79
40	1,151	28·77	1878	2,204	152	14·50
26	993	38·19	1879	1,491	113	13·19
24	951	39·62	1880	1,480	84	17·61
24	917	38·20	1881	1,026	57	18·00
37	975	26·35	1882	1,754	101	17·36
39	1,352	34·66	1883	2,077	94	22·09
40	1,361	34·02	1884	1,762	82	21·48
39	1,688	43·28	1885	2,199	117	18·79
52	1,846	35·50	1886	2,439	122	19·99
38	2,062	54·26	1887	2,078	97	21·42
58	1,886	32·51	1888	1,691	93	18·18
43	1,396	32·46	1889	1,019	44	23·15
52	1,476	28·38	1890	1,183	61	19·39
39	771	19·76	1891	973	58	16·77

BATTING				BOWLING		
Completed Innings	Runs	Average	Year	Runs	Wickets	Average
10	448	44·80	1891–2	134	5	26·80
34	1,055	31·02	1892	958	31	30·90
45	1,609	35·75	1893	854	22	38·81
44	1,293	29·38	1894	732	29	25·24
46	2,346	51·00	1895	527	16	32·93
50	2,135	42·70	1896	1,249	52	24·01
39	1,532	39·28	1897	1,242	56	22·17
36	1,513	42·02	1898	917	36	25·47
22	515	23·40	1899	482	20	24·10
30	1,277	42·56	1900	969	32	30·28
31	1,007	32·48	1901	1,111	51	21·78
32	1,187	37·09	1902	1,074	46	23·34
26	593	22·80	1903	479	10	47·90
25	637	25·48	1904	687	21	32·71
13	250	19·23	1905	383	7	54·71
9	241	26·77	1906	268	13	20·61
2	19	9·50	1907	—	—	—
2	40	20·00	1908	5	0	—
1,389	54,904	39·53	Totals {	— / 51,488	12 / 2,864	— / 17·97

Based on statistics by F. S. Ashley-Cooper and G. Neville Weston

W. G. GRACE IN FIRST-CLASS CRICKET AND IN MINOR MATCHES

CENTURIES:
First-class matches . 126 Minor matches . . 95

HIGHEST FIRST-CLASS SCORE:
344 for MCC v. Kent at Canterbury, August 11, 1876.

Carried bat through a completed first-class innings 17 times

Grand Total of W.G.'s figures in all classes of cricket

	Runs	Wickets	Catches	Stumpings
First-class matches:	54,904	2,879	871	3
Minor matches:	44,936	4,446	641	51
Grand Total:	99,840	7,325	1,512	54

HOW W. G. GRACE WAS OUT

Caught	760
Bowled	439
Caught and bowled	76
L.B.W.	54
Run out	27
Stumped	26
Hit wicket	6
Completed innings	1,388

HOW W. G. GRACE SCORED

0	83
1 to 9	345
10 to 19	251
20 to 29	190
30 to 39	148
40 to 49	96
50 to 59	90
60 to 69	56
70 to 79	49
80 to 89	34
90 to 99	25
Centuries	126
Innings commenced	1,493

MEN WHO HAVE CLEAN BOWLED W. G. GRACE IN FIRST-CLASS CRICKET MORE THAN THREE TIMES

20 Times.
Shaw (A.)
14 Times.
Richardson (T.)
13 Times.
Barlow (R. G.)
11 Times.
Morley (F.)
10 Times.
Briggs (J.)
Emmett (T.)
Hill (A.)
9 Times.
Peate (E.)
Shaw (J. C.)

8 Times.
Flowers (W.)
Southerton (J.)
7 Times.
Lohmann (G. A.)
F. R. Spofforth
C. T. B. Turner
6 Times.
Bates (W.)
Hearne (J. T.)
Martin (F.)
G. E. Palmer
Peel (R.)
A. G. Steel
Wootton (G.)

5 Times.
Attewell (W.)
Barnes (W.)
G. Giffen
Lillywhite (J. jun.)
Mold (A.)
Wainwright (E.)
4 Times.
Hearne (A.)
Mycroft (W.)
Tate (F. W.)
H. Trumble
Watson (A.)

FEATS, RECORDS, AND CURIOSITIES OF THE CRICKET FIELD

	Year.
The first authenticated mention of cricket is in evidence recorded in archives of the borough of Guildford Anno Elizabethæ 40	1597
First match between the Hambledon Club and England . .	1772
First Inter-County match (recorded), Kent v. Surrey . . .	1773
First match in which hit wicket appears, Hambledon v. England, Sevenoaks	1773
Stumps were increased from two to three about the year . .	1775
Leg-before-wicket introduced (about)	1775
First match supposed to have been played with three stumps, Hambledon v. England, Sevenoaks, June 18 . . .	1777
First tie match on record, Kent v. Hambledon, Hambledon, July 8 and 9	1783
First match at Lord's (original) Ground, Middlesex v. Essex, May 31	1787
First match recorded of M.C.C. (v. White Conduit Club, Lord's), June 27	1788
The first Colts' match was Surrey v. Hants, in	1788
First match (recorded) of Notts (v. Leicester), at Leicester, September 11	1789
First match registered in books of Marylebone Club, Middlesex v. Essex (Lord's), May 16	1791
Last recorded match of Hambledon Club (v. Twenty-two of Middlesex, Lord's), June 6	1791
First match recorded between Surrey and England, Burghley Park, August 5	1793
Five days' match between Surrey and England, Lord's . .	1795
First match (recorded) between Eton and Westminster, Hounslow Heath, July 25	1796
A match between two Elevens on Horseback was played in . .	1800
First match (recorded) between Eton and Harrow, Lord's, August 2	1805
Sawdust, it is believed, was introduced by Lord F. Beauclerck about	1806
First match between Gentlemen and Players, Lord's, July 7 .	1806
The first match on the present Lord's Ground was Kent v. M.C.C. and Ground, June 22	1814

First match in which a batsman scored two centuries. Epsom *v.* Sussex, with Osbaldeston and Lambert. W. Lambert, 107, not out, and 157, Lord's, July 2, 3, 4, 5 and 6 . . . 1817

First match with stumps of the size and height now used, B.'s *v.* England, Lord's, June 2 1817

First (recorded) score of over 200, Mr. W. Ward, 278, M.C.C. *v.* Norfolk, Lord's, June 24 1820

First match in which Gentlemen beat Players on even terms, Lord's, July 7 1822

First match between Harrow and Winchester, July 27 . . 1825

First (recorded) match, Kent *v.* Sussex, Brighton, June 1 and 3 . 1825

First match between Eton and Winchester, Lord's, August 4 . 1826

First (recorded) match between Oxford and Cambridge, Lord's, June 4 1827

First match in which wides appeared, Kent *v.* Sussex, Brighton, September 17 1827

First Laws of Cricket were published 1827

Mr. Tramfer and his sheep-dog played two gentlemen of Middlesex, and won. The dog stood at the side of his master until the ball was hit, and was so quick at fielding that their opponents had great difficulty in scoring a single run . . . 1827

First (recorded) match between Oxford and Cambridge, at Oxford, June 8 1829

First match between Sussex and Surrey, Midhurst, July 16 . 1830

First match in which no-balls were scored, M.C.C. *v.* Middlesex, Lord's, May 17 1830

First match between Surrey and Sussex, Godalming, July 8 . 1830

First match between M.C.C. and Oxford University, Oxford, May 21 1832

Mr. E. Winter, in cutting at a ball, hit the top of the wicket so hard that the bails were driven into the stumps, where they stuck, although the wickets were almost in a horizontal position. Batsman not out 1832

First match of Yorkshire County (*v.* Norfolk), September 2 . 1833

First match between Old Harrovians and Old Etonians, Lord's, June 16 1834

First match between M.C.C. and Cambridge University, May 27 1835

First match between Sussex and Yorkshire, Sheffield, September 10 1835

First match between Notts and Sussex, Brighton, August 27 . 1835

First match between North and South, Lord's, July 11 . . 1836

First match between Notts and Kent, Malling, July 27 . . 1837

First important match on Trent Bridge Ground, Nottingham (Notts *v.* Twenty-two next best of Notts), September 3 . 1838

The first match in which cards were printed was Gentlemen *v.* Players, at Old Lillywhite's Cricket Ground, Brighton, in 1838

The first Canterbury Cricket Week began June 1 . . . 1842

First match in which wides were counted (Gentlemen of Kent *v.* Gentlemen of England, at Lord's), June 17 1844

First match of I Zingari (*v.* Newport Pagnell), August 25 . . 1845

First match played on Kennington Oval, Mitcham *v.* Montpelier, July 17 1845

Surrey County Club formed, October 1845

First match of All England Eleven (*v.* Twenty of Sheffield, Sheffield), September 1 1846

Last match on Box's Ground at Brighton (Sussex, with Mynn, v.
England), September 27 1847
A swallow was killed by a ball bowled to the Earl of Winterton
in 1847
The telegraph scoring-board was introduced at Lord's in . 1848
The first match in which cards were printed at Lord's was Sussex
v. M.C.C. and Ground, June 26 1848
First match between Yorkshire and Kent, Sheffield, May 2 1849
Leg-byes first recorded, England Eleven v. Twenty-two of
Edinburgh, May 6 1850
First match between Westminster and Charterhouse, Vincent
Square, August 8 1850
First match between Surrey and Yorkshire, Sheffield, July 21 . 1851
First match between Surrey and Notts, Oval, July 17 . . 1851
First match of United Eleven (v. Twenty Gentlemen of Hants,
Portsmouth), August 26 1852
W. Caffyn, playing for the All England Eleven v. Twenty-two of
Ipswich, threw in a ball from long-off which passed through
the stumps and dislodged the bails at the bowler's end, and
then travelled to the other wicket, passing through the
stumps and dislodging the bails also 1853
Last match of Winchester at Lord's (v. Eton), August 8 . 1854
First match at Bramall Lane, Sheffield (Yorkshire v. Sussex),
August 27 1855
First match between Rugby and Charterhouse, July 4 . 1855
First match between Cheltenham and Marlborough, Cheltenham,
May 9 1856
First match between Rugby and Marlborough, Lord's, June 26 . 1856
First match between "All England Eleven" and "United
Eleven," Lord's, June 1 1857
Mr. Fiennes was given out, in the I Zingari v. Royal Artillery
match at Woolwich, for playing a ball into the folds of his
pads, which the wicket-keeper secured 1858
Mr. H. Payne, for Chalçot v. Bow, batted first in both innings,
and scored all the runs for his side (24 and 10), and was not
out both times 1859
First English Team (Parr's) sailed for America, September 7 . 1859
First match of First English Team in Canada (v. Twenty-two
of Lower Canada, Montreal), September 24 . . . 1859
E. M. Grace, playing in a 9 a-side match for Berkeley v. Knole
Park in Gloucestershire, scored 100 out of the total of 119, of
which 3 were extras, and took every wicket in the Knole
Park second innings, August 20 1861
First English Team (Stephenson's) sailed for Australia, Oc-
tober 20 1861
First match of First English Team in Australia (v. Eighteen of
Victoria, Melbourne), January 1 1862
Jas. Lillywhite played in every Sussex County match from 1862 to 1881
First match between Middlesex and Sussex, Islington, June 6 . 1864
Follow innings (if 80 behind) introduced 1864
First match on Old Trafford Ground, Manchester (Gentlemen of
Lancashire v. Warwickshire), August 30 1864
For Twenty-two of Castlemaine v. W. G. Grace's English Team,
in Australia, Mr. Easton was batting two hours for 3 runs . 1864
First match of "United South" Eleven (v. Twenty-two of Ireland,
Dublin), May 11 1865

First match of Aboriginal Eleven in England (*v.* Gentlemen of
Surrey), at Oval 1868
W. G. Grace and B. B. Cooper scored 283 for first wicket of
Gentlemen of South *v.* Players of South, at Oval, July 15, 16,
and 17 (record for many years) 1869
First appearance of W. G. Grace for M.C.C. (at Oxford, *v.*
University), May 13 1869
Mr. W. Yardley—130 for Cambridge in 1872, and 100 in 1870—
is the only batsman who has twice played an innings of 100
runs in the Oxford and Cambridge match
Mr. W. G. Grace, who has never been dismissed for a pair of
spectacles in a first-class match, bagged a " brace " in the
following matches : (1) For Twenty-two of Lansdowne *v.*
A.E.E. (Tinley the bowler), May 28, 1863 ; (2) For U.S.E.E.
v. Twenty-two of Cadoxton Club (Howitt the bowler),
May 21, 1868 ; (3) For Bedminster *v.* G. W. Ry., Swindon
(Laverick the bowler), May 7 1870
First match of Derbyshire (*v.* Lancashire, at Manchester),
May 29 1871
First match of Gloucestershire County Club (*v.* M.C.C. and G.,
Lord's), June 4 1871
First match on Derbyshire County Ground (*v.* Lancashire),
August 17 1871
Mr. G. Richards, for the Harrow Blues *v.* Civil Service, batted
77 minutes without scoring 1871
Mr. E. M. Grace averaged 142 runs per innings for Thornbury
Club in 1872
Mr. E. M. Grace hit 295 runs in 100 minutes, out of a total of
331, for Thornbury Club in 1873
Swallows flitting across the wicket stopped the Gloucester-
shire *v.* Nottinghamshire match for a short time, at Trent
Bridge, in 1875
Highest individual aggregate (up to this date) in season of first-
class cricket, W. G. Grace, 2739 runs 1876
W. G. Grace scored 344 for M.C.C. *v.* Kent, Canterbury,
August 11 and 12 (the record till 1895) 1876
First match between All England and United South Elevens,
Lord's 1876
Mr. W. G. Grace scored 400, not out, United South of England *v.*
Twenty-two of Grimsby, Grimsby, July 10 1876
Best throw with a cricket-ball in England, 132 yards, W. F.
Forbes, at Oxford, March 1876
Lowest total in first-class match, 12, by Oxford University (one
short) *v.* M.C.C. and G., Oxford, May 1877
Eleven members of the Messrs. Robinson, belonging to Somerset
and Gloucestershire, played thirty-five matches from 1878 to
1890, winning twenty-six and losing nine. Eleven members
of the Messrs. Lucas, Lyttelton, Grace, Christopherson,
Cæsar, Watney, and Brotherhood families have also played
matches at one time or another.
First match of First Australian Team in England (*v.* Notts), at
Nottingham, May 20 1878
First match of Australian Team in London (*v.* M.C.C. and G.),
Lord's, May 27 1878
First match on Leicestershire County Ground (Eleven of County *v.*
Twenty-two Colts) 1878

Mr. H. F. Boyle captured seven wickets with eight balls for the Australians *v.* Eighteen of Elland at Leeds in . . . 1878

First match between England and Australia, Oval, September 6 1880

Highest individual score hit for an Australian Team in England, 286, not out, by Mr. W. L. Murdoch against Sussex at Brighton in May 1882

Messrs. G. F. Vernon and A. H. Trevor made 603 for second wicket, Orleans Club *v.* Rickling Green, at Rickling Green, August 4 and 5 1882

Highest individual innings in first-class cricket in Australia, Mr. W. L. Murdoch, 321, New South Wales *v.* Victoria, Sydney, February 10 1882

In the England *v.* Australia match at the Oval, all the England Eleven bowled, August 11 1884

Highest individual innings on record, A. E. Stoddart, 485 for Hampstead *v.* Stoics, at Hampstead, August 4 . . . 1886

Highest individual score in Oxford and Cambridge match, 143, K. J. Key (Oxford), Lord's 1886

Four scores of a hundred in same innings, I Zingari (L. K. Jarvis, 152; Lord Dalkeith, 120; H. W. Forster, 107; and Lord G. Scott, 100) *v.* Bullingdon, at Bullingdon, June 15 . . . 1886

Shrewsbury, when playing for Shaw's Team *v.* New South Wales, in Australia, was clean bowled in both innings by Mr. C. T. B. Turner without scoring, February 18 and 19 1887

The largest innings in an important match up-to-date, 803, at Melbourne, by Non-Smokers against Smokers, March 17, 18, 19, 21 1887

An important match over in a day, Eleven of North *v.* Eleven of South, Lord's, May 30 1887

The only instance of two successive scores of over 200 in important matches, Mr. W. W. Read, 247 for Surrey *v.* Lancashire, at Manchester, on June 16, 17, 18, and 244 for Surrey *v.* Cambridge University, at Oval, on June 20, 21, 22 1887

The largest gate at an English first-class match was in the Surrey *v.* Notts match, at the Oval, when 24,450 paid for admission ; and the total for the three days was 51,607 exclusive of members, August 1887

Only instance of first three batsmen scoring a hundred in an Inter-County match, Ulyett, 124, Hall, 110, and F. Lee, 119, for Yorkshire *v.* Kent at Canterbury, August 3 . . . 1887

Yorkshire's 434 made for two wickets on final day of match against Lancashire, at Bradford, August 6 . . . 1887

Two English Teams in Australia (Mr. Vernon's and Shrewsbury's) left London, September 15 1887

Highest total by an English Team in eleven-a-side matches in Australia, 624, by Shrewsbury's Team *v.* Victoria, at Melbourne, December 18 1887

Highest score by English batsmen in eleven-a-side matches in Australia, 232, A. Shrewsbury for Shrewsbury's Team *v.* Victoria, at Melbourne, December 18 1887

The aggregate scores of W. G. Grace in first-class cricket have exceeded 2000 on six occasions—viz., 2739 in 1871, 2622 in 1876, 2346 in 1895, 2139 in 1873, 2135 in 1896, and 2062 in 1887

Twenty-two matches between England and Australia have now been played in England, and of this number England has won twelve and Australia four, the other six having been left unfinished. The third game in 1890 had, owing to continuous rain, to be abandoned without a ball being bowled. The highest total in the nineteen matches is 551 by Australia at the Oval in August 1884. England's largest is 483 at the Oval in August 1893. The lowest total in the series of matches is 44 by Australia at the Oval in August 1896, England's lowest is 53 at Lord's in 1888

The highest innings at Lord's, 735, M.C.C. and Ground v. Wiltshire, August 13, ... 1888

The highest individual innings on the Warwickshire County Ground, H. C. Maul, 267, Warwickshire v. Staffordshire, August 16 1888

First English Team (Major Wharton's) for South Africa left London November 21 1888

The rule empowering a captain to terminate his innings was first applied at Lord's in the M.C.C. and Ground v. Northumberland match, August 10 1889

The first English Team that visited India was Mr. G. F. Vernon's, which left London October 31 1889

The largest number of runs for second wicket in important match, A. Shrewsbury and W. Gunn, 398, Notts. v. Sussex, at Nottingham, May 16 1890

Highest individual score hit against an Australian Team in England, 228, by William Gunn for the Players at Lord's in June 1890

The highest innings against an Australian Team in England, 526, by Players, at Lord's, June 20 1890

Three hundreds in an innings in a first-class match, Cambridge University v. Sussex, F. G. F. Ford, 191, C. P. Foley, 117, and McGregor, 131, in second innings, Brighton, June 20 1890

Batsman dismissed for "handling the ball" (Chatterton, in Derbyshire v. Notts, Derby), July 28 1890

County match ending in a tie, Somersetshire v. Middlesex, Taunton, August 22 1890

Somersetshire went through season without losing or leaving unfinished a single match 1890

The highest innings for the Players against the Gentlemen, 169, W. Gunn (Hastings) 1891

The highest score for Winchester College (J. R. Mason, 147) v. Eton, June 24 1892

The highest aggregate in Oxford and Cambridge match, 1100, Lord's, June 30 1892

The highest individual aggregate in Oxford and Cambridge match, M. R. Jardine (140 and 39), for Oxford, June 30 . 1892

Highest innings in Rugby and Marlborough match, 432, by Marlborough, July 27 1892

Highest individual innings in Rugby v. Marlborough match, P. R. Creed, 213, for Marlborough, July 27 . . . 1892

Four hundreds in same innings, A. P. Lucas's Eleven (L. H. Gay 112, F. A. Philips 120, F. E. Rowe 107 not out, and H. M. Taberer 114) v. Free Foresters, Chelmsford, August 12 1892

The highest individual score in the Oxford and Cambridge match is 143 by Mr. K. J. Key for Oxford in 1886, and the next highest 140 by Mr. M. R. Jardine for Oxford in . . . 1892

Three hundreds in same innings in first-class match, Notts v. Sussex (A. Shrewsbury 164, W. Gunn 156, and W. Barnes 102), Brighton, June 8 1893

Highest innings (up to this date) in first-class match, 843, Australian Team v. Oxford University Past and Present, Portsmouth, July 31 1893

Highest innings up to date England v. Australia in England, 483, Oval, August 16 1893

Highest score for first wicket against Australian bowling in England : Mr. Stoddart and Mr. F. S. Jackson scored 176 for the first wicket for Mr. C. I. Thornton's Eleven against the Australians at Scarborough in September . . . 1893

Aggregates of 2000 runs in a season have been obtained by Gunn : 2057 in 1893 ; A. E. Stoddart, 2072 in . . . 1893

First match of a South African Eleven in England, Sheffield Park, May 21 1894

Mr. W. G. Grace's highest innings at Lord's, 196, M.C.C. and Ground v. Cambridge University, June 26 1894

First match of a Dutch Eleven in England, Gentlemen of Holland v. Norwood Club, Norwood, August 6 . . . 1894

Surrey played England (the first time since 1866), Oval, May 27 1895

The highest aggregate in a first-class match, 1410, Sussex v. Oxford University, Brighton, June 26 1895

Mr. A. C. MacLaren made 424 for Lancashire v. Somerset (the highest individual score in first-class cricket), Taunton, July 15 1895

A thousand runs scored by an individual batsman in May, W. G. Grace 1895

The highest innings on record up-to-date, 924, Carlton v. Melbourne University, at Melbourne, February 8 . . 1896

The highest innings in a first-class match, 887, Yorkshire v. Warwickshire, Birmingham, May 8 1896

Four hundreds in the same innings (F. S. Jackson 117, Wainwright 126, Peel 210 not out, Lord Hawke 166), Yorkshire v. Warwickshire, Birmingham, May 8 1896

Gloucestershire's highest innings in first-class cricket, 551 v. Sussex, Brighton, August 3 1896

Highest innings by Sussex in county cricket, 559, v. Somersetshire, Taunton, August 6 1896

Leicestershire's best innings in first-class cricket, 399, v. Lancashire, Leicester, August 6 1896

Mold, for Lancashire, bowled Lohmann with a ball that sent the ball 63 yards 6 inches from the stumps (Oval), August 22 . 1896

Highest aggregate in a first-class match up-to date, 1514, Australia v. Mr. A. E. Stoddart's English Eleven, at Sydney, December 1896

Highest individual aggregate for a season of first-class cricket, K. S. Ranjitsinhji, 2780 runs 1896

The aggregate scores of Robert Abel have exceeded 2000 runs in a season on four occasions—viz., 2057 in 1895, 2218 in 1896, 2090 in 1897, and 2053 in 1898

The highest innings at the Oval was Surrey (811) v. Somerset, May 30 and 31 1899

Three centuries in same innings in first-class match : Abel, 357
(not out); Hayward, 158; Crawford, 129; Surrey *v.*
Somerset, at the Oval, May 30 and 31 1899
A splinter broke off Albert Ward's bat and knocked off his bail
in match between Lancashire and Derbyshire, and he was
given out "hit wicket," June 1899
Highest individual score, A. E. J. Collins at Clifton College,
Clarke's House *v.* North Town, 628 (not out), June 26 . 1899
The highest score ever made in Gentlemen *v.* Players match,
647 by the Players at Kennington Oval, July 6–7 . . 1899

TWO HUNDREDS IN THE SAME MATCH IN
FIRST-CLASS MATCHES.

W. G. Grace, 130 and 102 (not out), for South *v.* North of the
Thames, at Canterbury, August 3 1868
W. G. Grace, 101 and 103 (not out), for Gloucestershire *v.* Kent,
at Clifton, August 25 1887
W. G. Grace, 148 and 153, for Gloucestershire *v.* Yorkshire, at
Clifton, August 16 1888
G. Brann, 105 and 101, for Sussex *v.* Kent, at Brighton,
August 24 1892
A. E. Stoddart, 195 (not out) and 124, for Middlesex *v.* Notts,
at Lord's, June 5 1893
Storer (W.), 100 and 100 (not out), for Derbyshire *v.* Yorkshire,
at Derby, June 25 1896
K. S. Ranjitsinhji, 100 and 125 (not out), for Sussex *v.* Yorkshire,
at Brighton, August 22 (in same day) 1896
Tyldesley (J. T.), 106 and 100 (not out), for Lancashire *v.* War-
wickshire, at Birmingham, July 5 1897
A. C. MacLaren, 142 and 100, England *v.* New South Wales, at
Sydney, November 12 1897
C. B. Fry, 108 and 123 (not out), for Sussex *v.* Middlesex, at
Brighton, July 25 1898
Major Poore 104 and 119 (not out) for Hampshire *v.* Somer-
set, June 1899

HIGHEST INNINGS IN FIRST-CLASS CRICKET.

887, by Yorkshire *v.* Warwickshire, at Birmingham, May 9 . 1896
843, by Australian Team *v.* Past and Present of Oxford and
Cambridge, at Portsmouth, July 31 1893
811, by Surrey *v.* Somerset, May 29–30 1899
803 (for nine wickets), by Non-Smokers *v.* Smokers, at East
Melbourne, March 17 1887
801, by Lancashire *v.* Somersetshire, at Taunton, July 15 . . 1895
726, by Notts *v.* Sussex, at Nottingham, May 17 . . . 1895
703 for nine wickets (innings closed), by Cambridge University
v. Sussex, at Brighton, June 19 1890
698, by Surrey *v.* Sussex, at Kennington Oval, August 9 . . 1888
692, by Essex *v.* Somersetshire, at Taunton, July 11 . . 1895
681 for five wickets (innings declared closed), by Yorkshire *v.*
Sussex, at Sheffield, July 12 1897
674, by Notts *v.* Sussex, at Brighton, June 8 1893

HIGHEST INDIVIDUAL SCORES IN A FIRST-CLASS MATCH.

424, by A. C. MacLaren, for Lancashire v. Somersetshire, at
Taunton, July 15 1895
357, by Abel, for Surrey v. Somerset, Kennington Oval, May 29
and 30 1899
344, by W. G. Grace, for M.C.C. v. Kent, at Canterbury,
August 11 1876
338, by W. W. Read, for Surrey v. Oxford University, at Kennington Oval, June 26 1888
321, by W. L. Murdoch, for New South Wales v. Victoria, at
Sydney, February 10 1882
318, not out, by W. G. Grace, for Gloucestershire v. Yorkshire, at
Cheltenham, August 17 1876
315, not out, by Hayward (T.), for Surrey v. Lancashire, at Kennington Oval, August 18 1898
311, by Brown (J. T.), for Yorkshire v. Sussex, at Sheffield, July 12 1897
301, by W. G. Grace, for Gloucestershire v. Sussex, at Bristol,
August 3 1896
300, by Brown (J. T.), for Yorkshire v. Derbyshire, at Chesterfield,
August 18 1898

HIGHEST INDIVIDUAL SCORES IN ANY MATCH.

628, not out, A. E. J. Collins (aged 14), for Clarke's House,
Clifton v. North Town, on June 26 1899
485, by A. E. Stoddart, for Hampstead v. Stoics, at Hampstead,
August 4 1886
419, not out, by J. S. Carrick, for West of Scotland v. Priory Park,
at Chichester, July 13 1885
415, not out, by W. N. Roe, for Emmanuel College Long Vacation
Club v. Caius College Long Vacation Club, at Cambridge,
July 12 1881
404, not out, by E. F. S. Tylecote, for Classicals v. Moderns, at
Clifton College, May 14, 19, and 26 1868
402, by T. Warne, Carlton v. Richmond, at Carlton, December 3, 10, and 17 1898
400, not out, by W. G. Grace, for United South v. Twenty-two of
Grimsby, at Grimsby, July 10 (the highest against odds) . 1876
323, not out, by F. E. Lacey, for Hampshire v. Norfolk, at Southampton, May 1887

ALL TEN WICKETS IN ONE INNINGS OF A FIRST-CLASS MATCH.

E. Hinkley, for Kent v. England, July 11 1848
J. Wisden, for North v. South, (all bowled) July 15 . . . 1850
V. E. Walker, for England v. Surrey, for 74 runs, July 21 . . 1859
E. M. Grace, for M.C.C. v. Gentlemen of Kent, August 14 . 1862
V. E. Walker, for Gentlemen of Middlesex v. Gentlemen of Kent,
for 37 runs, June 16 1864
G. Wootton, for all England v. Yorkshire, July 19 . . . 1865

V. E. Walker, for Middlesex v. Lancashire, for 104 runs,
July 22 1865
W. Hickton, for Lancashire v. Hants, for 46 runs, July 21 . 1870
J. C. Shaw, for Sixteen of Notts v. England, for 20 runs, Sept. 15 1870
S. E. Butler, for Oxford v. Cambridge, for 38 runs, June 26 . 1871
Jas. Lillywhite, jun., for South v. North, for 129 runs, August 7 . 1872
A. Shaw, for M.C.C. v. North, for 73 runs, June 1 . . . 1874
E. Barratt, for Players v. Australians, for 43 runs, September 2 1878
G. Giffen, for Anglo-Australian Team v. Rest of Australia, for 66
runs, February 16 1884
W. G. Grace, for M.C.C. v. Oxford University, for 49 runs,
June 22 1886
G. Burton, for Middlesex v. Surrey, for 59 runs, July 19 . . 1888
S. M. J. Woods, for Cambridge University v. C. I. Thornton's
Eleven, for 69 runs, May 12 1890
T. Richardson, for Surrey v. Essex, for 45 runs, July 19 . . 1894
H. Pickett, for Essex v. Leicestershire, for 32 runs, June 3 . 1895
E. J. Tyler, for Somersetshire v. Surrey, for 49 runs, August 22 . 1895
W. P. Howell, for Australians v. Surrey, for 28 runs, May 15 . 1899
C. H. G. Bland, for Sussex v. Kent, for 48 runs, at Tonbridge,
June 7 1899

THROWING THE BALL.

140 yards, by Billy the Aboriginal, at Clermont, Australia, on
December 19 1872
132 yards, by W. F. Forbes, Eton College Sports, March 16 . 1876
130 yards 1 foot 6 inches, by A. McKellar (of Glasgow), at
Dundee, August 5 1882
130 yards, by G. J. Bonnor, in Australia.
127 yards 1 foot 3 inches, by W. H. Game, at the Oxford University Sports, March 13 1873

DISTANCE BAILS SENT FROM WICKETS.

Mold, 63 yards 6 inches, with the ball with which he bowled
Lohmann in the Lancashire v. Surrey match, at the Oval, on
August 20 1896
H. Rotherham, 62 yards, with the ball with which he dismissed
L. C. Docker in the match Uppingham Rovers v. Gentle-
men of Derbyshire, at Derby, August 5 1881

BIG HITS.

W. Fellowes hit a ball 175 yards at Christ Church Ground,
Oxford, from a ball bowled by Rogers 1856
C. I. Thornton, 160 and 155 yards, at Brighton . . . . —
G. J. Bonnor, 160 yards, during practice at Melbourne . . —
W. H. Fowler, 157 yards, Somersetshire v. M.C.C. and Ground,
at Lord's, August 4 1882
G. J. Bonnor, 147 yards, at Mitcham May 1880

LOWEST INNINGS IN A FIRST-CLASS MATCH.

12, by Oxford University v. M.C.C. and Ground, at Oxford,
May 24 1877

TWO HUNDRED WICKETS IN A SEASON.

The following bowlers have captured over 200 wickets in a First-Class Cricket season :—

Date.	Bowler.	Wickets.	Date.	Bowler.	Wickets.
1870	J. Southerton .	. 210	1894	A. Mold . .	. 207
1882	E. Peate . .	. 214	1895	A. Mold . .	. 213
1884	F. R. Spofforth	. 218	1895	T. Richardson	. 290
1888	G. Lohmann .	. 209	1896	T. Richardson	. 246
1889	G. Lohmann .	. 202	1897	T. Richardson	. 273
1890	G. Lohmann .	. 220	1888	C. T. B. Turner	. 314
1893	J. T. Hearne .	. 212	1890	C. T. B. Turner	. 215
1896	J. T. Hearne .	. 257	1888	J. J. Ferris .	. 220
1898	J. T. Hearne .	. 222	1890	J. J. Ferris .	. 215

THE SIZE OF SOME OF THE PRINCIPAL GROUNDS IN ENGLAND.

Name.	Whole Ground.	Match Enclosure about.
Lord's	12 Acres.	6 Acres.
Oval	11 ,,	8 ,,
Gloucestershire County Ground . .	15 ,,	6 ,,
Old Trafford	7 ,,	5½ ,,
Brighton	10 ,,	6 ,,
Trent Bridge, Nottingham . . .	10 ,,	8 ,,
Bramall Lane, Sheffield . . .	11¾ ,,	8 ,,
St. Lawrence, Canterbury . . .	7 ,,	5¾ ,,
Mote Park, Maidstone . . .	5½ ,,	5 ,,
Birmingham	12 ,,	5½ ,,
Scarborough	7 ,,	6 ,,
Fenner's, Cambridge	8 ,,	6 ,,
The Parks, Oxford . . .	10 ,,	5½ ,,

INDEX